A FRIEND OF THE FLOCK

John McCormack

ALSO BY DR. JOHN MCCORMACK

Field and Pastures New: My First Year as a Country Vet

A F RIEND

OF THE FLOCK

Tales of a Country Veterinarian

John McCormack, D.V.M.

Crown Publishers, Inc. New York

Published by Crown Publishers, Inc., 201 East 50th Street, New York, New York 10022. Member of the Crown Publishing Group.

Random House, Inc. New York, Toronto, London, Sydney, Auckland
http://www.randomhouse.com/

CROWN and colophon are trademarks of Crown Publishers, Inc.

Printed in the United States of America

Design by Mercedes Everett

Library of Congress Cataloging-in-Publication Data

McCormack, John (John E.)
    A friend of the flock : tales of a country veterinarian / John McCormack. — 1st ed.
    1. McCormack, John (John E.) 2. Veterinarians – Alabama – Choctaw County – Biography. I. Title.
    SF613.M38A3 1997
    636.089'092 – dc21   97-14637
    [B]   CIP

ISBN 0-517-70612-1

10 9 8 7 6 5 4 3 2 1

First Edition

Dedication

This book is for the people of Choctaw County, Alabama. The first day my family and I set foot on your soil, you welcomed us with your genuine hospitality, accepted us as we were, and entrusted us with the health care of your pets, hunting dogs, and livestock. But I never cared much for your monkeys and snakes.

And in memory of a very special man, Mr. W. R. Lanier, and his family. He was not only a good client, he was also my friend, my advisor, and one of my biggest supporters. He gave much of himself to the betterment of Choctaw County.

Acknowledgments

I would like to express my appreciation to Pat Sheehan of Crown Publishers, Inc., for his gentle editorial prodding and his valiant attempt to understand Southern jargon and customs. He may soon be eating grits, greens, and barbecue. Also, a big thanks to my publicist, Elke Villa, and her associates. Not one time has she gotten me lost on a bookstore call.

Introduction

The voice on the two-way radio crackled out the late wintry night message into the warmth of the pickup cab.

"Fresh cow down, bloated, prolapsed uterus. They want you as soon as possible!"

As Jan's voice slowly recited directions to the scene of the emergency, I wondered aloud if this would be a DOA trip, and if not, which one of the problems I should attack first. Should I try to sit the cow up and see if she debloated by belching off the gas, or should I immediately go ahead and pass a stomach tube?

It would be tough trying to put a prolapse back into a bloated cow, down and stretched out in the icy mud. Perhaps I should give her some calcium gluconate intravenously immediately, if she had milk fever, and then concern myself with the secondary problems. To make matters worse, it was one of those cold and pitch-black nights that make ungloved fingers ache and long for the warmth of a roaring fire, or at least the warmth of a pickup truck's defroster vent. I wondered if any of those cold weather vets in Wisconsin had ever cleaned, manipulated, and replaced a bovine uterus while wearing gloves and coats. I surmised they had not.

Roaring down the gravel road, I spotted the light in the driveway too late and ran past the turn. As I reversed the vehicle, I could see a cloaked figure moving toward the road, frantically waving a kerosene lantern. As I drew closer, I realized the lantern waver was a young woman. Two little boys bundled up in

their heavy winter coats and wearing their red check-
ered caps, their earflaps pulled down below their ear-
lobes, were hanging on to her tattered coattail, and
both were crying.

"Brownie's dyin'!" one of them blurted out
between sobs and sniffles.

A quick patient history revealed that Brownie, the
family milk cow, had delivered a fine heifer calf that
morning. Late that afternoon they observed nothing amiss, but when they saw her about nine P.M., she
was down.

As my flashlight beamed over the prostrate bovine
figure, my first thought was that she was beyond help.
She was dangerously rotund from bloat, and from her
rear parts there flowed a seemingly endless quantity
of reddish-brown, inside-out uterus that blended in
with the half-frozen mud, which made crunchy noises
as I stalked around, deciding exactly what to do first.

Turning my attention to her head, I discovered
that she did have an eye wink reflex and was breathing. Assuming milk fever, I delayed any further exam
and hustled to the idling truck for stomach tube, calcium, IV set, and needle. The warm bottle of calcium
that I retrieved from atop the instrument panel felt
good to my tingling hands.

As the three family members huddled together
and watched helplessly, I passed the stomach tube,
relieved the gas, and then started the calcium flowing
into her jugular vein.

"Could you two young doctors hold this bottle for
me while the medicine goes into Brownie?" I asked.

Both boys charged toward the cow and carefully
took the bottle from my hand. As they took turns
holding it aloft with their ragged gloves, I offered
instructions on how to regulate the flow of the solution into the cow. Then I took a deep breath, stripped
off my shirt, knelt in the muck, and attempted to clean

up the prolapse as best I could. Cleaning a mud-, blood-, ice-, and debris-covered prolapsed uterus is not easy, as anyone who has tried it can attest. There is never enough water or clean drapes or old raincoats or whatever. But I eventually got the mass acceptably clean, and after much stuffing, pushing, and straining, finally had the thing properly inverted into its original position. I ran to the truck and warmed my hands, which I was sure were approaching frostbite status.

When I returned, Brownie had emerged from her near-coma state and was making attempts to get upright. Finally, we sat her up, cow fashion, and she burped off more gas, then answered two calls of nature. The boys went to the spring and brought two pails of water that I used to wash the icicles and other material from my arms.

As I cleaned up, the young woman explained that her husband worked the night shift at the textile mill in town and tried to farm a little on the side during the daytime. Brownie was their only cow, and she furnished milk for not only their family but for relatives down the road, as well. Everyone had plenty of milk to drink and butter for their bread. The family was poor, and Brownie was not only an important food producer, but also a friend.

As I stepped back through the gate to see if Brownie could get up, I closed my eyes and said a quick prayer. This family needed this cow! I stuck my knees into her ribs and yelled. Nothing happened. A second try was equally unsuccessful. On the third try, she shakily got up on her knees and rear end, like cows do, and rested there briefly before standing the rest of the way up.

As we watched her with lantern and flashlight, she started cautiously taking some steps toward the water bucket. She drank, then walked with confidence toward the hayrack. She looked great at the moment, but I was letting the possibility of a relapse nag at me. Even so, I realized I wasn't quite as cold as before.

After some discussion about milking out, feeding, and housing, I said goodbye and started for the truck. Suddenly, the older of the two boys rushed up, hugged my leg, and said, "Thanks, mister, for makin' Brownie well!"

Driving home that night I had this feeling of exuberance. Perhaps it was the toasty truck interior that was making me tingle all over or maybe it was the feeling that I had done something good and important. I knew it wasn't earthshaking or even worthy of mention on the back page of the weekly newspaper, but I knew that simple act would make a difference for at least a couple of families, and a lot of the area residents would hear about the cow that rose from the dead.

The practice did grow in Brownie's area, and I passed the farm many times after that night. If I saw the boys playing in the yard, I would honk the horn and they would rush to the edge of the road and wave until I was around the curve and out of sight. I also saw Brownie grazing contentedly in the small pasture beside the road, and each time I remembered that cold night, struggling with her life. Then I'd have that good feeling all over again. As far as I know, she was never sick again.

Even though the practice of veterinary medicine has changed a great deal over the years, every veterinarian needs a case like this from time to time to recharge his or her mental batteries. Fortunately, we don't have as many of these cases as in years past. Perhaps farm veterinarians make a greater contribution today by assisting owners in preventing diseases and improving the overall health of the herd or flock. But I know that I became a veterinarian because of the Brownies of the world.

When I was working with Brownie, little did I know that a few months later one of her neighbors would take great pride in constructing my veterinary clinic building, and at a very reasonable cost. A veterinarian never knows how his or her actions or a simple kindness will be repaid a hundredfold.

A FRIEND OF THE FLOCK

One

～ Choctaw County is a friendly place. My family and I had moved there in the fall of 1963 with a goal of setting up a veterinary practice and becoming valued members of the community. We were surprised at how the residents of the town of Butler had greeted us and how they had gone out of their way to make us feel welcome. In just a few weeks we had been invited to various community events and asked to attend social functions at the homes of clients, neighbors, and local leaders. The First Methodist Church and Pastor Hastings had quickly found committee assignments for both Jan and me. We had been accepted for who we were, almost as if we were natives of the area. No one asked about our pedigrees, political affiliation, or motives for being there. Like them, we were happy to be there and appreciative of that opportunity. After a few months, Choctaw County had become our home.

By May 1964 we had more calls for veterinary work than we could handle. The program drawing blood samples and testing the thousands of cows in the county for brucellosis was in full swing, which meant that I was running Choctaw's dusty county roads almost every day except Sunday. I politely refused to test cows on that day. Of course, I took care of emergencies and followed up treatments on sick patients as necessary, and there were always people who showed up on Sunday afternoons with their pets at my small, makeshift, garage animal receiving area, because that was the most convenient time for them.

In spite of the success of our practice, we desperately needed a nice clinic building, not only for the convenience of our clients and the proper treatment of their pets, but for our convenience as well. Clients who brought their companion animals to the house without an appointment were always disappointed when Jan told them that I would be in the country for several more hours. We needed a place where they could leave their animals in comfort and safety, and I could take care of them when I came in. Jan and I both were constantly looking and talking with the locals about available sites. It happened one afternoon in late May when I returned from a farm call in the southern part of the county.

"You've bought what?" I exclaimed, five seconds after I walked in the back door.

"A lot," Jan replied.

"A lot of what?"

"You know, a lot. A piece of land where we'll build our veterinary clinic," she declared.

"Did you pay for it?"

She nodded her head affirmatively. I was so surprised that I forgot to ask where it was located.

"What with? I didn't know we had any money!"

I had been busy working with the county's animals and their owners for almost a year, trying to establish the practice while Jan took care of the books, the daily bank deposits, those silly quarterly reports the IRS demanded, and other worrisome business matters in addition to her full-time duties of caring for Tom, who was five, and Lisa, almost four. Unfortunately, like so many other veterinarians, I didn't like the rigmarole of the business part of practicing. I wanted to doctor the animals and let somebody else take care of all that other stuff. But I knew that Jan couldn't take care of all the nonveterinary matters by herself and that it was not yet possible for our newly established small-town veterinary practice to hire additional help. I knew that I would be writing business checks, dealing with drug company representatives, and ordering drugs and equipment on a daily basis.

A veterinary clinic is a privately owned operation and must be run in a businesslike manner if it is to succeed. Unlike the West Alabama Regional Hospital and other hospitals for humans, there were no taxpayer funds involved in building or operating such a venture. Most veterinarians I had met were easy marks for people who had a litter of kittens that needed homes or had picked up a stray dog along the roadside, and since there were no animal shelters in most small towns back then, the veterinary clinic seemed to be a natural place to dump these unfortunate animals.

"I know Doc loves animals and he'll take these kittens in," was the oft-repeated phrase. But I had seen and heard of veterinarians who ran their clinics in such a manner, and the care and feeding of a kennel full of nonpaying strays was an additional expense, which they had to pay for by increasing the fees of the clients who did pay. The majority of my clients in Choctaw County thought their veterinary bills were already way too expensive and would not have appreciated higher fees in order to pay for the sorriness of irresponsible animal owners. I vowed that my clinic wouldn't become the county home for unwanted pets and that if I found myself in financial difficulty it would be for some other reason. At the time, I didn't realize how hard it was going to be to refuse to take in cute kittens, puppies, fawns that folks thought were lost from their mamas, and countless other injured or helpless animals who somehow found themselves in the wrong place at the wrong time.

"Well, I've been putting a few dollars aside because I knew that an opportunity like this was going to present itself soon," Jan said. Either Jan's extrasensory perception is highly developed or she has an amazing faith in the future. She is always uttering positive slogans such as "Just be patient, things will work out" or "I've got a feeling that the time is right for this," and she is usually right.

"Now tell me about it. What happened? Why didn't you call me on the two-way?"

"I tried to, about three o'clock, but you must have been away from the truck or out of range. Speed called and said that when people had heard about the availability of the lot they were calling and lined up wanting it. But he wanted us to have first refusal on it, so I had to make a decision right then. I just knew that you would want me to go ahead with it."

"Why was he even selling it?"

"Seems it belonged to someone out at Lisman who had planned to build a house on it, but due to some family problem they decided to build closer to home. The lot has even been graded, so there's very little site preparation necessary. Speed even told me about a reputable builder who specializes in small block buildings, if that's what you are sure you want." She was talking just like a contractor, but I was unaware that she had any previous building experience. Perhaps women are just born with the nest-building gene and it comes naturally.

I knew exactly how I wanted my clinic building to look. I had drawn the plans on notebook paper over and over while "studying" in veterinary school. It would be of simple concrete block construction, with the blocks stacked, not staggered, a flat-topped roof, and dimensions of approximately forty feet by twenty feet. Naturally, Jan's building genes told her that a building of only eight hundred square feet was much too small and that I would not be satisfied with such a "peewee" building. But I knew what I needed and I didn't want to waste a lot of time tromping around in a big, sprawling clinic. Besides, if I needed more space I could easily add more room later. She disagreed, of course, but we had agreed that the clinic was going to be my baby and the new house she had planned would be hers. I shuddered to think what she could do once turned loose to plan an entire house!

The clinic entrance would be on the right side and would open into a large waiting room, with a counter and reception area on the left. A short hallway led to the examination room, on the left, then farther down, to the bathroom and a darkroom. On the right was the pharmacy and lab, and just beyond was the surgery. The hallway gave way to the kennel room, which was a mirror image of the waiting room. The back door was on the left side, and I would park there, leaving the front for client and visitor parking. I had it all planned.

~

Mr. Speed Whitted, local wealthy businessman, hardware store owner, and exceptional dog lover, had been one of our best clients, supporters, and advisors. His pack of deer hunting dogs and nonhunting basset hound house pals was constantly in need of veterinary service, and my temporary clinic arrangement was unsuitable for some of the treatments and surgical procedures they needed. I frequently referred cases to my colleagues over in Meridian, some thirty-five miles to the west, where more modern animal hospital facilities were available. On several occasions Speed had expressed an interest in finding a way to help us build a proper animal clinic. Actually, he had offered to build a clinic building for us before we even moved to the town of Butler, but I refused his kind offer, primarily because I was uncertain whether a practice would survive there. I didn't want to be saddled with a new building and a mortgage that local business wouldn't support.

But in the past several months, numerous clients had inquired as to when the new clinic was going to be built. Even Carney Sam Jenkins, local homemade veterinarian, taxidermist, gifted seer, and trusted dirt road philosopher had been on to me about it, because he was bragging to his clients and friends about how he was "training me to take over his practice" when he retired, and how he was helping me to properly design the new first-class facility.

"Wish you'd hurry up and get that fancy building for all these here poodle dogs," he exclaimed one day at the barbershop. He was in the third chair, which was Chappell's station. Neither Chappell nor Carney Sam could hear very well, so it was cheap entertainment to watch and listen to their loud discourse. "I still got people all the time comin' up to the shop leanin' on the horn, wantin' me to give their dog a dose of somethin'. They just won't leave me alone." I'd heard all that before from my unlicensed competitor. He said he wanted to quit, but like so many retirees, he just couldn't seem to give it up. Even so, I enjoyed hearing him go on about how hard he worked and how he was helping his new colleague learn the animal health business.

"What'd he say?" yelled Chappell, who had his back to Carney, whipping up shaving soap in his ancient mug. He said these three words a lot.

"Wanted to know when Supervet here was gonna erect that poodle parlor," declared Myatt. "I heard that Speed Whitted was gonna build it and hand the keys to Doc free and clear on account of him saving that high-priced basset dog that got rattlesnake bit down at his deer camp on the river. Did you really save that dog, Doc?"

"Speed thinks I did. Maybe we just helped nature along a little," I answered, quickly flipping through a mangled, three-year-old *Sports Illustrated* magazine.

"It don't take no fancy degree to treat a dog with snakebite. All depends on how much his head is swole. If that head is swole up big as a watermelon, that dog's gonna die, don't matter how much of that antivenom stuff you shoot in the dog," Carney pronounced. All was quiet for the next few seconds, except for the sounds of Myatt's scissors attacking his victim's hair and the whining of the country singer on Chappell's radio.

"Is zat so, Supervet?" Myatt asked.

"I don't know. But I do wonder if Carney could cite me a reference on that. I'd sure like to read that article. Or did you get that out of the almanac that tells you when you ought to castrate a horse?" I knew I'd get a quick response to that. Myatt's customer giggled.

I could see the front of Carney's throat turn red and his jugular veins bulge out, but he couldn't dare squawk because Chappell had soaped up his neck from the ears back, had his head pushed over to the left, and had a straight razor busy scraping away just below his right ear. Any movement would surely result in a serious cut under that razor's keen edge.

"Aw, I was just jokin', Carney. Don't get all riled up or you'll get cut. I think you're exactly correct about rattlesnake bites. The bigger the swelling, the bigger the load of venom the dog got," I said. "Sometimes nothing helps." He cut his eyes over my way, wanting to nod, but still hesitated. Chappell was shaving slowly, humming softly and off-key.

"What about that dog hospital?" reminded Myatt.

"We're looking for a small piece of land now, but it's hard to find anything that's reasonably priced. We'll find something this year, I'm sure." Now I was using Jan's positive attitude.

∽

"Where is this land that we just bought, Jan?" I asked excitedly. Even though she had been using builder's language, I was a little concerned about her ability to walk a piece of land and envision a clinic building sitting there.

"It's about a quarter of a mile north of the courthouse, on the west side of Highway Seventeen. It's not the best lot I've seen, but it is very convenient and the price was right."

"Let's go look at it right now, before it gets too dark."

Less than a mile and two traffic lights later, we slowly drove down the hill to where I could see a yellow streamer hanging from a sapling on the west side of the road. Stopping in the road, Jan pointed to the streamer.

"See that marker? That's the southeast corner. From there it goes north along the road nearly four hundred feet, then west two hundred feet alongside that small branch, then due south about three hundred feet, and from there back to this starting point," she exclaimed, still pointing out the landmarks. I was surprised that she could remember each dimension with such accuracy. She was quoting figures, while I was thinking acres. "That must be close to two acres," I thought to myself. But then I realized the back dropped off into a ravine that would be useless unless filled in. Nevertheless, there was more than enough space on the level part for any structure that we would ever want or need.

As we proudly stood on the roadside gazing at our parcel

purchase, vehicles occasionally passed and the smiling drivers would honk their horns, obviously aware of what was transpiring. No doubt they'd been informed by the efficient Choctaw County information bureau, otherwise known as the barbershop and beauty parlor rumor mill. Unfortunately, the rumors were usually somewhat less than accurate, frequently downright humorous. I could just imagine the conversation.

"Yep, I saw Speed Whitted with this young woman and her hair fixed up real nice and her two kids looking at Bobby Joe Christian's property today. I could tell that Speed was pointing out land lines to her and she was writing it all down in a notebook, real official like. I wonder if she was from Mobile and is planning to come up here to open up a new beauty parlor or something," a native probably said that night at supper.

"Naw, I heard at the mill today that it was that vet's wife, and Speed is going to give them that land and build a huge animal hospital for 'em free of charge," his wife would reply.

"Free! Why?"

"'Cause Speed's favorite dog got bad snakebit and that vet stayed up all night with that dog, even went over to the hospital and got antivenom and lot of IV fluids and all. Speed was all tore up and begged the vet to save him, said it didn't matter what it cost. It took two weeks but he healed that dog. Carney Sam Jenkins said it was a miracle that dog lived."

"I ain't surprised. Speed's always been a fool about a dog, and it's for sure he's got plenty of money to spend."

I couldn't help but laugh to myself, because it wasn't the first time the bureau's information had been in error. An earlier rumor had circulated that I was going to run for sheriff, apparently because I already knew the entire county road system better than most anybody and was on speaking terms with all the farmers. Jan and I giggled for weeks about that rumor.

Suddenly a new Chevy truck pulled in behind our vehicle and the driver came over to where we were standing. When I saw that it was Clatis Tew, the world's greatest truck salesman, I refused to cast any more quick, lustful glances at the shiny new pickup he was driving. I didn't need the temptation of a new truck gnawing at me, especially after just buying a piece of land.

"Hey Doc, Miss Jan. How are you, Tom and Lisa?" Clatis greeted us, shaking hands and smiling. "Are y'all broke down out here or something? Can I help?" Oh, he was smooth.

"If he could bottle that public relations stuff he learned in truck-selling school, he'd be a millionaire in weeks," I thought to myself.

Presently, another vehicle coming from the north pulled over to the side. It was Loren Caudle, my pharmacist buddy.

"Hey, Main Man, what you doing out here, trading trucks?" He always called me Main Man or Vetran. But I also had a name for him.

"Naw, Farmist, we're just looking at this land here, thinking about putting a drugstore on it, or maybe a vet clinic," I replied.

"Well, Vetran, I'd suggest the latter, 'cause we already got too many druggists here now," he exclaimed. "There's no vetrans here except you and your sidekick, Dr. Jenkins, and I hear he's fixin' to retire."

"Loren, Jan bought this land from Christian today, and I hear that Vester Crowson is gonna start construction next week. Is that right, Jan?" announced Clatis.

"I believe that is one name I have here on my list," said Jan, consulting her big notebook.

My head was turning back and forth from Jan to Clatis to Loren. I just couldn't understand how so many people knew so much about my business, even stuff that I didn't know myself.

"Vester Crowson's real good, and as honest as he can be," declared Loren. "Do you have any plans drawn up?"

"Yeah, right here in the truck," I said. "You want to look at 'em?"

Minutes later we were staring at the crudely drawn clinic plans on the hood of a truck, when another truck pulled in behind the parked parade of vehicles. It was Harry Moore, one of the two dentists in town.

Other cars and trucks were now slowing as they topped the

hills to the north and south and observed the congregation of machinery. Some crept by, staring intently at the crowded truck hood conference. Others, probably out-of-countians, honked at the slow movers, urging them to clear the roadway so they could speed on their way.

By that time, the sun was low beneath the thirty-year-old pines to the west and darkness was hinting at its imminent arrival, but the review of my clinic plans was becoming an in-depth critique. I was being jostled to the rear by the team of so-called experts on veterinary hospital construction.

"OK now, where's your drug department?" asked Clatis.

"Well, I'll keep some out in the waiting room in shelves on that west wall. The rest will be in shelves in the lab there," I replied, trying to punch my pointing finger through the row of humanity standing in the way.

"Uh uh," Loren stated emphatically. "You need to write pre-scriptions for as much of that as you can so you can support your local pharmacist, who, by the way, needs that business."

"I don't see any place here for descenting skunks," Harry said.

"All skunk-descenting procedures will be done away from the premises or at Carney Sam's shop," announced Jan. "I just don't think there's nearly enough space here, and I think you're gonna be sorry you don't have two, preferably three, exam rooms."

I opened my mouth to protest such an absurd suggestion, but Harry got there first.

"Y'all need to remember now, this ain't Mobile, or even Meridian. We're not going to have the volume of traffic through here like those big multiman practices there." What was this "we" business?

"You oughta know, Harry. Your place is no bigger than a reg-ular living room," laughed Loren. "You'll never get an assistant in there to help you."

"I don't want an assistant! I'm doing exactly what I want to do, exactly where I want to do it," he declared. "I'll see y'all later.

Gotta run down to the curb market and get me a couple of packs of ready rolls."

"Look at this kennel room, Clatis," said Loren, his head down close to the drawing. "I think it would be better if it was on the other end. That way we could put the parking lot on the south side here where there's a lot more space, especially for those trucks and trailers bringing in horses and big boar hogs to cut. If they park on the north side, some fool's gonna back his rig into that ravine."

"Yeah, maybe. But I think we ought to make this a two-story building, put the kennels downstairs and everything else upstairs. Of course, that means we'll have to bring in a lot of dirt to fill in so that his customers won't have to go up a lot of steps." A two-story building! That was the last suggestion I wanted to hear. Not only was it almost dark, I was being overwhelmed by the fast-moving events of the day. I needed some meditation time to clear my mind of all the chatter I had just heard.

"OK, that's it!" I shouted. "The critique is over, ended, terminated! Thanks to each one of you for your input, but my plan as drawn is final." I folded up the dog-eared piece of paper and stuck it in the back pocket of my blue coveralls. Within seconds, lips were pooched out, arms were crossed tightly over chests, and best of all, there was blessed silence — except for the quiet hum of the city water pump a couple of hundred yards up the hill. Even Tom and Lisa, who were in the back of the pickup with their trucks and dolls, stopped to see what the sudden quietness was all about. Finally, I realized some feelings had been bruised and it was time for an apology.

"Look, I appreciate the interest y'all have in this project. But I have done my homework on this plan. I've visited lots of clinics and picked out things that I like and discarded things I don't like. I adapted this plan from a drawing of a clinic I saw in a vet journal. It's a plan that's simple and I like it. Now, is that all right?"

"Sure, Main Man, it's your life and your money. If I was you, I wouldn't listen to my friends either," declared Loren.

"Yeah, it is your place, but I guess I thought this was sort of a community thing. You know, sort of like a church or a library or a kids' ball field, where a lot of folks have suggestions," said Clatis.

"Yeah, I understand all that, and I do appreciate what you're saying. I'm sorry if I was a bit curt with y'all, but just remember, it's old John Edward who's gonna be making that mortgage payment every month, not the community."

About twenty-four hours later, my family and I were standing with Vester Crowson amongst the grass and small pine saplings of our property discussing exactly where the building should be placed.

"Doc John, you got a floor plan?" asked Vester.

"I'm sorry, I must have left it at the house. But I can sketch it out right quick. Got any paper?"

Shortly I was drawing and scribbling on a brown paper sack he found on the floor of his truck, while Jan, the kids, and Vester watched. I wasn't the least bit embarrassed that I didn't have fancy architect drawings, nor did I even know that I needed them.

"My friends all tell me that a twenty-by-forty building is too small, so let's go ahead and make it twenty-five by forty. Maybe that will give the kids a little more space for a play area, and I can figure out later how I'm gonna pay for all this," I stated. To me that two hundred more square feet was the equivalent of Mr. Rockefeller adding ten more floors to his skyscraper!

After only five minutes of sketching and going into some detail about the type of doors, windows, flooring, color of paint, kind of shelving, number of sinks, and so forth, Vester did some scribbling of his own.

"We'll have it ready to move into no later than August the first, probably earlier. And here's about how much it'll run you. I hope that won't be too much." He shoved the piece of brown paper bag across the truck's hood, and I peered at it with my mouth gaped open—not because the price was so high, but because it was much lower than I had expected.

"Mr. Speed said to make it as light on you as I could, so I'll

even find an old bathtub and put it up on stilts so you can shampoo those poodle dogs," he said. "And I'll also throw in some
cages that I'll make out of scrap lumber, and then stack 'em along
that back wall, if you'll paint 'em." I'm sure he thought I was
going to protest that his estimate was too high, but I stuck out my
hand and sealed the deal.

"When can you start?" I asked.

"We're just finishing up a job for Speed out Riderwood Road,
so it will be within the next few days. You'll see me or some of
my boys here doing something on this lot nearly every day from
now on until we finish the job. I hope you'll come by every day,
too, 'cause if I'm doing something different from the way you
want it done, you let one of us know right then," he declared.
"And I want you to know how much I am going to enjoy this job,
because of what you did for one of my neighbors over the Mississippi line. You came over to his farm one cold night this past
January and treated his old cow for milk fever. She was down,
bloated, and everything inside her was trying to come out."

"What was that cow's name?"

"They call her Brownie, and she gives a lot of milk for his
family. When you came over there his wife and them two boys
were scared to death that they were gonna lose that cow. But
thanks to you, that cow is up and walking today!"

Veterinarians never know when a good deed, performed
strictly in the line of duty, will be unexpectedly repaid some way,
perhaps tenfold or even a hundredfold. Like our M.D. colleagues, we have the opportunity to touch the lives of so many
people, but in a somewhat different way. People love their companion animals and treat them as valued members of their families, as do those individuals who own a cow or two. Even owners
of large herds of livestock realize that their animals must be
healthy and comfortable in order to be productive and profitable.
Regardless of the type of animal, owners have an appreciation
for a veterinarian who takes his or her job seriously and tempers
those sometimes difficult and dirty jobs with compassion and
sincerity.

I never knew whether Vester made any money on the job of

building my clinic. And I never knew whether Speed had anything to do with the deal. Some folks in town thought he did — but they were the ones who also got most of the other rumors wrong. All I can say is, within a few short months we had a new, modern clinic where the people of the community and the surrounding area could bring their animals.

Two

~ I knew that our county-wide series of rabies clinics would be the big event of our summer, and also the main event for many of the dog-owning citizens of Choctaw County. For many veterinarians and their clients, this happening is the equivalent of a sheep shearing or the day the rolling store comes through the area. Or perhaps it is akin to the excitement generated in some locales when the county inmates show up in their prison garb to work on the area's gravel roads.

From my previous experiences at rabies clinics in other Alabama counties, I knew it was a social event second only to church functions in enjoyment. It was a great opportunity for the Baptists to see the Methodists, and for the Church of Christ people to rub shoulders with the Church of God people without discussing doctrine. And, unlike church events, this was a time for everybody, from the blowhards to the meek, to boast about the prowess and intelligence of their canines. People love to brag about their dogs, and after a day or so listening to dozens of supposedly normal people tooting their dogs' horns, it was apparent that we were in the midst of great and productive coonhounds, foxhounds, squirrel hunters, bird pointers, watchdogs, and biscuit grabbers. It sure made me feel a lot of pride to be veterinarian to the world's finest dogs!

But this social event was more than a chance for dog owners

to brag about the superiority of their canines. It was also a time to talk with their neighbors who didn't get out much, because of infirmity or vehicular inconvenience. The health of elderly residents was discussed and lamented, as were the antics of the young. Some came just to observe the vaccinating action, perhaps secretly hoping that they might get to see one of the mean dogs of the neighborhood take a bite out of some portion of the dog doctor's anatomy. Some came for no other reason than to loudly announce to all present how many dogs he had personally vaccinated, cured of mange, rid of dreaded tapeworms, and how much smarter he was than any college-educated vet, especially the young incompetent one presently walking around needling all the canines.

County-wide rabies clinics came about many years ago for several reasons. First, the law requires that all dogs should be vaccinated annually against rabies. That led to the clinics, which meant that the county rabies inspector was authorized, perhaps even commanded, to travel throughout the county to make stops at predetermined, convenient stations. Since it seemed to be a common belief that rabies was more common during the summer months, it made sense to hold the rabies clinics in early summer, usually in June. Also, having the children home from school and in contact with the dogs a lot more gave the need for vaccination a higher priority. Many people in Choctaw County erroneously believed that obviously healthy dogs always carried the rabies virus in their saliva and that any contact with that saliva, whether from a playful nip or a bite, was a very serious matter. To my knowledge, dogs do not carry the virus around in their bodies unless they have recently come in contact with a rabid animal.

Second, decades ago, people in the country did not have the mobility they have today, and they weren't always able to get their dogs transported into town to the veterinarian's office. But they could hitch the mules to the wagon, load up the dogs, and make it down to the country store, their church, or a crossroads where there was a large tree onto which had been nailed a rabies clinic poster.

Now that Jan and I were the county rabies inspector team, we pored over the county map that Mr. Sexton, the county agent, had given us, trying to decide where to set up our stops. Because of the bovine brucellosis testing program and other farm calls, I was very familiar with the county roads and communities, and many of my clients had inquired about when and where the rabies clinics were going to be held. But I thought I should call Mr. Sexton to get his advice on how it had been done in previous years.

"I wouldn't deviate much from what Carney Sam Jenkins has done in the past if I were you," he advised. "You know how we are all creatures of habit, and if you miss a traditional stop folks will be upset with both you and me. I have a flyer here in my desk outlining his stops from previous years if you are interested." I could hear the sound of a drawer being slammed shut. "Also, you might call Mr. Clyde McDuffie down at Melvin, and Mr. Jack Adams at Gilbertown, and get their advice on any additional stops you should make in their communities. I'll make you a quick list of other local leaders if you'd like." I could have just called Carney, but he was not real pleased with the selection of his successor. Asking how I should do his former job would be like pouring salt in a wound.

"What would we do without Mr. Sexton?" I said to Jan.

"Starve," she replied.

I knew that Carney Sam had been the rabies inspector for years in Choctaw County, and he had done a good job of getting an unusually high percentage of the county's dogs vaccinated. After his first round of rabies clinics, he went back around a month or so later, checking to see if the yard dogs he saw had the proper vaccination certificates and tags. If there was no proof of vaccination, he injected the vaccine, but at a higher fee, and gave a stern lecture as to its importance. If the owners refused to let him vaccinate, the rabies inspector had the "dirt road" authority to confiscate or destroy the dog. It was widely believed that his county authority was exceeded only by that of the high sheriff and perhaps the county commissioners. He even carried a pistol, strapped to his side bounty-hunter style, on his "dog patrol" rounds, and was reported to be a crack shot whether shooting at snakes or at distant dogs foaming at the mouth. Nobody messed with Carney Sam, everybody said. That could pose a problem for me, because I was not in the dog-shooting business, nor did I feel as if I had the authority to do such things.

We decided to start at the south end of the county, for no reason except that it had always been done that way. Our first stop was on a warm June morning at the Cullomburg store, some thirty miles away, right on the Washington County line. We arrived promptly at nine A.M., just as promised in the half-page newspaper ad and on the hundreds of flyers that the Future Farmers of America boys had distributed and nailed onto roadside trees, power poles, and every country store in the county. For this companion animal treatment duty, Jan and I had put on our white scrub shirts at the suggestion of my buddy, one Happy Dupree, a livestock owner, hunting and fishing companion, and self-appointed supervisor of my veterinary career. I suppose today Happy would be called an agent or a publicist.

"Doc, them blue coveralls are OK for foolin' around out here on the farm, but when you start workin' on people's dogs and cats, you gotta put on somethin' nicer lookin'. You know, one of them white or light green loafin' jackets like Loren Caudle wears down at the drugstore," he ordered. He was right about Loren. He sure did look nice and professional when he stood behind his counter filling those prescriptions in his outfit. But the way the Cullomburg crowd was staring at us, I wasn't sure we'd made the right decision, and I briefly mentioned something about peeling off the gleaming jacket and retrieving my coveralls from the back of Jan's white station wagon.

"No, remember what Happy said about looking nice," she said sweetly. "I've been trying to tell you the same thing, but you won't listen to your wife. We're strangers to most of these people and it's natural for them to stare at us." She was right, of course.

There were some two dozen vehicles parked haphazardly around the store. As we arranged our table and Jan's chair, pleasantries were exchanged and a few of the people began to open sedan doors and disentangle dog chains and long leashes as sud-

denly liberated canines strained against their collars. Their slobbery tongues lolled out and they made harsh, raspy breathing
noises as they tried to bark out their joy at being out of confinement. Other dogs in other vehicles saw their released colleagues
and began barking and excitedly bounding back and forth from
seat to seat, or trying to climb the sides of pickup truck enclo-
sures. Their owners tersely issued disciplinary orders, but to no
avail, for the thrill of the canine bedlam overrode all sense of
canine reason.

As the owners lined their pets up in orderly fashion for their
vaccinations, a fight broke out between a mangy red mongrel
and a hotheaded, tick-infested black cur, complete with a lot of
head shaking, flying hair, and loud, vicious-sounding growling.
I could see the hair on the backs of their necks standing straight
up as their owners frantically yelled and tugged at leashes.

"Heanh! Heanh!" the owners exclaimed, almost in unison,
now jerking and snatching leashes with more authority. "There
ain't no need in this, Rover! Behave yourself or I'll wear you
out!" They directed threatening hand gestures in the general
direction of the ill-tempered brawlers and further rebuked their
dogs until the fight broke up. Sometimes, after dog fights are broken up, human manners prevail and apologies are offered all
around as soon as order is restored. Usually, however, the owners can't wait to get home to tell everyone within earshot how old
Rover whupped the daylights out of that sorry cur from over on
the other side of the highway.

The vaccination and record-keeping procedure went as fol-
lows: I would greet the dog, call it by name, then carefully and
slowly attempt to make contact by rubbing my fist over his or her
head. I have been bitten by dogs many times, as have other veterinarians who have vaccinated thousands of animals. But I have
found that a dog will not bite a fist nearly as often as an open
palm. By watching the dog's eyes during this greeting, you can
usually tell whether or not it is a biter. I seldom ask the owner if
the dog bites because of the obvious response.

"He's got a mouth, ain't 'e," is the usual answer, followed by
a gang giggle. Like the nondog-owning observer out on the

periphery of the crowd, an occasional owner secretly hopes the vet will get bit so he can rush home and brag about it to all the neighbors and store sitters for the next several years. If I decided the animal was a biter, I applied a muzzle, even if the owner claimed that he could easily handle any necessary restraint. Those are the kind of assistants who immediately drop or release the dog at the first yelp of pain, and one tenth of a second later the vaccinator has several teeth imbedded in his hand, fingers, or arm.

After I had administered the vaccine, another head rub, and a few words praising the dog, I said a word or two to the owner about his outstanding ability to restrain such a fine specimen of canine flesh. This was also a time for an occasional brief consultation on some health problem.

"I notice Buster has a pretty severe-looking case of red mange there on the side of his face," I declared to the owner of the second vaccinatee at the South Choctaw High School stop.

"Naw, that's not the mange, it's just where he got scraped when he was in the woods huntin' a couple of weeks ago," he declared. "If it don't clear up pretty soon I'll smear some burnt crankcase oil and sulfur on it." I knew this home remedy for mange would probably be recited at every stop, and that statement would be followed by a related question that I would hear over and over again: "Tell me this, veteran, you got anything better for this here red mange than used crankcase oil and sulfur?" This question usually came from a bystander whose dog was so completely anointed with oil and yellow powder from nose to tail it was difficult to find a likely spot for the injection.

Early on in my career, I'd try to explain about demodectic mange, commonly called red mange, and how it was caused by a small, cigar-shaped mite called *Demodex canis*, which was different from the sarcoptic mite, which could be readily transferred from pets to humans. It was common to see shirtless youths clawing at inflamed sarcoptic mange lesions on their bellies, obviously caused from lugging a mangy puppy around. I explained how the mite burrowed into the skin and caused intense itching, which obviously caused the dog to be constantly scratching himself. About that time some people would begin to uncomfortably wiggle around, trying to secretly scratch themselves with an elbow or a toe to the back of the leg. I'd rattle on about individual immunity and the role of the pup's mama and daddy, and the difficulty in treatment, and that scientists didn't completely understand it, and why it was important for them to permit me to perform delicate skin scrapings to be sure of the correct diagnosis. Then I would recite the funny names of some of the newer miticides and go into various treatment protocols and how much time it took to do it right, and that home remedies are sometimes dangerous, and how it was the humane thing to do, and so on. By this time, most people were wishing they had never asked the question and were looking at their watches and slowly easing backwards to the pickup, now openly scratching arms, bellies, and other places that were itching intensely, and knowing for certain that they, too, had the dreaded dog mange.

That approach didn't work. So as I began to mature as a country vet, I would decide whether that questioner really wanted to know the answer or already had his mind made up and was just testing me to see what my response would be. Most wouldn't use anything besides used crankcase oil anyway, and wouldn't have used my medicine had I donated it to them. So, often I'd just answer "Naw" and go on to the next dog.

After I had done my thing with the patient, the owner would proceed over to Jan's table, where she would make up a certificate of vaccination, which contained all pertinent information, such as name, address, and proper identification of the dog. Some folks didn't like giving out all this information, while others simply didn't know important things, such as the age, sex, and weight of their animal. This often led to a mild family dispute.

"What sex is your dog?" Jan asked a man at the Bladon Springs stop. She was in a writing frenzy because the line was long and our allotted time was about up. We wanted to try to stay on schedule as much as possible.

"It's a dog," he replied.

"Yes, sir, I know that, but what sex is it?" Now she was getting impatient because the line was getting longer.

"I tole you, lady, it's a dog!"

Jan soon understood that in some areas a male is referred to as a "dog" and a female is called a "gyp."

When she asked the next man the age of his dog, he hemmed and hawed, rubbed his chin as if in deep meditation, but was obviously completely in the dark about such unimportant things. Then, as most men would do, he yelled for his spouse.

"Lorene, how old is this dog? Ten or more than that?" he yelled, scanning the impatient crowd. But Lorene had endured enough dog noise, bragging owners, and standard rabies clinic commotion, and had seated herself in the relative comfort of their pickup truck.

"Git over here, Lorene! It's your dog!"

"What?" she screamed when he finally got her attention. Presently, she was stomping over to the administrative table, mumbling to herself, obviously in a dirt road snit. I could tell that Jan was about to lose her patience, since her nostrils were beginning to flare and the pen in her fingers was atwirl.

"I said, is this dog ten years old or what?"

"You know that dog ain't no ten years old, Lamar!" Lorene exclaimed. "He come up to the house the summer that Uncle Milfred's mule fell in that well. Was that '57 or '58?"

"Naw, naw, that's not right! That was the summer before. We found the dog out in the hall of the barn when we came home from the rodeo in Montgomery. Now, what year was that?" was Lamar's retort.

Now the neighbors were getting into the debate, because they were trying to be neighborly. But they, too, began arguing among themselves, and then voices were raised and the dogs began to bark.

"NEVER MIND!" yelled Jan. "I've already written down TEN!" She ripped the certificate from the pad and shoved it toward Lamar. "It's not that important!" Almost instantly, tranquillity descended upon the gathering, except for a few undisciplined canines who continued their irritating racket. Lamar took the certificate and peered at it intently for a few seconds.

"Well, it ain't right," he said softly. But when his gaze met Jan's steely official eyes, and he beheld her tightly pursed lips, he quickly crammed the paper into the bib pocket of his overalls and took his leave.

"Next!" cried Jan. There were no more problems with dog ages at the Bladon Springs stop. We soon finished there and drove on to our next stop.

In minutes the Aquilla church came into view, and we could see a great crowd gathered under the pines and lining the sides of the road. There were several mule-drawn wagon loads of dogs, cars with dogs hanging out of car trunks, a number of pickup trucks, and one John Deere tractor with a small dog box rigged up on the back. Dogs of all descriptions were wagging their tails, scratching themselves, and looking for fights. As had been the case at the other stops that morning, some were suffering from mange and also had large ticks, some the size of plums, sticking to their skin. Many of the animals were secured to their wagons and trucks by log chains big enough to snake out downed pine trees, while others were tied with brand-new well ropes or plow lines at least fifty feet long. Still others had long quantities of thin kite cord secured around their necks and they were writhing, cutting flips, and yelping, all the time being dragged along by grimy, teeth-clenched urchins. It was a sight to behold. Jan and I stared in wonder as we drove right up to the front door of the church and were soon immersed in our work.

"Yes sir, Doc, these here rabbis shots are just wonderful things. Since y'all started shootin' all our dogs with this serum, they just don't have as many of them runnin' fits anymore," announced one coonhound enthusiast.

I had been taught in veterinary school that rabies definitely did not cause "running fits" and that the cause was probably nutritional, or a deficiency of some obscure vitamin or mineral. But I refrained from giving another canine health lecture on this day.

"Yes sir, this vaccine I have this year is a new type and they claim that it is better than ever. I'll bet none of these dogs will have fits after these shots," I declared while injecting a yelping and snapping mutt. I couldn't beat them, so I just joined them!

It interested me that many of the ladies were apparently snuff dippers. Their lower lips were swollen and pooched out, and some even had streaks of the juice dribbling down one or both corners of their mouths. But their remarkable ability to expectorate quickly and accurately amazed me.

"What's your dog's name, please?" Jan asked one such snuff pro.

The lady turned her head away from Jan, and in the length of time it takes to bat an eye, and with a quick backward flick of her head, discharged a long arching ribbon of the brownish juice, which cleared by several inches a number of dogs and small children before precisely splattering a disease knot on a loblolly pine several paces away. I noticed a shudder run through my wife as she watched the exhibition out of the corner of her eye. Jan has never been a spitter.

"Spote," replied the lady, wiping her mouth with a small rag she was carrying around — obviously for that specific purpose, because it was the same general color as the juice now trickling down the tree trunk.

"I beg your pardon?" Jan replied with teeth clenched.

"I said Spote. The dog's name be Spote," she repeated with a degree of impatience.

It was a common name for dogs in the area, and Jan quickly scribbled "Sport" on the form and daintily placed it in the lady's extended and smelly palm, being very careful to avoid any of the wet spots.

The entire event was a demonstration that I would witness many times in the future, and I always marveled at the amazing lip dexterity of these users of smokeless tobacco. After studying this feat for several years, I realized that it was accomplished with the teeth clamped tightly together and the lips only slightly apart at the instant of juice ejection. I didn't understand how this could happen until I had observed it being done over and over, and then I realized it was due to a gift of nature, made possible by an abnormally wide space between the two upper incisors and a very agile tongue. These two oral features, combined with years of daily practice, made it possible to become a respected expectorator of Olympic quality. I also noticed that even though some males also used snuff, they didn't possess the necessary skills to become great spitters. The technique they used lacked any particular kind of delicacy, and it seemed they just expelled their oral overflow at random, never taking the time to develop any kind of form or style. And a man would never be caught dead holding a silly hanky in his hand. Instead, he would simply smear his shirtsleeve across his lips and chin — or, if it was summertime, the back of his hand.

When all the dogs had been vaccinated, one elderly gentleman came forward with a request.

"Doc, Mrs. Shirley is a semiinvalid lady just down the road who can't bring her dog up here. Do you reckon you could go by her place and vaccinate old Buster? Carney Sam always helped her out."

"Sure, we'll be glad to do that. We'll follow you down there."

"One thing, Doc. Buster's real mean. You may need to use your choke stick on him. Mrs. Shirley will probably get mad at you, but it's the only way to get it done."

The dreaded choke stick was actually a hickory hoe handle through which had been drilled two holes some sx inches apart on the end where the hoe would have been. A rope was first passed through the hole closest to the holding end, then through the hole closest to the hoe end. A fairly large knot was made in the free end of the rope. This allowed the user to slip the loop over the dog's head and then, using restrained force, tighten down on the free end and subdue him for an injection. I hate using the device, but sometimes such restraint is necessary.

Buster was forty-five pounds of black hair and meanness. The instant I spotted him chained to the chinaberry tree, I knew he was going to be the most vicious dog I had ever dealt with. There was a ring of gray hair around his eyes and nose, and when he snarled and showed me his teeth, I could see that many of the incisors and all the canines were broken off, probably from biting strangers and slow salesmen, I surmised.

He lunged at me, growling and barking before I ever invaded his space, and whether I went left or right, he kept leaping and snapping, just hoping that he could somehow bite off a big chunk of man flesh. I was hoping the chain would hold.

As I made my way around the tree, Buster followed me, continuing to show his fury at the stranger invading his space. After a couple of clockwise revolutions I realized that his chain was getting shorter and shorter, until finally, he had wound himself up like a yo-yo. I quickly popped the syringe and needle crossways into my mouth, Tarzan style, grabbed him by the end of his tail, and stretched him out until both feet were off the ground. Now he was more than mad, he was livid! He was barking, growling, and desperately trying to snap at his tormentor, who had him stretched to the limit. At the same time he was expelling foul-smelling anal gland material from his rear parts. In between wiggles, I was able to plunge the needle into a hip and deposit the vaccine, just seconds before he choked completely down. Then I reversed my direction around the tree and he followed suit, staggering but still vociferating loudly, if somewhat hoarsely, and spraying the area with droplets of saliva. Unbeknownst to me, Buster's owner had watched the entire show from her living room window.

"Ma'am, I apologize for having to be so rough on Buster. But I didn't know how else to get the vaccine into him," I said.

"Young feller, you got it done in a fraction of the time it always took Mr. Jenkins to do it. And he used that horrible choker pole. I'm so happy that you didn't use that inhumane device," she exclaimed. "It's obvious you know your business! I'll look for you again the same week next year."

"Yes, ma'am, I've had some training on how to handle mean dogs. Not that Buster is mean, he just has a lot of spirit," I heard myself say. But I was already dreading next year.

With my first Buster episode under my belt, we headed for

our last stop of the day. I was still shaking from the scary encounter, and by then my adrenaline level was quite high.

"Honey, you were mighty rough with that one. I hope you won't have to do that very often. Was the lady upset?"

"No, she was very complimentary about my restraining skills, and was delighted that I didn't have to use the choke stick. Said I did a lot better than Carey Sam," I bragged.

"Well, that's a first. Maybe we're on the right track," Jan declared. "By the way, I watched you give that injection, but I couldn't tell whether you gave it intramuscularly or subcutaneously. Which was it?"

"Neither. I gave it intradog!"

By the time we arrived at the last stop of the day, at the country store in the small town of Isney, I was almost back to normal. I knew many of the folks there, and even the names of some of their dogs, because I had recently spent a lot of time there testing their cows. The dogs were all well-behaved and we enjoyed a lot of good, small-town bantering.

"Yeah, I told 'em up at the bank just last week that they better add on to that vault they got, 'cause it won't hold all the money this here vet's makin'," asserted one prominent citizen as he handed me a twenty-dollar bill. The entire group chuckled, nodded their heads in agreement, and jabbed their associates in the ribs.

"Just barely gettin' by," I whined. "Just barely gettin' by." This complaint brought forth more chuckles, even a couple of guffaws.

Just as we had packed up the table and were about to leave, a car with a Mississippi license tag drove up and the driver spoke. "You that feller what shoots dogs?"

"Yes, I vaccinate dogs."

"How 'bout shootin' this 'un here in the car. I'm afraid he might get away from me if I let him out."

"Be glad to," I replied. Things had gone so well since we arrived in Isney, I wasn't thinking about the possibility of a biter. I quickly opened the rear door of the old DeSoto, sat down, and closed the door, only to be rudely greeted by a half-bulldog, half-chow looking thing whose ill-tempered behavior was legendary in the area, I later learned. Before I could retreat, he had all four of his sharp incisors through the outside skin of my right forearm and was holding on with the tenacity for which his ancestry is famous. It takes a lot of willpower and fear to resist the urge to jerk away and risk serious injury, so in a panic, I found myself trying to needle him left-handed. I'm sure the outside-the-car observers were aghast at the growling and yelling that was being emitted from inside the car. Paws and handprints were making slobbery streaks all over the windows, and the car was rocking back and forth. The bitter wrestling contest between man and beast extended from back seat to front, then onto the floorboard. The dirty windows began to steam up in spots from all the heavy breathing and loud throaty expletives being shouted and growled by both contestants.

Finally, I was able to plunge the needle into the cantankerous cur, using the "intradog" route of administration. When he opened his mouth to yelp, I needed no encouragement to extract my gnawed-up arm from his mouth and beat a hasty retreat out the door, which the laughing owner had opened at just the right instant. I heard teeth click together an instant after my rear parts cleared the open door, but I felt no pain back there; he had missed. I glared at the jerk owner and we exchanged insults, but several of the bystanders intervened just as fisticuffs seemed imminent. He thought it was great sport to see the vet get bitten, but he was upset because I had somehow slung blood over a considerable area of the cloth interior of his aged car.

Since we were a long way from a physician, I found a teat cannula and flushed my wounds with bull penicillin. It was the same formulation they had over at West Alabama Regional Hospital, it just came in bigger bottles. My arm healed well, but I still have the battle scars to remind me of a well-learned lesson.

Country rabies clinics were a big part of veterinary practice and country living—and still are in some areas. Vaccinating a dog out in front of a country store with a huge crowd of onlookers may not be the textbook scenario desired by many veterinarians, for the obvious reasons of the time involved, cleanliness, and the inability to properly examine each patient presented. But it produces a special bond between the owners of those pets and the veterinarian who comes around at the same time and to the same place every year.

I suppose that once you've been on one country rabies clinic, it's like having malaria or some other recurring disease. You have it in your system and it tends to flare up during periods of warm weather stress. Even now, every summer I get this spiritual inner urge that tends to draw me back to country stores, old churches, and huge roadside oak trees with scars on them. I also have a strong urge to call up veterinary pharmaceutical houses and order several thousand doses of rabies vaccine and a like quantity of little red or silver tags in the shape of fireplugs, hearts, or doggie bones.

All veterinary students should have the opportunity to participate in an intensive two-week countrywide series of rabies clinics. They could learn more about human and animal psychology and see more medical problems, plus learn more about the back roads of the county than they would any other way, and in a short period of time. In fact, I think everybody should be required to go on at least one rabies clinic. Perhaps then they would have a better appreciation for veterinarians!

Three

〜 It was the week following on our two-week-long, nine A.M. to three P.M., combination rabies clinic tour and continuing education sessions. Not only had we vaccinated thousands of dogs from the southwest Alabama area, at each stop we also learned new and interesting "facts" about preventative medicine as well as never-before-heard therapeutic measures for canine health problems. But this morning I was driving west, making an unusual small animal call. It was to Mr. Dickey's honky-tonk on the Mississippi state line.

Mr. Dickey owned a pen of fine dogs that he wanted "vetted" — or vaccinated, dewormed, and generally checked over. He had not phoned me, but instead had sent word by one of his "regulars."

It should be noted here that Choctaw County was a dry county. This meant that bonded whiskey or alcohol of any kind could not be legally sold or purchased within its boundaries. Of course, there was always moonshine liquor available from a number of moonshiners and bootleggers.

The nearest legal beer was over in Mississippi. There were several roadside taverns just inside the Mississippi state line whose primary customers were Choctaw Countians. On any passing trip, Choctaw County cars and trucks could be seen parked out front in abundance, especially if it happened to be on a weekend. In addition, there would be other vehicles wearing Alabama license plates parked around back, away from the prying eyes of preachers and other teetotalers passing by out on the country road.

If state line beer wasn't spiritous enough, legal "red" government whiskey could be purchased in a state-owned "green front" store in the town of York, in Sumter County, just to the north of Choctaw, but it was scorned by longtime advocates of the more potent, woods-distilled local varieties. Some people complained that the store-bought stuff lacked the quick kick and awesome knockdown properties to which they had become accustomed. I was amused that you could obtain "red" whiskey from a "green" front store, but you could buy homemade "white" whiskey from what could be called the "black" market. I reckoned that either one would make you feel "blue" the morning after...

It was frequently said that the preachers and bootleggers were in cahoots to keep the county dry. Some said that the proprietors of the honky-tonks were also instrumental in maintaining the status quo, although their alliance with the clergy was somewhat uneasy.

One of the problems associated with the wet-versus-dry situation was how some people, especially the dry forces, judged every citizen in the small community in regard to his or her imbibing habits. You were either a complete teetotaler or you were a drunken sot. There was no in-between category for a person who might have an occasional brew or who kept a bottle in a brown paper bag under the front seat of the pickup for emergencies.

Some felt strong drink was indicated in case of snakebite or a scorpion attack, for instance, while others believed that a nip was necessary in case of accidental exposure to various killer viruses such as the ones that cause the common cold.

My own position on alcohol was somewhere in between the teetotaler category and the sot set, probably closer to the former. I kept no brown paper bags under the front seat of the truck, but we did have something available at home for an occasional libation. Also, we were beginning to socialize more as we made new friends in Butler, and we wanted to be sure we filled our roles as proper hosts when our friends came to call. Some guests brought their own white liquor of the homemade variety because they couldn't bring themselves to consume the watered-down legal red whiskey dealt by the green front store. Also, there was a question of loyalty. If an imbiber's Unca Bubba, who was a backwoods distiller of wide repute, found out that his nephew was partying around drinking some weak Canadian blend or that tasteless Russian stuff, there would be some hurt feelings. Not only had the thoughtless nephew violated a family loyalty, he was also buying foreign goods.

It wasn't long before a petition was brought around for signatures in an effort to allow voters to decide whether they desired the opportunity to purchase legal alcohol locally. I signed the petition, not because I was in favor of the free flow of booze but because I felt people had the right to register their personal preference in the form of a secret vote. In spite of that, some of my dyed-in-the-wool dry clients acted right ugly when they found out that I had signed it.

"How do you know I signed that paper?" I asked. "Who told you?"

"Well, the preacher knows who signed," they bragged.

"What happened? Did it come to him in a vision, or did he break into the courthouse?" They'd purse their lips and then leave with their noses in the air and their little dogs under their arms.

But the honky-tonk folks had pets and livestock too, and they frequently required the services of a veterinarian. I looked carefully at the dollar bills they gave me at the conclusion of our animal health appointments, and I couldn't find any evidence that anything was wrong with them. The bank in town, and the First Methodist Church of Butler, readily accepted as much beer garden money as I could bring in without any complaints whatsoever.

That's why I found myself uneasily pulling into the parking lot of Dickey's roadhouse on a beautiful June morning. I parked right next to an old beat-up white 1953 Buick, detrucked, and with head lowered, shuffled toward the front door. The neon signs in the tiny blackened windows above my head announced the brand names of several beers and their logos, blinking in an attempt to fling a craving on parch-mouthed passersby.

As I approached the entrance, my steps grew slower and my legs seemed reluctant to move in the direction of the open door. But I knew why. Even though I was a full-grown adult, I was hesitant about darkening the doors of a beer joint. It was because my momma's words echoed through my head every time I got anywhere near a saloon.

"Stay out of beer joints and honky-tonks," she'd always preached. "Nothing in there but trash drinking old nasty beer, cursing, and smoking cigarettes. Besides, you're apt to get cut."

But I was making a professional call, not paying a social visit. Surely it would be all right to be there as long as I didn't partake of the various mind-impairing beverages — and no one drove by and recognized my truck.

That could be a problem. Just as I realized that everybody knew my truck, a car passed by honking its horn enthusiastically.

"Oh no, who is that?" I mumbled, trying to kneel down in front of the toothy grill of the Buick. As the slow-moving vehicle eased its way on past the beer joint, I peered over the left front fender of the Buick in an effort to identify the driver in the plain black Ford sedan.

"That head looks like Chappell, the barber! And he does drive a plain Ford just like that one," I said to myself. "Now he'll spread the word that the vet was at the beer joint!"

Good old Chappell! When you left his barbershop you felt as though you had just been briefed on local, regional, national and international events, rumors, and predictions. He and his associate, Myatt, knew everything about everybody and disseminated that information profusely all day long while cutting hair and shaving off whiskers. Of course, there were usually several other citizens there occupying the bench who could for sure give the answer to any question on the off chance that Chappell or Myatt faltered.

As I entered the door of the establishment, the late, great Hank Williams was finishing up his sad tearjerker tune about his lovesick blues on the jukebox and was quickly replaced by a twangy-voiced female singer who wasted no time going into a tirade complaining about the sorry state of the opposite gender and how she'd personally been done wrong by at least half of all males under the age of thirty.

As my eyes became accustomed to the near darkness, I could make out the shadowy appearance of numerous cheap tables and chairs, which were arranged in haphazard fashion. I wondered if the furniture disarray was planned or if the place just hadn't been straightened up after the last brawl.

I could distinctly feel the stares of the two early morning drinkers at the most remote corner table, as they silently double dog dared the coveralled stranger to invade their tippling privacy. Each held on to a long-neck beer bottle with one hand, slowly peeling the label with the other, occasionally moving a cigarette back and forth from mouth to ashtray. Smoke slowly ascended toward the ceiling in proper barroom fashion.

"Hey, Doc, come on in here, boy!" yelled someone. It was Mr. Dickey, the proprietor, bartender, fight breaker-upper, and owner of the pack of dogs that I was there to check out. After exchanging pleasantries with him and waving toward his two customers, we left the bar unattended and walked out to the dog pen.

There were some twenty-odd canines lounging around in the first-class dog pen. The six-foot-high hog wire fence enclosed some two thousand square feet of real estate, complete with fancy self-feeders, a washtub for their drinking water, and several doghouses and empty fifty-five-gallon drums. Two drums were mounted sideways on posts, one atop the other town-house style, and each had one end removed and was bedded with a small amount of straw for the additional comfort of the dogs. There were several of these condos, and the dogs seemed to especially enjoy the lounging privacy of the elevated drums. Some dogs were coiled up back in the drums asleep, while others were hanging halfway out, obviously enjoying the scenery from their vantage point.

The dogs were typical southwest Alabama and southeast Mississippi crossbred deer dogs. The fifty- to sixty-pound athletes were of walker hound, bluetick, and redbone ancestry, and exhibited colors ranging from reddish brown, brindle blue, and black and white to anything in between. There was no segregation of the sexes, although a sturdy cross fence created a small isolation area on one end of the pen that I assumed was for females in heat—or "cuttin' up," as the locals described it.

As we entered the gate, the reactions of the dogs varied considerably. Some went into a frenzy, baying, jumping, and wagging their tails with such intensity that their entire hind ends were sashaying. Others would calmly come up and sniff our trousers as if to collect our smell and run it through their cranial computers for identification. Several drum and house dwellers paid us no attention other than to raise their heads briefly, observe the goings-on, and then return to their former state of inactivity. Dogs are like their human masters; each has a different personality.

No dog resisted when addressed by Mr. Dickey. He spoke quietly, patted each dog's head, then rubbed on his fur before latching onto the collar and presenting the patient to the doctor for treatment.

Generally, hunting dogs such as deer dogs, coonhounds, foxhounds, and bird dogs are not difficult to deal with when examining, giving injections, or poking pills down their throats. The ones that cause veterinarians a lot of grief and finger pain are the little Chihuahuas, Pekes, and other lap-type dogs. They are hard to restrain because they are so squirmy and difficult to grasp solidly.

No dog attempted to bite my hands, nor did any of them resist having large pills poked down their gullets. A few yelped from the sting of the rabies needle, but Mr. Dickey was a good restrainer. It was obvious that he spent a lot of time with his dogs.

"They sure are nice dogs," I declared. "Do you get time to hunt with them?"

"Doc, I rarely ever hunt," he said. "I stay right here at this nightclub, working while everybody else plays. It's pretty tough dealing with drunks, breaking up fights, and keeping all those Baptist preachers over in Choctaw County off my back. But when I get a bait of it, I just come out here to the dog pen, sit down, and feed 'em dog biscuits."

"I'm sure that's very soothing and relaxing."

"Yep. Some folks drink, others play golf. I play with my dogs!"

After he paid me with cash money from a long leather pouch that he had chained to his belt, we walked back up the path to the joint.

"Come on in, Doc, I'm buyin'," he declared. "You need something cold to wet your whistle after all that work."

"Thank you, but I believe I'll pass this time. I've probably got more work to do. Most of my clients don't want me doctoring on their animals with a beery breath."

He laughed and agreed that he surely wouldn't have wanted a drunk working on his valuable dogs.

"May I use your phone? My two-way radio is on the blink and I need to check in with Jan."

"Surely. It's right over there by the jukebox."

Shortly, Jan was on the line. "Things are pretty quiet here," she said. "Have a couple of people with dogs for you to look at, the Upjohn salesman came by, and the diagnostic lab called. They said your test charts from the sale barn had too much manure and blood on them again."

"What else?" I asked, trying to keep from exploding. "That lab crowd ought to have to spend just one day testing cows with me at Livingston Stockyard. They'd never say another word about a little gunk on a test chart," I mumbled to myself.

"Oh, yes, the preacher just now called," she continued. "He said to not forget about the board meeting tonight at the church. That is, if you get back from that state line beer garden in time."

"I knew it! He must have just visited the barbershop. By now Chappell has trumpeted the news in all directions," I thought to myself. "Why can't people just tend to their own business and leave me alone?"

By the time I arrived at home I had cooled down and was ready to take care of the work there. A half dozen cars were parked out front, some of which contained friendly, tail-wagging dogs. The first patient was a new Mexican Chihuahua puppy, not much bigger than a rat.

"What's his name?" I asked, trying to read an unfamiliar name on the record.

"It's Tequila!" the puppy's mama proudly announced.

"How do you spell that?" I asked.

"Well, I'd think you'd know, as much time as you spend at those state line roadhouses!" the lady answered haughtily.

"Now, how did you arrive at that conclusion?" I asked.

"Well, everybody knows it," she replied. "Why, they were just discussing it down at the Dairy Queen!"

And so it went for the next week or two. The matter wasn't really earthshaking, nor did it cause me any loss of sleep, but in retrospect, it did demonstrate a truism.

On visits to state line roadhouse honky-tonk beer joints, a small-town veterinarian should always park behind the shack and out of sight. Vehicles parked out front are too vulnerable to the prying eyes of passersby, one set of which might belong to the barber.

I have noticed that interesting news and gossip travels much faster and more efficiently in a small town. This is probably because there is not much going on there and when something does happen it is the main topic of discussion at every place of business in town. On the other hand, perhaps it is because people care more about their neighbors in a small town and they check on each other a lot closer.

Four

~ As much as I was enjoying the excitement of finally being on my own and making a success of the practice, watching our new clinic building being constructed was even more exciting. Vester Crowson, our builder, had started construction in late May, and he and his crew had worked in short spurts in between his other jobs, sometimes even showing up at daylight or right at dark for a few hours of concrete block work and board nailing. I visited the site nearly every day, sometimes peering at the day's effort by truck headlights late at night. Jan had always been interested in the construction business, and her constant presence on the site relieved me of many of the dozens of small decisions that had to be made.

Since it was my introduction into the construction business, I was amazed at all the small problems and questions that arose. The colors of the walls, what kind of floor tile, bathroom fixture design and color, even the height of the shelves in the laboratory, were things that I hadn't thought about and really didn't care about, but they had to be dealt with. Jan loved dealing with all this minutia and thrived on it. I just wanted it finished so we could start bringing in the patients. Folks were already calling for appointments — "As soon as that dog hospital is finished," they said.

A lot of visitors took it upon themselves to stop by the clinic and offer suggestions on how to proceed with certain aspects of the construction. They all claimed to be experts in their own right, and they all had carved-in-stone opinions of the building, usually pointing out some minor flaw that only their trained and expert eyes caught.

"Doc, you're not gonna put the front door there, are you?" one inquired, seemingly shocked.

"Yeah, why not?"

"'Cause it's too close to the end of the building. You ought to have moved it over to the left about two or three inches."

"Why? What difference does it make?"

"'Cause the door won't open up as wide. It'll hit the wall. I'd make him do it over, if it was mine. 'Course, it's yo' clinic...." He sighed, his voice trailing off.

Others didn't like the flat roof, the location of the building on the lot, or the light tan paint on the blocks, but they all suited me just fine, and I practiced my tact by brushing off those unpaid and unwanted consultants with a word of thanks and a smile of appreciation.

"Let's have a grand opening," suggested Jan one night. "Vester told me today the building will be ready for occupancy in a few days, as soon as the parking area is graveled and the inspector looks over everything. We'll have some punch and homemade cookies in the lab, and let people wander through — or even conduct tours, if they'd like that."

"I didn't know the town of Butler had to inspect my building before I could move in. What business is it of theirs?" I asked. "At home, if we wanted to build a barn or shed, we just did it. It wasn't anybody's business but our own."

"John, you know very well that things like construction have regulations and red tape, especially in town. It's for the protection of the consumer. If you didn't have inspections, there's no telling what kind of shoddy job a jackleg electrician or plumber might get by with," Jan replied. "Don't worry about it, because I'm coordinating all that with the proper authorities." I wondered how she knew all that red tape stuff when she had never been through a building program before. But I knew she was thorough with any project she undertook, as evidenced by the copious notes of price estimates, dates of delivery, and direct quotes from various equipment and supply salesmen.

"Now," she said, peering into her book of notes, "I was thinking that we'll probably have everything moved from our little office here into the new place within two or three weeks if we do it at night and between appointments in the daytime. I think our daily clinic routine should be well established before we have the grand opening celebration, so that our guests can see the dogs in the kennels, flea powder on the counter, and observe us in actual operation. That will put the grand opening in the early fall, but before the football season really makes everybody crazy."

"Do you really think anybody will show up?" I asked.

"Of course they will! The AVMA has done surveys and found that folks love to see what goes on in animal hospitals. It's documented!" It was obvious I couldn't argue against the American Veterinary Medical Association's "documentation."

"OK, let's do it," I declared. "You pick a day, then clear it with your authority chums just to be sure there isn't some kind of festival or rat killin' on the same day."

"Daddy, can our kindergarten class come too?" Tom asked.

"Why sure. That would be a great idea," I declared. "But do you think that would be all right? I mean, some kids might not like the smell of B vitamins and whipworm medicine."

"Mrs. Minsloff has already spoken to me about bringing them by for a tour. I'm just sure they'll love it," replied Jan. "It will be very educational for them, and it will impress upon them the necessity for taking care of the health needs of their pets. I doubt if any one of them has ever seen a veterinary clinic."

"Can I go too?" asked Lisa. She was almost four years old, but thought she was much older, and wanted to go wherever her five-year-old brother went.

"You sure can, Lisa Bug. You can help me feed the dogs. How's that?"

"I wanna help you operate," she answered.

"You're too young, Lisa. You have to be five to do that," retorted Tom.

"Uh uh! I can too help!" she answered. Both of them enjoyed climbing up on their observation stools near the surgery table and watching my every move when I did surgery. Their favorite procedure was a cesarean section on a dog or cat. I handed them the fresh newborns, and their job was to briskly rub them to stimulate breathing. Unfortunately, many of the mama dogs and cats had been in labor too long and it was too late to save the little ones. I was impressed by their despondency in that situation, and proud of their concern for animal life.

"There's a bleeder, Daddy. Better get it!" Lisa had exclaimed one day, pointing at a small artery that I had just severed while trimming the ears on a boxer puppy.

"I see it, Lisa. Now, you let me do the operating, OK?" I said. It was nice of her to notice, but no surgeon, whether country vet ear cropper or world-famous cornea transplanter, wants to be told how to perform surgery.

"Lisa, don't tell Daddy what to do. That's my job," chided Jan, smiling.

"Y'all are just gonna have to get out of here if you don't be quiet and behave," I warned.

But then, in typical small-child fashion, Lisa whispered very quietly to herself about what I should be doing differently, and then held her tiny forefinger up close to her nose, privately pointing in the general direction of the patient. I couldn't help but be amused, yet proud of how both she and Tom seemed to be taking such an interest in the work that we were doing. I looked forward to the day when they could help around the clinic and on farm calls.

After a few weeks and several long nights of hauling furniture, equipment, drugs, and other supplies from our house and the homes of our friends, we opened the clinic for business. Then the pets started arriving, just as Mr. Sexton, the county agent, and all the others had predicted. In addition to the house pets, there was a daily invasion of hunting dogs coming in for worm checks, vaccinations, and free ear tattooing. Good hunting dogs were frequently lost on deer hunting drives but usually showed up later at a farmhouse, on the side of the road, or at a country store. If they were wearing a collar ID, most people would contact the person listed there, which would result in dog and master being soon reunited. Unfortunately, there were a few dog thieves in the region who simply removed the collar and claimed the dog as their own, even if the rightful owner knew the dog was his property. But if the owner's three initials were tattooed in the dog's ears, he had some evidence to back up his claim.

The floor plan and traffic pattern of the clinic was working out fine, just as I'd known it would. Jan still thought the clinic was too small, but I liked having everything kind of centralized. That way I didn't waste a lot of time walking. But I had to admit that I was already looking out the back window, wondering if I could expand the kennels and add runs back there if the practice grew so large that I needed another veterinarian or two. That was a long way down the road, however. Right now I wanted to enjoy practicing in a building that I could afford. It sure did offer a lot more than a closet in the garage.

Five

〜 I never thought I'd be considered a sheep specialist. All my relatives back home raised a few sheep, so I knew more than the average man on the street about their husbandry and daily living requirements. But after a surgical incident with Sir Alfred, a "companion" sheep from whom I surgically removed a kidney stone, who was owned by the wealthy Mrs. Vanlandingham, I was suddenly looked upon as a great savior of the ovine kingdom. Actually, the surgery was quite minor. But unfortunately for Sir Alfred, it required him to change his wool ribbons from blue to pink, and visit the ladies' room rather than the one that was marked "Men." Nevertheless, due to Mrs. V's widespread proclamations of my sheep-saving expertise, I began receiving phone calls from the few local sheepherders as well as those from surrounding counties and from out-of-state residents. The calls ranged from free information requests to deworming, vaccinating, and foot-trimming appointments.

"You're the only one around here that cares about doctoring sheep," they all declared. That was probably true, since Carney Sam Jenkins had let it be known in no uncertain terms that he didn't have time to "mess with sheep."

So it was for that reason that I was at Ronnie's place early one morning observing his efforts to pen his 800 ewes. As I watched from a distance, I figured there must have been 798 sheep rushing into the pen, but as usual there were a couple that just had to show off.

The renegade, an old high-headed West Texas ewe, seemed to be grinning and pleased with herself as she led her lamb in an easterly direction, away from the flock now peacefully assembled in the corral.

I was sitting in my truck at the edge of the pasture, watching intently, and wondering whether I should help or stay out of the way. When the ewe went into a gallop, I could not sit idly by without at least trying to head her off.

"Dang you, ewe!" I yelled, then snickered at what I had just heard myself say.

I cranked the truck, dropped the gearshift lever into low, and rocketed after her, throwing dry red-clay clods and a cloud of dust into the air.

Her three-month-old lamb was matching her stride for stride, never leaving his position on her left side and slightly to the rear. I knew all the running was melting off the valuable pounds that Ronnie had worked so hard to feed onto his young carcass.

In seconds I had maneuvered the truck up to the right side of the wooly beast and had commenced yelling and banging on the side of the door with my hand, thinking that she would turn back and do the right thing. But suddenly she veered right into the left front wheel.

Whump! Bump! Whump! The initial hits were followed by a series of smaller-sounding *whumps* as she apparently entertained the underside of my vehicle. Her lamb continued aimlessly on, occasionally looking back and bleating.

"Oh no!" I lamented. "I've just bought myself a sheep, and a physically mutilated one at that!"

I slid to a stop on the side of a terrace, hopped out of the truck, and fell to my knees in order to peer up under the vehicle. I was expecting to see material suitable only for the emergency room and trauma team, or else Easter dinner, but luckily all I observed was the intact ewe lying on her side. She was very still, but I saw her eyeball move and her chest was heaving up and down. Her wool was frying on the hot muffler.

"I've got to get her out from under there before she burns herself up, and this truck with her," I mumbled. I was tugging at her hind legs with all my might, but it wasn't easy lying on my stomach and trying to avoid all the things that are hot under a truck. About that time Ronnie arrived, puffing and asking questions.

"Did you run over her, Doc? Is she hurt? What's that I smell?"

"Help me get her out from under here before we're all fried!" I yelled.

"Looks like she's tryin' to sull," Ronnie exclaimed.

When animals sull, they usually get down and refuse to get up. Sheep, Brahman cattle, and Jersey milk cows seem to be very susceptible to sulling attacks. Usually, no amount of sweet talk, begging, threats of bodily harm, or foul language will produce the desired results.

Some people declare these animals "sulled up," muleheaded, balky, sulky, or malingerers. Other synonyms, somewhat more rustic, yet absolutely descriptive, are commonly used by the herders and owners of these intensely aggravating beasts. I have never understood why sheep sull at such inappropriate times. It's almost like they plan the event.

"Hey, I think I'll just sull right here," this particular sheep was probably quietly bleating to herself. "I'll wallow over on my side, roll my eyes back in my head, and irritate these idiot humans as much as I can. They'll think I've croaked and will feel guilty." I'm sure she was entertaining herself, silently chuckling even as I was tugging on her limp carcass.

With a little difficulty, Ronnie and I finally extracted the irritating ovine from underneath my vehicle.

"She ain't dead, is she?" Ronnie asked. She did seem mighty quiet.

"Naw, she's breathing. Sit her up on her side and let's see what she'll do." Her lamb was about two terraces over, hollering like he'd never heard of the word *sull.*

She must have just been semisulling, because at the sound of her lamb's voice she sprang to her feet and beelined it in his direction, barely limping or swaying in the hind end.

Ronnie looked at me through slitted eyes and gritted his teeth. "Why did you run over my sheep, Doc? She's my best one!"

Why is the animal that I'm always fooling with the farmer's "best" one? It's always his "best" cow, even though she hasn't had a calf since the Korean War. It's always his best sheep, even though she produces a knotty lamb every other year and her fleece is the quality of drought-stricken oat straw.

"I didn't try to run over her, Ronnie. You know better than that," I replied.

"Yeah, sure. She just ran right into your old truck," he sneered.

"That's exactly what she did! It wasn't my fault! Besides, you were up at the corral fiddlin' around with that old gap."

"Well, just forget about it. Let's try to get around her and get her to the pen," he exclaimed.

"Heck no," I yelled. "Leave her alone. Let's get what we have. I've wasted too much time already!"

Reluctantly, he agreed, but he couldn't help looking back over his shoulder as we drove back up the hill toward the corral. He was muttering and mumbling under his breath, saying rather unkind things about the escapee and how she would be on the next truck to the abattoir when and if he did get her corralled.

As the pen full of sheep came into view, my first thought was that the group appeared smaller than it should have been. It looked more like 58 sheep, rather than 798. Then I saw the collapsed gap on the opposite end of the pen and sheep streaming down the driveway, some walking, others running. Even though I couldn't hear a thing over the racket of the truck I knew they all were bleating out sheep freedom slogans to each other.

When Ronnie spotted the breakout, he bolted from the truck in a full run, shakily yelling all sorts of orders, all of them having to do with halting, stopping, or retreating. But it was too late, since at least 400 of them were already out on the main road, heading toward town. When I stopped the vehicle and turned off the ignition, I could hear horns honking and diesel trucks gearing down.

"Why? Why do I keep getting in these messes?" I asked myself as I trotted way behind Ronnie, trying to figure out what to do. He was now galloping parallel to the driveway fence like an Olympic sprinter, kicking up little puffs of red dust each time his worn-out tennis shoes scratched the cloddy earth. He was gaining on the second wave of ovines when he suddenly scissored over the fence and skidded to a stop at driveway's end, then turned and faced the sheep in a typical gunfighter's stance.

"Uh oh," the sheep all appeared to be saying as they stopped in mid-trot, mid-bleat, and mid-chew. "Now we've had it. The man's mad!"

The face-off continued while Ronnie was gasping for air and trying to look mean.

"Bring a bucket, Doc!" he puffed, cupping his hands around his mouth megaphone style.

Some two or three minutes later, I handed him an empty five-gallon plastic bucket. He immediately commenced slapping his hand vigorously on the side of the bucket and making sheeplike noises.

It appeared to work, since each time he slapped all the sheep bleated in unison, kind of like the responsive reading at a Methodist church service. Each ovine nose was pointed in the direction of the suddenly beloved shepherd; each set of eyes was riveted onto the magic bucket as if under a hypnotic spell. Even the large group that was headed for the nearby cold drink mart had heard the news, reversed its direction, and headed back up the driveway as if its members had just been identified as lottery winners and the bucket man had the dough.

I couldn't believe it! Ronnie was awash in a sea of wooly creatures as he held the bucket high overhead and walked unsteadily amongst them, attempting to get them back into the corral. Surely one faulty step and he'd be trampled underneath thousands of knifelike hooves.

Minutes later, the entire mob had raced back into the pen through the west gap and were again trapped. Even the old "hit-by-truck" ewe was bleating at the east gap, begging to be admitted to the meeting.

"Gotta say I'm impressed," I told Ronnie. "Never thought I'd see that pen full again this day."

"I reckon it proves you can catch more flies with sugar than with vinegar," replied Ronnie. "I call it bucket psychology."

Folks who consider themselves experienced lifelong "cow-hands" are puzzled when they first try to work sheep. Ovines don't respond well to being driven, nor do they respect a speeding truck, but they do stick together for the most part, and they are almost hypnotized by a banging bucket and a familiar voice. Occasionally, I wish cows were as smart as sheep. Not often, just occasionally.

~

The purpose of Ronnie's ovine roundup was to deworm the flock, vaccinate the lambs, and trim feet. Also, there were a few late-born lambs who needed their tails removed in order to prevent their rear ends from getting excessively soiled, which would invite blowfly attack. Ewes needed their eyes, teeth, udders, and general health quickly checked to be sure they were vigorous enough to remain in the flock for another year.

To say that sheep need a preventative health program would be an understatement. No animal, other than the human, needs to have such an intensive, ongoing health program. The fact is, there are textbooks chock-full of descriptions of sheep diseases, the names of which are essentially unpronounceable and which are usually undiagnosable except on postmortem examination. To be blunt, a sheep is a pathologist's dream but a practicing veterinarian's nightmare, unless all these diseases are kept under control.

"Sick sheep seldom survive," Carney Sam Jenkins had declared one day in his daily seminar to the regular store sitters at Mrs. Ruby McCord's General Store and Serv. Sta. "A sheep is born lookin' for a place to die."

Carney's comment about sick sheep seldom surviving had some validity. Sheep possess a natural flocking instinct greater than that of most other animals, and this flocking instinct keeps them tightly within the group, even when they are seriously ill. The shepherd may not observe any signs of illness until the disease has advanced beyond a treatable stage. Most other animals tend to isolate themselves when sick or giving birth.

I have long held the opinion that there are several chores in which all people should be forced to participate before they are privileged to benefit from the "good life." Chores such as cutting off fence rows, catching a few thousand broilers out of a dusty henhouse, cutting pulpwood for a week in August in a south Alabama pine woods, and hand-picking cotton for a spell on rocky terrain, just to list a few. Deworming a flock of sheep and trimming their feet should be added to this list.

If it were just a matter of asking the wooly patients to open their mouths for a couple of short shots of a somewhat objectionable worm-slaying potion, then it wouldn't be a chore at all. But sheep simply don't want their mouths messed with, so when the deworming gun approaches the proximity of their cheeks, they cease bleating and then pretend to have a severe case of lockjaw. In addition to the fake lockjaw, their wool coats are wet in the winter, hot in the summer, and covered with dozens of needlelike cockleburs in the fall, all of which makes for a mighty uncomfortable experience when wading in amongst the animals and wrestling with them for an hour or two.

Trimming sheep feet is an exercise that requires the animal to be flipped up in such a manner that she is sitting on her hind end, Buddha fashion. Naturally, she is just as annoyed with this procedure as she was with the mouth-handling experience, so she engages in all sorts of wiggling and struggling in an effort to return to a normal four-legs-on-the-ground position. Fortunately, an experienced and tight-lipped sheep thrower can usually convince a sheep that it is in her best interest to remain quiet while receiving her pedicure. If the feet are not trimmed at least yearly, especially in the southern United States, the claws grow long and troublesome and the animal has difficulty walking. Long, overgrown hooves also predispose sheep to contagious foot rot, a disease that causes severe lameness and can occur in epidemic proportions.

I was glad to see that Ronnie had two hired hands present, Ed and Calvin, to assist with the work that morning. Unfortunately, both of the pool room–inhabiting teenagers had soft, lily-white hands that had never even heard of palm calluses, nor had their eyes ever gazed upon sheep before, except for some pictures in the Sunday school literature down at the Free Will Baptist Church.

I quickly gathered my deworming and foot-trimming paraphernalia and vaulted over the fence into the waving sea of wooly creatures. Ronnie followed suit and immediately captured the first sheep to demonstrate to Ed and Calvin exactly what they were supposed to do.

"Git on in here, boys. They won't bite!" announced Ronnie. When the two started looking for a gate rather than climbing over the fence, I knew then it would have been better to have left them in town shooting billiards. Sometimes it's easier to just do it yourself rather than have slow-witted, inert hands standing around in the way.

While Ronnie did most of the catching, I did all of the yelling at Ed and Calvin.

"Grab that sheep, Ed! Don't let her get away!" I hollered.

"Let's go, Calvin, don't stand there pickin' your nose! Time's awastin'!" Ronnie yelled.

"Doc, you got some of that worm medicine on my hand, will it hurt me?" cried Ed as he tried to wipe the green stuff off on a sheep's hide.

"Naw, it might even help you to shoot pool better!" I declared. "Reckon you're wormy?"

"What? I ain't got worms!"

"How do you know? I heard there's a fellow over in Mississippi had a big tapeworm ten feet long in his small intestines. The doctor said they'd have to use sheep-worming medicine on him, and it might kill 'im or it might cure 'im."

"What happened?" asked Ed, still scraping wormer off his arm.

"Oh, he lived. He's gained fifty pounds!" Ronnie testified.

I kept my head down and worked fast so I wouldn't burst out laughing about the tapeworm and sheep drench tale.

Actually, the green dewormer was called phenothiazine and it had little or no tapeworm-killing properties. But it was mildly irritating to humans, especially to redheads and others with sensitive skin. It seemed that every time I dewormed a group of cows or sheep with the product, the backs of my hands and my face turned bright red from the phenothiazine fumes. Then the skin would flake off and the itching would commence. I often wondered if the mucosa of a sheep stomach became as uncomfortable as my forehead.

Sometime later the last sheep was dewormed, and we all stood upright for the first time in the last hour or two and observed the antics of the sheep. Some were slinging their heads and licking their lips in a full frown, while others were trying to nibble at grass under the fence in order to get the bad taste out of their mouths.

"Awright, you boys, start throwing 'em and trimmin' feet," declared Ronnie, handing each a pair of trimmers that appeared to be tree-pruning shears. "Now, here's how you do it."

With that, Ronnie grabbed the nearest 150-pound ewe around the neck with one hand and flanked her with the other. Then, using his knees as a fulcrum, he lifted her off the ground and quickly balanced her on her hind end. In seconds, the expert sound of shears snipping and clipping excess hard hoof tissue echoed around the corral fences.

Calvin and Ed quietly stared at the proceedings, then stared at each other. I knew they were not at all sure of their ability to successfully duplicate the maneuvers they were witnessing. Presently, Ronnie completed the job, straightened up, and released the sheep, then watched as she scrambled to her feet and angrily butted herself into a mass of her colleagues, quickly blending into the sameness of the crowd — except for the red crayon mark that Ronnie had striped down her back.

"Y'all boys git a sheep, I told you!"

Both boys immediately made tentative advances on the nearest beasts, but they were surprised at how evasive the sheep were, even while packed in tight. Finally, Calvin captured an ancient, slow-moving ram, wrapped his arm around the cooperative animal, and commenced making throwing and grunting movements while tossing his grimacing face backwards with each attempt. Even though the ram was old, worn out, and sick, he weighed at least a hundred pounds more than Calvin.

"You gonna rupture yo' sef!" declared Ed, who had wisely used his common sense by seizing a lightweight yearling lamb as his intended patient.

We all watched and giggled as Calvin's potential patient soon tired of all the hassle and began marching in circles because of his temporary connection to the hapless human being. Suddenly, the clumsy Calvin lost his footing and his carcass disappeared into the furrows of wool — except for his hands, elbows, and knees, which were occasionally bobbing up and down between the squirming wooly coats.

When Ronnie and Ed quickly waded in shooing and shoving sheep apart, they found Calvin on his back with the ram's front feet planted on his chest, and their eyes locked. It was the first time I had witnessed a sheep carry out a throw down.

As Calvin tried to brush off his clothes and empty his pockets of cute little oval-shaped pellets of sheep excrement, he and Ed suddenly realized that they were both late for important engagements in the town of Meridian, some twenty minutes away by hitchhike. After Ronnie handed them a few dollars they sheepishly sauntered out to the farm-to-market road, never looking back. We saw the first truck heading west pass the boys, then suddenly screech to a stop a hundred yards down the road and begin to back up. The boys trotted halfheartedly toward their newfound ride, but from their reaction it was apparent that they were not thrilled about arriving in the big city riding low and uncomfortable in the back of an old bumpy pickup.

"Reckon where they're headed?" I said, throwing a sheep.

"The rasslin' matches," declared Ronnie. "They're always goin', whenever they can hitch a ride."

"They like that fake rassling, do they?"

"Oh yeah, they like it a lot. They believe it's on the level, Doc."

Since it was getting late in the day, we decided to postpone most of the other work and trim feet only on the lame animals. So as we trimmed feet we discussed the work patterns of Ed and Calvin and their colleagues, and how little the general populace knew of agriculture and where the food on their dinner tables came from.

Later, as the sheep filed out the open gate and beelined it to the big pasture, Ronnie came up with the thought of the day.

"Doc, why is it that a lot of folks think rasslin' is real but think that lamb chops and sweet milk magically appear on grocery store shelves?"

I wish I knew! Sometimes it's enough to make a grown man sull!

Six

〜 One of the surprises of practicing veterinary medicine in Choctaw County was the number of hobby livestock people and investor-owned cattle farmers in the area. Many of my new clients were not farmers by any stretch of the imagination, but instead were jewelers, stockbrokers, doctors and dentists, teachers, wealthy retirees from up north, and others who might have good jobs in town but cows in the country. These nonfarmer clients were different from the regular farmer clients who called on me for veterinary service and advice because they listened intently and hung on every word that escaped from my lips.

Sometimes the first call they made to my office was a request for "Dr. McCormack to come out and vaccinate the cattle for everything." Naturally, being a businessman, I complied with their request for a total vaccination program, even some of the vaccine-covered diseases rarely seen in the region. Unfortunately, good management skills don't come packed inside a vaccine bottle, and you cannot purchase an instant package containing the basics of animal husbandry, "cow know-how," and bovine restraint. Those things must be learned the old-fashioned way.

One such client was John Harlow, whom I met at a monthly meeting of the Choctaw County Cattlemen's Association. Since I knew most of the cattlemen, I wondered why I didn't recognize his face and name. But when I shook his hand I knew this man was no cattleman. Anyone with hands that creamy soft did little except handle a telephone and lightly grip the smooth steering wheel of a nice car. I suspected that he even drove with those fancy driving gloves.

"Do you have a farm around here, John?" I asked. "I don't recall ever seeing you at any of our meetings."

"Oh, I'm over west of here, just into Mississippi. Recently bought a two-hundred-acre place just across the county line," he said proudly. "It's part of the old Stanford place." I had not been in the county long enough to know the pedigree of all the farms, so I was not familiar with the location of the Stanford place.

"How many cows do you have over there?"

"None yet, but by next week I'll have fifteen, all with calves at their sides."

"So you are just getting into the business."

"Yes," he said. "I'm a stockbroker with offices in Atlanta and Meridian, but I've been reading a lot about the livestock industry, and I plan to get at least fifty to seventy-five head of good Angus brood cows, breed them to Brahman bulls, and then sell those F-1 crosses to a buyer in Texas." At the time many buyers and ranchers were looking for crossbred cattle, especially those with "a little ear on them." This meant they wanted a little Brahman blood in them, in order to take advantage of the "hybrid vigor" inherent in that line of breeding. Supposedly, hybrid vigor makes cattle more efficient breeders, increases weaning weights, and makes them more robust and disease resistant. These hybrid vigor theories are often vigorously debated wherever livestock people congregate. Cow folks are never bashful when it comes to expressing their opinions.

"I hope you have good fences and a strong, high-planked catch pen."

He didn't seem to understand the meaning of my statement, and that concerned me somewhat. What I was trying to say in an amusing way was that the Brahman influence would also create cattle with a greater tendency toward disorderly conduct. They seem to take delight in jumping fences and demolishing the typical shabby cow-handling facility that would ordinarily contain the native animals of the Hereford, Angus, and piney woods varieties.

"Actually, the primary reason I came tonight was to meet you," he said. "Dr. Carney Sam Jenkins recommended you very highly, and I was hoping that you would agree to be my consulting, as well as working, vet."

"Sure, I'll try to help you any way I can."

"What I thought I'd do would be to send you a check for, say, seven hundred and fifty dollars, and when your fees use up that amount I'll send you another check," he stated in a very professional manner.

I blinked my eyes and pinched my leg to see if I was dreaming! Did he think he was dealing with a lawyer? I'd never heard of a cattleman doing business with a veterinarian in such a fashion, except for some of those fancy white-coveralled vets way up north. But I knew without a doubt that I could adjust to it without any difficulty whatsoever. Perhaps these nonfarmer clients weren't too bad after all.

"Certainly, John. My accountant is setting up our books to more easily accommodate those clients who prefer being on a monthly retainer basis," I allowed with the straightest face I could muster. But I almost choked on the chunk of sirloin I was chewing. I couldn't believe what I was saying, but I congratulated myself for the way I said it. Jan would have choked if she had been there. She *was* the accountant.

"John, I have a question. If you are going to be in town most of the time, who is going to look after the cattle?" Now I was beginning to think like a working vet.

"I have engaged the services of a man named James, who will be a part-time manager, and also two younger men, "Bubbahead" and "Tennessee." One or all three of them will check the cattle daily. James is an old cowhand, and Bubbahead is ox-strong and willing to work hard to learn the livestock business. Tennessee will probably be more useful just opening gates and doing heavy lifting, because his attention span is very short.

They're there putting up cross fences this week, and I just hope they can get those fences up straight."

I wondered why it would take three men to handle a few cows. I reckoned, however, that there would be a good bit of fencing to be done, plus clearing additional land for pasture and putting up hay. For some reason, the thought occurred to me that three men working without owner supervision might be tempted to goof off while on the job, perhaps even participate in the consumption of alcoholic beverages. Perhaps similar situations I'd observed in the past triggered that thought.

About a month later, John asked me to make a call to the farm in order to examine the first load of cattle. He had been regularly using his retainer by calling for consultation, sometimes more than once a day, whenever a question arose in his mind. He was a voracious reader of farm magazines and extension material, and he was a very fast learner.

When I turned off the main road, I observed huge rolling fields of green clover and coastal bermuda, fenced with the latest type of electric fencing. There were several areas of tall pine trees, which were not only aesthetically pleasing but would also provide shade for the cows on the hot summer days. Farther down the hill, I could see a meandering creek, the banks of which were covered with sweet gum, oak, and other shade-giving trees. Working with landowners was giving me a greater and greater appreciation for the land and the things that sprouted from it.

I came back to veterinary reality shortly, however, when I spied what appeared to be a corral of sorts up on the hill, but as I drove closer, it became obvious that the structure was nothing more than a memory of a once-nice cow-handling facility, perhaps fifty or more years old. John was waiting for me there in his new, white, imported sports car. He was wearing weird-looking gloves, just as I had suspected.

"Where are the cows?" I asked, looking around.

"Down in the pasture by the creek," he announced. "Come on, hop in."

Presently we were hurtling down across the field at break-

neck speed, the driver seemingly without any thought concern-
ing the small stumps or sunken stump holes that were certain to
be hidden among the lush grasses. I was holding on to the dash
and door handle for dear life even as I flopped up and down on
the seat, and I wondered if some research professor in France had
ever investigated the possibility that donning expensive driving
gloves leads to driver insanity. However, we escaped serious
injury and soon slid to a stop where three men were stretching a
strand of barbed wire between two posts with an old pickup
truck.

John didn't seem to notice the preponderance of empty
twelve-ounce aluminum cans in the back of the truck, nor the
fence posts that were tamped into the ground at less than the
proper perpendicular setting. But I was sure that something from
those cans was interfering with their fencing performance.

"That's James, Bubbahead, and Tennessee. If they call you for
help, I'd appreciate you helping them out."

When we arrived at the creek minutes later, most of the cows
were keeping cool by standing in the water. They peered up at us
with indifference while contentedly chewing their cuds and
occasionally checking on the location of their offspring. Now and
then a calf practiced a juvenile bawl, which was immediately
echoed by a more mature bellow. They were fine Angus cows, all
nursing calves four to six months of age. John recited each animal's pedigree from a large leather notebook.

"Do you think she's pregnant?" he asked, pointing toward a
particularly nice cow.

"Well, no farther along than she is, I can't tell by looking, you
know," I said with a grin.

"Oh, I thought you told me the other night at the meeting
you could tell for sure if they'd been bred thirty-five days or
more," he stated with some degree of disappointment.

"That's true, but you'll have to put them through a chute so
that I can examine their reproductive tracts," I replied. "I'm sorry
I didn't make that clear."

"Oh, I see. So you can't just do it out here in the field then?"

I tried very diplomatically to explain to John that proper restraint of animals was important for their safety as well as for the safety of the humans doing the work. I promised to send detailed drawings for a corral.

About two weeks later he called and reported that calf number 39-A was lame on her right rear foot, and that James and his associates would meet me at the pasture. I requested that the calf be corralled, but I knew that was wishful thinking on my part.

Turning in at the pasture gate later that afternoon, I observed the fence-stretching pickup and crew down in the middle of the pasture. One of the occupants opened the passenger side door and motioned for me to come that way.

As I approached the truck, a twelve-ounce aluminum can came flying, end over end, out of the truck window. I could see flying droplets of foam being slung out of the hole in the open end, and then I noticed the word *Milwaukee* boldly printed on the side when it came to rest a few feet from my vehicle. I knew that I was in for an interesting event.

"Where's the heifer?" I asked.

Immediately, as I had expected, each of the three occupants grinned and pointed in a different direction. Tennessee hiccupped and then belched loudly, timing the two rude noises just a split second apart. Then he let loose with one of those "I'm-right-proud-of-myself" giggles.

"Doc, we wore ourselves plum out runnin' that fool, and still couldn't get 'er up to the pen. We was hopin' that you could rope 'er up yonder in that thicket," declared James in an almost coherent manner.

"Yeah, when you rope 'er, I'm gonna tho' 'er!" allowed Bubbahead, grinning and with head weaving back and forth. He was also sweating profusely, and the aroma he presented was most unpleasant.

"Bubbahead, that calf's half Brahma and weighs at least four hundred pounds," warned James. "That thing'll half kill you."

"Naw, I'll git 'im."

I knew James was right. A semiwild four-hundred-pound

heifer calf is faster on her feet than a normal human, and a whole lot faster than a human tanked up with response-altering beverages.

After a short search, we located the herd at the back corner of the farm, where they were lounging in the shade of several red oak trees and chewing their cuds. We angled both vehicles into the fence as sort of a makeshift pen, and I crept up into the crowd with lariat ready. Luckily, the loop fell right over the head of 39-A on the first try.

The heifer was up like a shot, however, and commenced bucking and bellowing as if the end of the world was on the other end of that rope. I quickly encircled a tree with my end, just as my beery-breathed helpers arrived and took over. Finally, the four of us were able to get the patient close enough to the tree for our calf wrestler to do his bulldogging trick.

"Go to it, Bubbahead!" hollered James. "She's all yours."

Immediately the unsteady but determined young man fell upon 39-A as if he were a blanket. Unfortunately for him, the smart beast saw what was coming and quickly used her nonlame rear foot to pop her attacker twice in the right kneecap before he could react or even figure out what had happened. The two loud cracking noises did not discourage him from his assault, but instead seemed to make him more determined than ever. But they made me wince, because bovine kicks to the knee area are painfully "hot."

Now the calf was breathing heavy, raspy breaths and bellowing loudly with tongue lolled out while jumping up and around in the manner of an enraged rodeo bull. Poor old Bubbahead was hanging on but was being tossed around as if he were tied to an out-of-control pogo stick. He was trying to get a flank hold but couldn't because of the slippery antics of the patient.

"Git 'im! Git 'im!" slurred a spectating Tennessee. "Don't let that lil' ole calf whup you!" But I noticed that his cheerleading efforts were being conducted at a safe distance from the violent activity.

"Grab 'im by the leg!" cried James.

Dust was flying and chunks of denim cloth were being

tossed around into the air like confetti. Actually, Bubbahead was being stripped of his clothing by the continuous churning of the knifelike hooves of the young calf. All of a sudden, a belt buckle zipped past my left ear, and I saw a leather belt disappear like a writhing snake in the dirt under the combatants. Bubbahead's pants quickly hit his feet as if jerked downwards by a giant rubber band. His shirt was stripped of all its buttons, the buttonholes had been ripped out, and the tail looked as if a first grader had attacked it with a large pair of shears.

Finally, accompanied by a throaty yell, the calf was hurled to the ground with a dull thud, with Bubbahead, molasseslike, sprawled atop the confused beast. Both were utterly exhausted, exhibiting the same frantic breathing and having the same wild look in their eyes.

"Do yo' work, Mr. Doc," hoarsely whispered Bubbahead. "I got 'im now."

I quickly examined the sore foot, applied my homemade foot rot concoction, injected an antibiotic, and got out of the way.

"Let her go!" I yelled.

The patient scrambled to her feet and was soon flying down the side of the hill, in spite of being "three-legged-lame." The three men then turned their attention toward Bubbahead, who was totally without clothing from the waist down, and because of the tattered condition of his shirt, he wasn't much better up there. His legs were covered with bruises and the kind of deep scrapes that burn unmercifully. There were several imprints of the calf's hooves on his legs, rivulets of blood were flowing from his forearms and the backs of both hands, and there was a knot the size of a pullet egg in the middle of his forehead.

"Are you hurt, Bubbahead?" I asked. I immediately thought about what a silly question that was.

"Naw. Why?" I then noticed that his eyes weren't focusing properly. I didn't know whether it was from the trauma or the alcohol. I had noticed the stout stench of rotgut whiskey sweat and the unmistakable aroma of clothing that had not been removed from an unwashed body for at least a month. Like many of the poor laborers I have known and worked with, Bub-

bahead rarely changed clothes. Instead, he just molted his garments, in the same manner a laying hen loses her feathers.

"Well, you're kinda beat up. Reckon we better get you to the
doctor?"

"Naw, I ain't goin' to no doctor," he allowed. "They scare me
to death with all them needles and stuff."

"You're gonna be mighty sore tomorrow," warned James.
"I'll bet you'll be asking for some pain dope then."

Sure enough, when the painkilling effects of the alcohol wore
off late that night, Bubbahead was transported to the emergency room for treatment of his multiple injuries. But the nurses
wouldn't let him inside their treatment room until he had been
semifumigated with a garden hose at the ambulance garage.
They thought he had been in a terrible highway crash or had
encountered a band of professional ruffians at a state line
roadhouse.

Something good did come out of the 39-A incident. After
paying Bubbahead's hospital bill, John built a fine new catch pen,
complete with squeeze chute, cut gates, and funneling fences.
From then on, it was a pleasure for me to work the cattle on that
farm. However, I don't think that James and Tennessee enjoyed
themselves quite as much as before. Sometimes they were even
completely sober and acted completely normal.

I never saw Bubbahead on the farm again. Someone said he'd
claimed medical disability and was working part-time in the
back of a liquor store somewhere in Mississippi. That was handy,
because it put him much closer to what he loved the most.

My association with so-called rich city slickers, such as John
and others, proved that, regardless of their level of "cow sense,"
they really could become excellent cattle raisers. They want to
know as much about their new farms as possible and therefore
leave no stone unturned in seeking out that information. They
are usually voracious readers of farm magazines and extension
pamphlets, and will phone professional livestock specialists for
their advice. And they take the advice of their local veterinarian.
It's called protecting your investment.

Seven

⌒ The phone was ringing with increasing frequency each day at our new clinic, much to our relief. Not that we were delighted with finding out about ill or injured animals, but that the citizenry was recognizing our financial commitment to a needed community service and their responsibility to the health of their pets and livestock.

It is obviously necessary for the phone to ring regularly if a practitioner is going to stay in business. Starting a new business venture of any kind in new territory is always a gamble, and it takes gumption and enthusiasm — and the timing has to be right — for it to succeed. Jan and I felt like we had those three items covered, but we were still going on a lot of hope and blind faith. We hoped the phone would ring and we had faith that it would. We knew that convenient veterinary service was unavailable in the county, unless you counted Carney Sam Jenkins and the several other homemade veterinarians who were part-time practitioners. They tried to help their neighbors and did the best they could, but without formal training on animal diseases and surgery, there were so many things they didn't know. And as livestock became more valuable and pets took on the role of highly regarded companions, people expected accurate diagnoses and a treatment plan more substantial than splitting cow tails, lampblack on dog wounds, and turpentine on the navels of colicky horses.

One of the more frequent phone calls we received was a request for assistance with a coughing dog.

"Is this the veterinary speaking?"

"Yes, it is. May I help you?"

"Yeah, I got this dog that's coughin' an' gaggin', and I was just wonderin' if you could tell me what to do for 'im," was the typical response. The urgency of the request always seemed to be directly proportional to the lateness of the hour. If a call came in during daylight hours the purpose was usually to obtain a free and quick one-word diagnosis and the name of some inexpensive, sure-cure medication available from the feed, drug, or hardware store that would quickly put an end to the family's misery. It was apparent that the dog's coughing was disturbing the peace of the household, and often that was more important to the caller than the actual health of the pet.

When the canine coughing disturbed a family's sleep, the call might come in at any hour of the night, but the preferred time seemed to be from eleven P.M. to one A.M. This would be an urgent request for the dog to be seen immediately, and the owner would declare the poor dog was racked with pain and would surely be a corpse in just hours if not treated. Of course, the feed, drug, and hardware stores were all closed at that hour, so hauling the vet out of bed was the only available option.

"Well, why don't you give him two teaspoons of cough syrup and call me about seven in the morning," I drowsily suggested one Saturday night. "Then we'll take a look at him just before you go to church."

"Oh, he's plum bad off. I don't think he'll make it that long, 'cause I'm afraid he's got a chicken bone hung in his goozle," was the predictable reply. I could hear an annoying moist coughing in the background and the voices of children who should have drifted into dreamland hours before. The cough was definitely not a chicken-bone-in-the-goozle cough. Even though the sound was being transmitted over miles of telephone wire, I was sure the poor dog's problem was located deeper in the chest cavity.

"Besides, I've got somethin' else I gotta do in the mornin'," the owner concluded. "I can be over there in ten minutes." I then understood the true urgency for the emergency call. He was going fishing, golfing, or hunting in the morning and wouldn't have time to fool with the dog then. It was a lot more convenient for him to inconvenience a stranger than to have a dog and a stranger inconvenience him. Trying to remember that my profession was one of service, I slowly hauled myself out of bed, put on my working clothes, and drove the mile to the clinic, all the time thinking about how nice it would have been to have an emergency veterinary clinic in town.

An hour or so later, an old dented-up, muddy, and mufflerless Jeep thundered into the peace and quiet of the little community and pulled into the gravel driveway of the clinic.

"I guess the neighbors have all been jarred awake," I mumbled to myself. Several who lived nearby, but weren't dog and cat enthusiasts, mentioned to Jan how odd it was to hear trucks coming in at all hours of the night, frequently hauling barking or coughing dogs.

"Why, this is just like living next door to the hospital, except there's no sirens," one neighbor had said. "How come folks aren't in the bed asleep at midnight, instead of fooling with their dogs?" I wondered why, too. But persistent late-night noises, such as loud rasping coughs and fits of floor-thumping scratching, seem to last for an eternity when one is lying flat on one's back, hopelessly insomnolent. It's no wonder the owners were furiously dialing the sleepy vet.

Minutes later the dog was on the exam table, surrounded by a disheveled vet, three small children, and a mama and poppa in their mid-twenties.

"What's wrong with your puppy here, young man?" I asked the oldest child. He was about seven, the other two not much less.

"Daddy said he's got a chicken bone hung up in his goozle," he replied. I noticed all three of the kids had runny noses and grime-stained faces. *Goozle* means "throat," and it is one of those words that always makes me want to laugh. Sort of like the words *guffaw* and *corruption*. I bit my lower lip and stifled a giggle.

"What's his name?" I asked, rubbing my hands over the crossbred cocker spaniel's dry black hair. He was halfheartedly wagging his tail.

"Rover," one quickly replied.

"What an unusual name," I declared, trying to be amusing. No one smiled but me. "And how old is he?" I noticed the hair on his muzzle was gray and his eyes were showing signs of cataracts. He didn't attempt to bite when I lifted his lips and peeked at his nubby teeth.

"He's around eighteen year old, I guess," answered the man. "My granddaddy gave him to me when I was in the second or third grade." Some folks never put an *s* on the word *year*.

"That's pretty old for a dog. Has he ever been sick before?" I asked.

"Naw, not that we know of," replied the wife. It was the first thing she'd uttered. But then she clammed up. I fiddled with my stethoscope, killing a little time, knowing full well that the silence would cease once I had the earpieces in my ears and was trying to listen to the interior of the thorax. Sure enough, as soon as I began my chest examination I started to hear bits and pieces of the conversation in between lung and heart sounds.

"When did you…chicken bones?"

"…last Tuesday."

"Remember last summer…car hit him?"

"…gave him them worm pills."

But when I removed the earpieces, the room again became silent, except for the heavy breathing of the dog. I knew that if I again tried to use the stethoscope, the talking would recommence. It must be a game, just to see how much the vet can hear all at once.

"I'm afraid he has heart trouble," I declared, prying open Rover's mouth. "See, there's no chicken bone down there." Everybody tried to look, as if I surely had erred in my diagnosis.

"I woulda swore he had a bone in 'nere," declared Daddy. "What's wrong with 'im then?"

"I'm afraid he has heart trouble," I repeated, trying to pronounce the words just right.

"HEART TROUBLE! I didn't know dogs had heart trouble!"

"Oh, yes, especially old dogs. Old Rover here is like a hundred-year-old man," I pronounced. "He has what we call congestive heart failure. His heart isn't strong enough to pump his blood effectively, and that's causing congestion in his lungs. That's why he's coughing so much."

"I never heard of such! Do dogs have heart attacks?" Mama asked.

"Sometimes they do, but most of the time their hearts just keep getting weaker until everything else fails," I said.

The boys were wide-eyed, partly because of the diagnosis, but mostly because of all the instruments, the medicine on the shelves, and the stethoscope.

"That heart hearer thing is just like the one that real doctor uses over at the hospital," I heard one of the kids whisper to the others. I handed the older of the three the stethoscope.

"Want to listen to your heart?" I suggested. That would keep them occupied for a few minutes.

"Is there anything you can do?"

"Yes, we need to get him on some heart pills and a diuretic. We can't cure it, but we can make what time he's got left a lot more comfortable."

"Yeah, my granddaddy's got the same problem and he's on them pills. When he takes that diabetic pill, it makes him run off at the kidneys real bad."

"Well, it's called a diuretic, and it gets rid of all that extra fluid that builds up in his lungs," I asserted. "Is Rover an inside dog?"

"Uh huh. Is it gonna make his kidneys run off?"

"Yes sir, it will. So you'll need to let him out more frequently or he's liable to mess up the floor."

"We'll figure out something. I might just put him in the shed."

"Naw, Daddy, please. I'll walk him a lot. Don't put him out there in the shed!" begged the older child. The other two were busy pretending to be veterinarians.

I counted out the medication and made some suggestions about how to get the pills down old Rover. Soon they were headed out the door toward the truck.

"Heart trouble? I can't believe it! I would have swore that dog had a chicken bone hung in his goozle!"

Ten minutes later, I was back home and quietly easing into bed, trying not to awaken Jan.

"What was it, honey?" she asked.

"Oh, I'm sorry, I didn't want to disturb you," I whispered. "It was a coughing dog with a heart problem. I think I fixed him up, at least temporarily."

"That's good. Nighty-night."

"Good night, dear."

I laid there in the dark, thinking about all the coughing dogs I had seen since vet school, and I thought it was strange that over half the time the owner was certain the dog had a chicken bone hung in his throat. I decided there were two questions I would someday like to ask an expert veterinary psychologist who specialized in canine coughing.

First, why is it that folks with a coughing dog always just know for sure that the cougher has a chicken bone hung in his throat? Why isn't it ever a fish bone, or a small screwdriver, or a piece of plow line, or a small child's toy? Anything but a chicken bone.

Second, I'd like to ask that psychologist to explain why the coughing always gets worse as the midnight hour approaches, especially if it's Friday or Saturday. I suspect that it is due to the same force that causes equines to suffer from colic more often between midnight and one A.M. and cows to experience breech births during Wednesday evening choir practice.

I wondered if canine psychologists might someday be available for consultation. Would they use a couch, and hypnotize dogs? What else did the future hold for the profession of veterinary medicine? Would people actually take their dogs to a veterinary dentist? What about funerals for dogs, cats, birds, and other unusual pets? I could just see some vets I knew becoming veterinary morticians, funeral directors, and grief counselors. Maybe I'd become a respiratory specialist, working only a couple of hours every night. Then I'd play golf every day. I would have laughed out loud, but I didn't want to shake the bed.

~

It was only hours later when my next throat case surfaced, and it altered my dogmatic view about dogs' never having bones hung in their throats.

"Doc, I'm gonna let you take a look at an old dog with a bone hung in this throat," a know-it-all aluminum siding salesman said on the phone the following Sunday afternoon. Naturally, he had called just as the football game came on.

"I'll be happy to examine him, but I'm sure there is no bone in there," I retorted, somewhat peeved at his arrogance.

"Well, he ain't been able to eat for a week," he said. "I got some penicillum from the drugstore and gave him a shot of it last night, but he still can't get anything down. Dr. McCormack, I wouldn't take a five-hundred-dollar bill for him."

An hour later his son drove up in a clean, used Dodge pickup with dealer tags on it. In the back was a lemon-and-white bird dog that appeared to be somewhere between "pretty pore" and emaciated.

"Where's your daddy?" I asked the young man as I patted the beast's head. "Didn't he come along?"

"Aw, he wanted to watch the football game, so he made me do it," he allowed, obviously bored and put out.

The dog was holding his head straight out, his pharynx was swollen, and his jaw was dropped. I was concerned about dumb rabies, so I slipped on some gloves and attempted to pry his mouth open. He reacted in pain, and I caught a glimpse of a huge foreign body deep in his throat. The odor was terrible.

After a little pentothal and much prying and pulling, I was successful in extracting a large swine cervical vertebra from the poor dog's pharyngeal area.

"I'd better keep King here a day or two," I ordered. "That throat's in bad shape and he's gonna need some treatment. Tell your daddy I'll call him."

"Daddy ain't gon' like this," the boy said weakly. "He don't believe in spendin' money on no dog."

At this point, I flew hot. I think there are times when the great keepers of the temper book are willing to forgive a minor flare-up of hotheadedness. I've also noticed that those who are burdened with more than the standard issue of gumption and take their jobs seriously seem to get written up in the book much more frequently than do those who have a gumption deficiency.

With hands trembling and face hot, I attacked the defenseless telephone and viciously dialed the number of the dog's owner. Presently, a sweet-voiced lady answered on the other end.

"May I speak with Cyrus, please?" I asked with nostrils flared, but still in control of the smoldering rage inside.

"Boy, I'm gonna bore this idiot's hollow horn," I muttered to myself. "Anybody who'd let a nice bird dog get in this shape needs his horns sawed off — without anesthesia!"

"Oh, hi, Dr. McCormack," Cyrus said a few seconds later, "so good of you to call. I appreciate it more than you know, you taking the time to see King on a Sunday afternoon and —"

"Well, he had this huge bone hung in his throat," I said, still moderately steamed.

"Oh my, I was afraid of that," he exclaimed. "That dog actually belongs to my father. Papa's crippled up bad with the rheumatism up on the mountain, you know, and he can't see after his animals like he should. I went up there yesterday and found old King in this shape."

"The man is actually trying to be civil," I thought. "Guess I'll put the dehorners down." I was breathing slower now.

"Yeah, I started to call you last night about midnight when I got home, but I knew you would be asleep, so I went ahead and gave him the penicillum. Actually, John, I wouldn't take a thousand-dollar-bill for this old dog."

I thought I could hear sniffling noises being transmitted into my ear from the other end.

"Well, I'm glad you sent him on in when you did. Even though he's mighty sick, I think he'll be all right, but I need to keep him a few days."

"Anything you say," he agreed, "you're the good doctor! By the way, do me a favor. Give him a worm treatment while you have him there. I figure he'll weigh about a hundred and fifty pounds."

"Sure will," I replied.

"Another thing, John. Could you put that chicken bone in a jar for me? I know you see dogs every day like this, but I want to show it to Papa."

"Sure will," I repeated, and then hung up the phone, shaking my head. Now I had items three and four to add to my list for the canine psychologist.

Item three has to do with the financial appraisal of the dog. Frequently, the initial call indicates the dog is worth five hundred dollars. But once the diagnosis is established, the value escalates. Or if the dog dies, the value skyrockets. Why is that?

Fourth, it seems like a lot of dogs weigh 150 pounds, according to their masters. It takes a lot of canine flesh to weigh that much. Perhaps an expensive, coughing dog at night just feels heavier.

I often think about the perceived value of dogs and other pets. Rover, for instance, obviously had no value as a hunting, working, or guard dog. Yet, a dollar value cannot be set on the emotional bond between Rover and his family, and to suggest such would be foolish. It has been shown that the mental well-being of humans is greatly influenced by the companionship of pets. On the other hand, King was a working bird dog, probably with a long pedigree, and his value could easily be established in the sporting dog marketplace.

Sometimes it is a little difficult for a large animal practitioner to make the change into small animal practice without having to make adjustment in animal value. On the farm, livestock have a dollar value, and all decisions regarding veterinary treatment have to be weighed against that sale value. If it can be shown that a certain surgery or vaccination can positively influence the production of the individual or the herd, then the owner may elect to carry out that procedure. It must be cost-efficient. But when that practitioner returns to his small animal clinic and dons that clean white coat, the economics change. Maybe that's why a general practice is never boring.

Eight

〜 Country vets spend a lot of time on the road traveling to, from, and between farm calls, which provides a lot of time for thought. On my way home from an especially rough day of roping cows in dilapidated pens and being jostled around in stalls full of cattle, I began to think about a better way of restraining cattle for veterinary procedures. The rough-and-tumble, near-rodeo methods that I had been using were eventually going to cause an injury, perhaps not only to me, but to the cattle, one of the workers, or one of the frequently present know-it-all bystanders.

At the last two stops of the day there had been one such alleged know-it-all by the name of Safford, and after watching him in action for a couple of hours, I was almost convinced that having someone around like him was necessary for working cattle. There was nothing he didn't know, especially in the world of cows. He had an answer for any question, whether it was on foreign affairs or the present state of the sugarcane crop in south Louisiana.

"Yap, I've done this myself, many a time," he bragged as I dehorned a yearling heifer. "Ain't nothin' to it, long as the sign's right." Most farmers in that area wouldn't think of dehorning, castrating, or performing any elective surgical procedure on their animals unless the stage of the moon or the sign of the zodiac was prechecked in the almanac. That was fine with me, just as long as the sign was right for getting paid.

"Yap, I've had to help break in young veterans before," he bragged. "I helped Doc Williams over yonder in Waynesboro get started and now he's one of the richest men in town. Drives a big car and works out there in that big, fancy dog hospital." Then he went into a lengthy dissertation about the proper way to treat red mange in the canine species, how to trim bulldogs' ears, and why it's necessary to let female dogs have a few litters of puppies before they are spayed. "Yap, I'm sort of a veterinary myself, you know. Took a course on veterinary once."

"Really? Where was that, at Auburn?" I asked.

"Well, it wasn't no real vet course, you see, sort of a cattlemen's meeting over in Waynesboro put on by the county agent. He told us how to cut calves." That's what I'd figured. But I knew that he had some good information, so I tried to listen carefully to what he said as I hurried through my job of testing the cows.

"You know Carney Sam Jenkins?" I asked while checking the teeth on a cow.

"Yap, taught him ever'thing he knows about cows," he replied proudly. That's what I'd figured. "Don't see him much anymore. We kinda fell out with one another about how to treat the hollertail."

"Oh, is that right?" I perked up my ears. I always wanted to hear a treatment variation on this so-called folklore disease.

"Yap, he wanted to use black pepper after he split that cow's tail, but any fool knows you have to use red! At least that's what I was taught down here. Maybe he learned a different way when he got up there in the north end of the county. But he's wrong." I smiled to myself, just thinking about the two guys in a heated argument about which color of pepper to use on a sick cow's tail. My stern vet school professors would have had a fit, and probably would have flunked out any student who even mentioned the word *hollertail*. But I found myself wishing they had at least mentioned that we new graduates would be faced with the belief in such outlandish diseases and treatments. I was brought back to the present by a question.

"How old is that cow, Doc?" asked another of the bystanders.

"Looks like she may be old enough to vote," I declared. "Take a gander at the nubs she's got for teeth." Five men instantly bent over and stuck their seed-corn-capped heads down within inches of the elderly bovine's mouth as I held her by the nose with one hand and peeled her lower lip down with the other. The patient had her mouth gaped open, baby-bird style. Had a normal town-person passed along the road and observed the odd sight of a group of men peering down into the gaped-open mouth of a cow, it would no doubt have stuck in the "strange" category of his memory bank for life.

"No wonder she's so po'," stated Safford. But his mind was stuck on a different subject. "Yap, what you need to do, young feller, is get you one of them squeeze chutes on wheels to pull from farm to farm and handle these here cattle. You gonna get yourself hurt rasslin' around with wild cows, especially when you get on up the road around Needham and Gilbertown. Yap, that'll be just the ticket for you. Yap, I helped Doc Williams get his'n." I noticed that he started most of his pronouncements with "Yep," but from his lips it sounded like "Yap." I found myself calling him "Safford the Yapper" — in the privacy of my own mind, of course.

By the time I had pulled into my driveway, I had decided to take the Yapper's advice. I would not only purchase a chute, but I would also encourage the cattle owners in the county to construct better handling facilities. It would help in carrying out the program, as well as providing a place for them to more easily perform the routine chores that need to be done, such as vaccinations, dewormings, and so on. I knew this idea would be met with resistance from some of the cattlemen, especially those who resented anyone telling them what they ought to do. But I'd tell them that the notion came from both the Yapper and Carney Sam, and that way it would be a lot more palatable, since it came from someone who was a native.

"I'm gonna get a portable squeeze chute, if I can find one for a reasonable price," I told Jan that night as I ate my late supper.

"I'm so glad!" she said enthusiastically. "I've been so worried about you getting badly hurt out there. Also, maybe you can get through testing quicker and get home before dark. You'll have more time for me and the kids."

It was true that I didn't spend nearly enough time with my family. I frequently left the house before they got out of bed and arrived home after they were asleep. Jan and I both wanted to be busy, but for the past several months there had been more work than we'd bargained for.

After a few phone calls, I located a handyman three counties over to the east who had built a chute for a respected colleague and classmate, Dr. "Whip" Wilson. Whip was pleased with his, and called the handyman for me.

His design was simple. The chute was built over an axle and two-wheel chassis, and was about ten feet in length, which was long enough to accommodate two full-grown cows, one behind the other. The sides were made of two-inch by twelve-inch treated pine lumber, and they were angled in a funnel shape, eighteen inches wide at the bottom but widening to thirty inches at the top. The "head gate" was also made of the same type boards as the sides, stationary at the bottom but opening up at the top to make a large V into which the cow would put her head, to be caught by the operator. To close the head gate, the operator had only to yank down hard on the rope, which was attached to a vertical metal bar, some cables, and a turnbuckle. But it was necessary that this action be done at the precise time the curious cow stuck her head between the two upright boards; otherwise the cow would force her shoulders through and escape. Also, when pulling on the rope, the operator had to avoid serious injury by being sure his head wasn't in the line of descent of the metal bar.

Most other chutes on the market were made of steel, with vertical metal rods along the sides. But once the cows started into the new wooden chute, they could see daylight and potential escape only at the front part, nothing out the solid sides. The design was reported to work well when backed up to the partially opened door of a barn full of cattle.

It took only a month of part-time work for the craftsman to construct my chute. On a Sunday the four of us drove over near the town of Evergreen in Jan's station wagon to trailer it back home. It also gave us an opportunity to visit Dr. Wilson and his family. While he and I talked about the practice of our profession, which was the standard conversation whenever veterinarians met, our wives shared information on how to get green stains out of coveralls and T-shirts and other female spouse discussion that was characteristic of the early 1960s. In the 1990s these spousal discussion roles are frequently reversed. The ladies are talking about their veterinary practices while the men exchange recipes and ideas for handling childhood misbehavior. That day all the children had a great time chasing each other through the yard, and I'm sure they compared notes in their juvenile ways about their fathers and the animals they doctored.

But the socializing was over way too soon, and before long we were on our way back to Choctaw County, the car accelerating a little slowly because my new toy was being towed behind. As we became accustomed to the chute's being close behind us, Jan and I talked about the visit that day with another veterinary family, and even though we had made many friends in Choctaw County, it was great to be with others who shared our unusual means of livelihood. I especially enjoyed our independent lifestyle, but I frequently longed for the professional company of another veterinarian, with whom I could consult on difficult cases or reminisce about those difficult vet school courses, not to mention share emergency and Sunday duty.

∼

The next morning I drove back and forth through town several times with the chute trailing behind my truck, just showing off the new contraption and killing a little time before my first appointment with the meanest herd of Brahman cattle in south Choctaw County. I intended to give the wonderful convenience a stiff test the first day. I was going to show those cattle owners how cattle should be handled.

I waved, tooted the horn, and grinned as I passed Choctaw Drug Store, Doggett Hardware, and the people standing on the east steps of the courthouse, waiting for the doors to open. They scratched their heads and peered back and forth at each other, wondering what kind of combat equipment was arriving in town. I threw up my hand when I passed by the barbershop, intentionally going real slow so the traffic light would turn red just as I arrived. Turning my head, I could see both Myatt and Chappell, along with their caped customers, standing at the window, pointing their scissors and straight razors in my direction. One of the customers was so interested in the sight out on the street that he had jumped from the chair half shaven, one half of his face profusely lathered with Chappell's shaving cream. I knew then that my early morning tour of the town square and business area was a complete success; by nightfall the barbershop information networking system would have dispatched the news of Doc's new thingamajig throughout the county and into portions of adjacent counties. I was constantly in awe of the news dissemination power of Chappell's barbershop!

With my mission accomplished, I pointed my truck southward and headed for the community of Water Valley and my appointment with the Brahmans, flushed with great confidence. It was fun driving along the farm-to-market roads, honking at people working in their yards and gardens, and observing their actions as I passed by. Some just stared while leaning on their hoes or shovels, while others, especially younger children, ran to the road and watched in wonder until I was out of their sight.

A few minutes later I arrived at the ranch, wheeled into the barn lot, and with one hand on the steering wheel while looking out the back window, expertly backed the two-wheeled chute up to the barn door as Mr. Green, his crew of hands, and even the cows peeking through the cracks watched in silence. I could tell they were impressed with my trailer-backing ability, which was a skill or perhaps an art learned from my years of teenage practice backing a four-wheeled manure spreader into the hallway of a narrow Tennessee mule barn. I had this crowd where I wanted them, and with my new equipment, new clinic, and a great spouse for a partner, nothing was going to stop me now from becoming the finest practicing veterinarian in all of southwest Alabama.

As we shook hands all around, all present bragged on my up-to-date equipment, my clean coveralls and boots, and even the cleanliness of my blood tubes and charts as I removed them from the back of the truck and placed them in proper order on a brand-new worktable. After setting the chute down on the ground, I carefully secured it to the barn posts with two new chains, then shook it to be sure it was ready to hold wild cattle.

"I guess I'm ready if y'all are," I declared, with the lever poised high over my head.

Presently, I saw the first cow creep into the open rear end of the chute. I slid and shuffled my feet around, being sure I had good footing in the moderately muddy lot, then braced myself and regripped the lever again and again. I was like a nervous golfer, addressing and readdressing the ball, until finally one of his partners screams out "For Pete's sake, Marvin, hit the dern ball!"

Suddenly, the cow plunged forward with the speed of a recently discharged bullet, and I jerked down on the lever with all my quickness and strength the instant I saw her hit the head gate. I vaguely remember a noise that sounded like a cross between a far-off explosion and two pickup trucks colliding head-on, and then a split second later I saw lots of stars of varying sizes and heard some teeth click together. Apparently, in my state of euphoria I had forgotten about the steel bar above my head, and when it came down, it created a furrow in the middle of my skull deep enough to plant cottonseed — or so some of the hands so stated.

Momentarily, or perhaps it was several minutes later, after a couple of face bathings with pond water, I came to and realized I was supine in the mud and had the worst headache of my life.

"DOC, DOC, ARE YOU OK?" someone was saying. Then another voice said, "Man, look at all the blood!" Hearing the word *blood,* I tried to sit up, but everything seemed fuzzy and then went dim.

I recall something about a fast truck ride and then being in a small medical office. I clearly recall asking where I was and being told it was Gilbertown, then I remember the feeling of sutures being squeaked through the laceration on my scalp and trying to explain to the nurse and other medical personnel about what I thought had happened. But I might as well have been speaking to deaf children from Mars.

"A squeeze shoot! What's that? What were you trying to catch a cow for?" they said, looking at me as if I was the strange one. Hadn't they ever heard of veterinarians and cows and deworming and such?

I left the chute there on the Green Ranch for a couple of weeks, until I got up the nerve to ask them to recorral the cows and show my face there again. The same group of hands welcomed me back with a lot of enthusiasm and pats on the back. I thanked them for taking care of me and apologized for being such an idiot.

"Bring me a cow!" I yelled. "But not the same one as before. I can't stand another trip to Gilbertown!"

The Green Ranch cattle worked through the chute just like the doctor ordered. Unfortunately, several of them were infected with brucellosis, which necessitated multiple return trips to the farm to brand and tag the reactors and retest the survivors at thirty-day intervals. But I never conked myself out again, even though my hired-hand buddies were constantly encouraging me to do so — because they would then get the rest of the day off, again.

Even though I still have the healed furrow in the top of my head from the chute lever and several other noggin scars, I love my squeeze chute. There have been times when I thought other squeeze chutes were also going to be responsible for my premature checking in at that great veterinary clinic in the sky. Nevertheless, I would like to shake hands with the gentleman who designed or invented the first portable one. By making it possible to safely restrain cattle for routine veterinary work, the device has made my life a lot easier and much safer. Without a chute, I would have wasted a lot of time in wild roping episodes and trying to corner the beasts up between the corncrib and the feed bunk.

And since I was no longer chasing around after cattle and getting home a few minutes earlier every day, Jan was a lot happier too!

Nine

Jan and I were pleased that the practice kept us busy doing things that we knew were important, but it left little time for the two of us to engage in nonwork activities, such as evenings at the movies or a quiet dinner at one of the nice restaurants in Meridian, a thirty-five-minute drive away to the west. Golf, hunting, and civic work were my primary away-from-the-practice recreational activities, but I was nearly always accessible if I was needed for an animal health emergency. Jan enjoyed her occasional bridge game, and she also enjoyed her work with the Civiettes, a women's club that sponsored various community projects.

A mixed country practice is very demanding and time-consuming when you're the only veterinarian in the county, since there is no one else available to share the nighttime and weekend emergency duty. And there is always the anticipation of knowing the phone is going to ring at any moment, often bringing the news of some strange animal malady and asking for a diagnosis and treatment. But in spite of this excitement and the need to be available for one's loyal clients, it is frequently nerve-racking when the veterinarian and his or her spouse attempt to leave the kids with a baby-sitter and spend a few hours just enjoying themselves. For several months Jan had been suggesting that we find the time to go see a movie, but for various reasons we had never found the time.

The local movie theater was owned by Mr. Garvis Allen, a local businessman and store owner. He had appropriately named the theater the Gala, using portions of both his given name and his surname. Garvis ran the Gala in a rather informal manner. One afternoon Jan called the corner store that Garvis owned and inquired about the evening show.

"What time does the first show start?" she asked.

"Oh, I don't know exactly. Whenever they all get there, I reckon," Garvis replied.

"What time will that be?" she then asked.

"About six or seven, I reckon. Would that be convenient for you and Doc?" he asked.

Being from a somewhat larger Southern town where the theater schedules were more rigid and not operated with concern for the convenience of the local animal doctor and his spouse, she was taken aback by his style of management. She preferred a more businesslike approach and more punctuality for a starting time than "whenever they all get there." I thought it indicated a pretty relaxed way to approach life, even if it wouldn't work in the big city. I reminded her that maybe this slower pace of life was one of the reasons we were living in a small town rather than Memphis.

Garvis owned a beautiful white spitz dog named Sambo who was one of our more frequent clinic guests. One of Garvis's handymen would bring Sambo in almost every week for a shampoo and comb out, and sometimes Garvis himself would show up with his beloved companion for us to check on minor ailments. I always thought that bringing Sambo to the clinic was just an excuse for him to get out of the store and go for a ride, because after the examination and treatment, Garvis would pull out of the driveway and head north, in the opposite direction of his store and the Gala.

"Miss Jan, y'all have never been to a movie. Why not?" he asked one day while at the clinic with Sambo, who was wheezing and coughing from an attack of bronchitis.

"How do you know we haven't been there? Are you always there?" she asked. "And when are you going to get some good films instead of all those shoot-'em-up-Pete westerns?"

"Of course I'm there. I own it, you know, and I know who comes to the show and who doesn't," he stated proudly. "Next year we're gonna order more films that you and all those good Yankees out at the paper mill will enjoy."

"Why don't you talk about it to my man while he cleans Sambo's ears. I can't get him to come home in time for supper, much less go to the picture show," she complained.

"What's playin' tonight, Garvis?" I queried.

"It's a good one about a big battle in the Pacific, with that John Wayne in it."

"You mean *The Sands of Iwo Jima*?" I exclaimed. "That's my favorite movie, Jan, let's go! I'll try to get through here early and put off any calls that I can."

"John, you've seen the thing three or four times. Don't you get tired of all that carnage and gore?"

"Sort of, but it makes me think about how much so many people sacrificed and how lucky we are to be alive and well in the good old USA. It makes me feel patriotic and want to join the marines!" I half shouted.

"Well, you can't join until you get all the cows tested and this clinic paid for. Besides, they won't take older men who need glasses," she declared with a chuckle, glancing at Garvis, who also enjoyed her good-natured put-down. I quickly injected Sambo with his antibiotic and then counted him out a week's supply of triple sulfa tablets. The duo headed north, as usual, when they left the clinic.

Jan agreed to the evening out, though she couldn't match my enthusiasm for seeing the World War II movie again. In minutes she had the baby-sitter lined up and a proposed schedule for the evening.

"We'll get to the Gala around seven, and we'll have popcorn and Cokes for supper, then after the movie we'll go to the Dairy Queen and have a sundae, if they're still open," she detailed.

"What if they're closed? I think that's a long movie, and the DQ closes before eleven if it's a slow night."

"I guess you can stop at the curb market and get a Moon Pie and a Dr Pepper. I'll just have some buttermilk and corn bread when we get home." The menu didn't sound too appealing for a night out with one's spouse, but just being together without phone calls did.

Several hours later we arrived on the south side of the town square, parked in front of Bedsole's Department Store, and strolled hand in hand the forty steps to the little cubbyhole where the tickets were sold. There sat Garvis, his back turned while he thumbed through some sort of film catalog. When I tapped on the window, he whirled around and grabbed a roll of tickets as big as a hubcap.

"Good evenin', Doc, Miz Doc," he declared as he stood, exhibiting his proper Southern manners. I'm sure if he had been wearing a hat, he would have taken it off, or at least tipped it in the presence of a lady. "How many, please?"

I looked around, but there wasn't a soul within ten paces.

"Two, I guess. How many do I need?" I asked.

"Two, since there's just two of you," he stated, looking all around to see if there were others. "And by the way, Miz Doc, you might like to know that next year we'll be getting some great ones, including the one about this Russian feller who wrote poems. I think it's called *Dr. Vivargo* or something." He held up the brochure for Jan to see.

"I heard about that, but I believe it's called *Dr. Zhivago*, from Pasternak's book," Jan answered. "I hear it's going to be great." From the sound of her voice I knew she was on the verge of a huge chuckle. *"Dr. Vivargo"* did sound a bit amusing.

We made a little more small talk and then slowly made our way into the lobby, pausing long enough to read the large posters announcing coming attractions. When we arrived at the ticket-taking spot, there sat Garvis on a stool, patiently awaiting our arrival.

"You sell 'em and take 'em up, too?" Jan asked as he examined the tickets briefly before ripping them in half and returning our portions.

"Would y'all care for some popcorn?" he asked, rising from his stool and stepping behind the adjacent snack bar.

"You bet! Two bags of popcorn, a medium Coke, and a large Dr Pepper."

"Sorry, we just have Cokes," he apologized.

"All right, a small Coke and a large Coke, please."

"I don't have any large cups, Doc. What if I just give you two small ones?" He fumbled around in a box of junk on the floor, apparently searching for a large cup.

"Two small cups will be fine. I ought not be drinking a large one anyway since I'm on a diet." He drew our three drinks but never smiled as if he had caught the silly diet quip.

I didn't dare cut my eyes toward Jan for fear that we would both explode in laughter. I knew she was also trying to avoid looking my way, so she mercifully moved over to the top of the aisle and out of my peripheral vision.

"Doc, there's your patient over there," he said, pointing toward an old sofa near the balcony staircase. It was Sambo, lying there asleep and taking up the entire seating capacity of the sofa. He seemed to be breathing normally. Maybe the injection had given him some relief from the bronchitis.

"Sambo! Wake up, boy! Doc wants to look at 'chu," Garvis yelled. He paid no attention to the people sitting just a few steps away in the auditorium and seemed to lose all interest in snacks, tickets, and other moviegoers who were arriving at the ticket office. It was obvious that Sambo was his pride and joy.

The dog sprang to a sitting position the instant his name was mentioned, probably thinking it was popcorn time. When he saw me heading his way, he grinned and his tail began to wag. Dust and dog dander billowed from the sofa as his tail beat out a neighborly rhythm on the dilapidated cushions. He hacked out a couple of polite, closed-mouthed dog coughs, his cheeks puffing out with each hack.

"Hello, Sambo," I said softly while patting and stroking his head. "Sounds like you've been smoking them old nasty cigarettes." Now his tail was really putting a whipping on the seat, and a cloud of hairy dust was engulfing both our heads as we both hacked in unison. Then, out of habit, I checked his gum color, opened his mouth, and checked the condition of his tongue and throat.

"Is he OK, Doc?" Garvis asked, as if Sambo hadn't seen his doctor in weeks.

"Yep, he looks fine to me, as well as I can tell in this bad light."

"Honey, the movie. Remember?" Jan interjected. "Come on, let's sit down. I'm sure the movie will be starting soon."

We made our way down the aisle, Sambo's respiratory symptoms echoing in our ears. There were thirty or so people scattered throughout the theater, including the obligatory three young ten-year-old boys fidgeting around in the front row, giggling and having a contest to see which one could hit the other on the shoulder the hardest. I recognized "Little Buddy" Clark, Stink's younger brother, as one of the fidgeters. He seemed to be winning the scuffling contest. Like his older brother, he was big for his age, and in comparison to the smaller lads, he appeared to need a good dose or two of dewormer.

The Clark farm had been the scene of one of my first bovine surgical procedures, several months before, just a few days after our arrival in the county. Stink, the oldest son and a strapping young man of fourteen, already had his own herd of cattle and made all the decisions about their husbandry. His recently purchased prize bull had swallowed a long piece of baling wire and was suffering the consequence, which is usually severe peritonitis resulting from the wire's perforating the second stomach. I performed the surgery under the red barn with Stink's able assistance, and the bull went on to perform the services for which he was purchased.

After some searching, we located two unbroken seats about halfway down on the right side of the left aisle. I requested the outside seat so I could have more legroom and could get out easily if the need arose.

"Where's my popcorn?" I asked Jan. She was filling her

mouth with the buttery stuff, her hand movement from bag to mouth resembling the cadence of an assembly line lady working in slow motion. "And my Cokes? Can I have some of yours?"

"No siree! Go get your own," she whispered, jerking the bag away. "When Garvis left to play with you and Sambo, I just went behind the counter and got mine. I guess you'll have to go back. And while you're there, wash your hands. You've got dog all over them."

"No, I'll just wait. He'll deliver mine, I guarantee you, because he'll want to talk about the dog."

As I sat and waited on the delivery of my refreshments, I inspected the interior of the once-attractive building. Like most small-town theaters, it had seen its best days and was in need of a great deal of refurbishing and new paint. The tall ceiling showed signs of peeling plaster and dark concentric water stains, but otherwise appeared sturdy. The musty-smelling, red velvet chairs needed to be ripped out and taken to the dump since many of them had broken armrests, seats that wouldn't work, and screws that had worked loose from the floor, which allowed them to flop back and forth. Of course, this defect delighted the ruckus-raisers in the front row, and they wasted no time in trying to rock the remaining hardware apart.

There was a large hole in the screen just to the right of center, probably having been created by an accurately hurled missile by a disgruntled viewer when the film broke or the reel changer dozed off. I had heard that it was routine procedure for the audience to be presented with a blank screen for a few minutes while reels were being changed. I could just imagine the whoops and hollers from the impatient teenagers who were always in a rush. I often wondered why young folks were always in such a hurry and the old folks just poked along. Since the young have sixty or seventy years ahead of them and the oldsters may have only a few short years left, it seemed that the wrong people were doing the rushing.

I waved at several of our friends and clients, but I then purposely scrunched down in the seat in an effort to hide from animal owners who I feared would interrupt our evening of relaxation with requests for free advice.

Presently, the lights dimmed and images of coming attractions jumped out on the screen, with the volume cranked all the way up to "ear-split." A few yells from the small crowd resulted in the decibel levels being reduced several notches. It appeared that Garvis wasn't going to bring my snacks as I had predicted, so much to the delight of Jan, I reluctantly went back up the aisle, scooped up my own popcorn, and poured my own Cokes. Sambo was observing my every move and began to lick his chops when I passed his station. I had not been back in my seat but a minute or so when I felt a cold dog nose bump my elbow, and out of the corner of my eye I could see Sambo's sad, begging eyes glued to my bag of popcorn. His gaze followed the hand that was moving from bag to mouth, and his tail-thumping on the seat brace intensified each time he heard the sound of fingers rattling the paper bag. Ignoring the coughing, tail wagging, lip licking, and drooling antics of the begging dog wasn't easy, so after a few minutes I weakened and started handing him an occasional kernel, which he immediately vacuumed off my fingertips with the relish of a half-starved backwoods cur. Finally, when the bottom of the bag began to appear, the bored Sambo flopped down in the aisle and took a nap.

It had been reported that Sambo had seen *Gone With the Wind* twenty-seven times, but he liked Road Runner cartoons even more, walking all the way down front for better viewing. Regular customers said that he stood there looking up at the screen, wagging his tail, and occasionally woofing out encouragement to the inept coyote. However, he showed no interest on that evening, possibly because the cartoon wasn't a Road Runner.

Later, John Wayne and his platoon of marines up on the screen were giving their lives for their country on the far-off island of Iwo Jima. Even though I wasn't a movie buff, tough John Wayne types were my kind of men, and I enjoyed the action they created. Amid all the clamor of machine gun fire and the exploding of incoming mortar shells, I heard a voice yell in the rear of the building.

"JIMMY, YOU GOT A PHONE CALL!"

A man on the opposite side of the room slowly stood and trudged out. Evidently, if a phone call came in asking for someone suspected of being in the audience, a loud cupped-hands-around-the-mouth announcement was made from the top of the nearest aisle. Jan and I looked at each other and shook our heads. We were thinking the same thing: "I wouldn't have believed all this, but I'm glad we're here to see it!"

The behavior of the boys up front was getting out of hand. The earlier mild-mannered giggling, scuffling, and tousling had escalated into borderline fisticuffs, which resulted in a lot of squeaking and squawking of the antique seats. Finally, after several "SHHH"s had been issued in their direction, I had heard more out of them than I had the war, so I marched down to their seats and kneeled in front of them. Blessed quiet descended upon the trio.

"OK, you boys," I said sternly, "we can't hear anything in the back except your racket. Quieten down or I'm gonna get Mr. Allen and he'll call your daddies. Do you understand?"

"Yes sir," they declared in unison, their necks rigid and eyes so wide they reflected weird images from the screen. Sambo had followed me down and was sniffing Little Buddy's leg, no doubt smelling the scent of the Clarks' fine redbone coonhounds. I returned to my seat, hoping there would be no more interruptions.

Finally, there was peace in the movie house, except for the war effort, and everyone there knew even that would end in peace before the film ended. The boys were so still and quiet they wouldn't even turn their heads to stare at each other. I should have known it wouldn't last.

"LET'S GO, LITTLE BUDDY!" a deep voice bellowed from the back.

I knew the voice well. It belonged to James Clark, Little Buddy's father. I noticed the young lad didn't move, obviously trying to milk the last few minutes out of his visit with his now squirming again associates. Minutes later, the booming voice repeated the order.

"I SAID, LET'S GO, LITTLE BUDDY! DON'T MAKE ME COME DOWN THERE AFTER YOU! This time the voice reverberated from the thirty-foot ceiling, even drowning out the orders of my hero on the screen. It was an impatient and potentially dangerous voice, and it obtained the desired result.

The youth bolted from his seat and lumbered up the aisle, narrowly missing Sambo, who was sprawled across the aisle and soundly sleeping. He then paused briefly at our row, turned around, and watched the movie as he walked backwards.

"What next?" I whispered to Jan. "All these extracurricular activities are almost as entertaining as the show!"

"More," she said. "With the movie you know what's going to happen next."

It wasn't long before I detected the distant ringing of a phone. Seconds later, I heard Garvis's voice.

"HEY, DOC, TELEPHONE!"

I looked around to see if anyone else called "Doc" responded to the page by slowly arising and heading for the exit. If he was there, he wasn't stirring.

"Better go, honey. It might be the baby-sitter," Jan advised.

Without saying a word I started for the phone, wondering what mysterious excitement awaited my ears this time.

"Hello…"

"Mr. McCormack, this is Agent Robinson with the New Life Insurance Company. How are you this evening?"

"I'm just dandy," I said. "How about yourself?"

"That's good, Mr. McCormack," he replied, sounding just like a recorded robot. "I would like to take a few minutes of your time this evening to explain an exciting and innovative new concept in the area of financial protection for your beloved family in the unfortunate event of your demise. What is your age, Mr. McCormack?"

"The very idea of this unknown jerk calling me this time of night, and while out on the town with my wife!" I ranted to myself. I wondered whether he'd been drinking moonshine liquor or eating Jimson weed seeds. But as I seethed, I told myself this call was good practice for future idiotic calls that I was sure to receive.

"My age is confidential, sir," I said. I could feel my face burning and my heart skipping beats. "Let me ask you, do you have a dog or cat?"

"I beg your pardon? Uh, yes, I have a dog and a cat," he replied.

"Give me your phone number, because I'm gonna need to call you back." He recited his long-distance number.

"Sir, do you actually think you can call an unknown person and sell him some life insurance over a long-distance phone call? I kinda doubt it."

"Sir, it's for the protection of your loved ones and —"

"Sir, I'm practicing on how to talk to thoughtless callers over the phone, and right now I'm practicing hard on how not to yell at people like yourself for calling me out of my favorite John Wayne movie. I am now going to bid you a good night and hang up this phone before I say something ugly to you. Good night!"

"But don't you want your loved ones protected in the event of your unfortunate..." I could hear him pleading as I gently cradled the phone. I knew I was improving my telephone manners, because the old telephone John in that situation would have blessed the man out and then smashed the phone down. On my way out of the ticket booth Garvis stopped me for a chat.

"Y'all enjoying the movie, Doc?"

"Oh, yeah. Some of the most fun we've had since we've been in Butler," I declared. I was amazed at my newfound diplomacy.

"I knew you would. Y'all need to come back at least once every couple of weeks. Don't wait for that *Dr. Vivargo* film," he suggested. "By the way, do you think Sambo's cough is any better?"

"Glad you brought it up. I know exactly what's causing his bronchitis."

"What, pray tell? It's worms, ain't it?"

"No, it's that nasty sofa. Get one of your men in here tomorrow and haul that thing to the dump," I advised. I also wanted to say, "And take all those old theater seats, too!" But I denied myself the pleasure out of tact.

"His sofa?"

"Yeah, he's allergic to it. Get rid of it and get him a new one," I said, walking away. "Gotta go see the end where Big John gets killed."

"I know. It's so sad I can't watch it anymore. We've never given our World War Two veterans the honor and credit they deserve. Y'all hurry back, Doc. I gotta go check on the projector." He pulled a hanky from a rear pocket and honked his nose into it a couple of times.

"Who was it, hon? It wasn't the baby-sitter, was it?" Jan queried when I returned to the seat.

"Just a nice fellow from Mobile trying to sell me some insurance for the protection of my family," I replied. Inwardly, I was seething and wished for a few grenades. Those things were working mighty well for Big John and his soldiers.

"Why did he call here? Couldn't it have waited?"

"No, I reckon not. He seemed to think I was gonna croak right away. Maybe you ought to drive home."

The remainder of the show passed in relative calm. The film broke once, and there was a brief pause a little later when the reels were changed. The fire engine went south, its siren screaming, which caused most of the audience to rush out to see if it was headed in the direction of their property. A few sprinted for their cars and trucks to head home.

When the movie was mercifully over and we started for Jan's station wagon, I realized that the relaxing evening had been anything but that.

"Next time, let's just stay home," I suggested.

"What a marvelous idea," Jan agreed. "That is, until *Dr. Vivargo* comes to town. I hear it's gonna be real good."

We laughed all the way to the Dairy Queen, but our laughter was cut short when we turned in and found all the lights out and the doors locked.

"Boy, I was looking forward to that fudge sundae," I declared. "It was going to be our reward for spending the evening at the Gala."

"Just stop and get that Moon Pie. It'll have to do," Jan said.

Later, I came out of the curb market with paper bag in hand.

"Did you get it?" Jan asked.

"They were out, so I got us two pints of milk and two Butterfingers. Ted said there's a shortage of Moon Pies."

"Probably because of you. I saw a whole bunch of wrappers in your truck the other day," she said. "I like Butterfingers better anyway."

Later we found out that the Gala and its laid-back atmosphere had grown on us, and we returned for more of its pleasures on a regular basis. One must be open-minded about new adventures. When *Dr. Vivargo* came to town, we went both nights!

Ten

◦— I've always liked cats. That's why it seems strange to me that some people think that just because a veterinarian spends a lot of time on farms treating horses, cows, and pigs, he has no feeling for small animals, especially cats. I don't know how they reached that conclusion.

Most of the livestock farms I have visited over the past forty years have a cat or two around the house and outbuildings, not only for the purpose of mouse and rat eradication but for companionship as well. Dairy farmers aren't thought of as cat lovers, but every dairy has a passel of cats around the premises. I'm sure they're not there just for the purpose of lapping up surplus milk, since many have proper names and their own designated lounging area. I've also noticed that when I'm on a farm call there is always at least one feline that wants to be involved in the treatment of the large animal patient.

It can be distracting, even frightening, for a veterinarian bent over in deep concentration while examining a downer cow in a darkened stall to have a fellowship-seeking cat suddenly pounce from the rafters and land with a thump on his back. Such an act guarantees the vet will make a hasty return to upright posture, which is often accompanied by a bloodcurdling yowl as the cat flies across the stall.

After years of observation and study, I have decided that pets and people are basically the same. People in general are pretty good folks, although I try to avoid the mean and two-faced ones if at all possible. Those are the ones who will be smiling at you while sharpening the knife that they'll later use to stab you in the back. There are some dogs with those same characteristics, too.

Good dog friends and good human friends are a joy to be around. They are loyal, considerate, consistent, and are concerned about your family's well-being. Both will go down the river with you, and for you, if necessary.

But what about cats? Do they exhibit the same good and bad traits of their human and canine colleagues? Perhaps it's because I slightly favor cats over dogs, but I believe cats are more stable, exhibit fewer mood swings, and are more independent than most dogs and people. Cats think for themselves, don't rile easily unless trifled with, and don't go off half-cocked when things get hectic and crossways in the road. They do want to determine the conditions under which they will be fooled with. Cat lovers are a different sort also. I can't put my finger on it exactly, but they aren't the same as dog lovers.

Before Jan and I moved to Choctaw County, we considered all kinds of veterinary practices. We looked at an exclusive small animal practice in Memphis, considered going back home to middle Tennessee, and even exchanged letters with a practice in Alberta, Canada. The Canadian practice sounded great until I read the part about the snow starting in October and still being on the ground in May. I still wonder if the long snow season wasn't mentioned just to keep some of us information-seeking wimpier types in the Deep South where we belonged.

We even visited colleagues at work in their veterinary clinics to see how they conducted their practices, as well as to try to pick up ideas on how to treat certain diseases or pathological conditions. Their patients, I noticed, were always well mannered while they were being examined and treated. They just sat there on the examination table, stoically allowing their ears to be otoscoped, their eyes ophthalmoscoped, their chests stethoscoped, and every portion of their bodies probed and scrutinized. I noticed that none of the cats squalled, bit, scratched, or tried to make life miserable for everybody within a hundred-yard radius of the hospital. We were almost convinced that we should open a feline practice in one of the larger Southern cities. But I hankered for a small-town, rural atmosphere, where I could be outside at least half the time, working on farms with real farmers and waving wildly at them when our pickup trucks met on the farm-to-market road. Also, in spite of my cat-loving attitude, I soon found out that restraining and treating a resisting cat was more difficult in my clinic than it was at my colleague's uptown clinic in Memphis.

Even in spite of our occasional difficulties in handling and treating these furry companions, our fondness for the feline species was apparent to local, as well as more distant, cat owners, and they quickly allowed us to take care of the health needs of their beloved pets.

Our most frequent cat-owner client was a middle-aged lady by the name of Josie Rainey. Josie had worked in Indianapolis for some thirty years, and when she tired of the hustle-bustle of big-city life, she had returned to her birthplace in the woods of northern Choctaw County, some fifteen miles north of Butler, to live out the rest of her life in peace and quiet with her growing family of cats. According to reports from Chappell's barbershop, Josie had apparently made real good money up north, but nobody knew how. I believe the exact words were "Somehow or 'nother, she raked in a passel of jack." Apparently one of the barbershop sitters or waiters had seen her unloading rolls of greenbacks at the teller's window on several occasions at the Choctaw Bank.

In spite of her apparent wealth, she didn't have a car to drive — or a telephone, running water, or electricity. Nor did she desire those modern conveniences of life offered in the second half of the twentieth century. But she did want the best in veterinary care for her cats.

A week or so after our new clinic building was opened to the public, she called from a phone in the nearby community of Pennington, requesting an appointment sometime in the next few days. It was a little unusual for someone to call that far ahead and actually set up a date and time. Usually what happened was a lot less formal.

"The doc gonna be in for the next little bit?" the caller would say.

"Yes, I think so. What could we do for you?" Jan would politely ask.

"Well, I got to run to town sometime this afternoon to get a part for the tractor, so I thought I'd run old Rover by y'all's shop and get him wormed and a rabies shot. I was gone the day y'all were out here vaccinatin' dogs."

"Yes sir, we'll be looking for you within the hour," Jan said.

"Well, I ain't sure exactly when I'll get there, 'cause I might stop by Chappell's and get a haircut if the wait ain't too long. Reckon he'll be there all afternoon?" It was for sure that Jan handled these calls more tactfully than I did.

From their first conversation, Jan knew that this Miss Josie lady had been used to dealing with big-town vets because of the way she asked about the appointment. Jan had often tried to convince me of the advantages of changing the small animal practice to the appointment system, but like most people, I disliked it and preferred the walk-in, "How y'all been doin'" system.

"It's more businesslike," she argued, "and it's a more efficient use of your valuable time. You can't go to the doctor, dentist, or even Lucille Skinner's beauty parlor without an appointment! That drug salesman yesterday told me you even have to schedule a haircut now in some of those fancy barbershops in Mobile."

"But what about the drop-ins? They might be driving down the road with their deer dogs and have a few free minutes. They can just whip in here to get 'em all checked for heartworms or whatever. What are you gonna do about them, refuse 'em service? And besides, it'll be a cold day in Mobile Bay when I call a barbershop to ask 'em what time I can drop by to get clipped," I replied.

"Yeah, they'll have to wait if you have people here who have used the good sense to call ahead. And yeah, you will someday schedule a haircut just like you do a visit to the doctor. And I'll tell you something else I've noticed. People who own cats want a businesslike approach to their pets' health matters, and that includes the scheduling of appointments."

I knew she was right, but I didn't want to admit it. In veterinary school we spent thousands of hours learning about anatomy, physiology, pathology, and how to deal with animal diseases, but nothing about how to deal with the business aspect of a practice.

Josie Rainey showed up at the appointed time in a hired truck. I suppose it was technically a taxicab, but it had no meter or license, and there were no taxicabs in the community of Pennington. It was just an old rattletrap truck, with high sides on the back, owned by an area jack-of-all-trades kind of guy named Junior, who hauled trash, firewood, goats, manure, and anything else he could get to stay on the back of that truck. He would even haul people if they didn't mind the leftover smell of live goat.

I frequently passed Junior on the road while making large animal calls. He was a small runty fellow who looked ridiculous sitting down so low in the butt-sprung driver's seat of the old truck. All an approaching driver could see in the cab was a barely visible hard-billed chauffeur's cap some three or four inches above the top portion of the steering wheel. His hat size was probably about a seven, but the cap he wore was almost a full size larger, and he always kept it pulled down over both ears, with the bill almost covering both eyes. I often wondered if he went to bed with the cap on, or if he had worn it so long it had grown to his head.

The appearance of the rear half of the truck was equally screwy. The side panels extended normally backward the length of the truck bed, but they stuck up much too high. So high, in fact, that when he was not loaded the sides swayed freely in the wind, giving oncoming drivers the appalling notion that the conveyance was on the verge of taking off in the manner of a gigantic, slow goose, or flipping over. If he was loaded with trash, pine straw, or other wind-sensitive material, the truck would not only be leaning to one side or the other but it would be losing its load at an alarming rate because of the wind currents created by the truck's forward progression. Meeting large log trucks was cause for Junior to stop dead in the road and pray for relief from the imminent truck-rocking blast of wind. The "blow-off" problem was partially solved when Junior engaged the services of three neighborhood teenage boys to lie spread-eagled upon the load. Unfortunately, two Cadillac-riding, do-gooder ladies from Meridian fell in behind the trash-laden truck one summer day, and they were horrified at the sight of the young lads, clad only in ragged blue jean cutoffs, sprawled atop the smelly garbage. Junior was reported to the sheriff's office, and the sheriff quietly suggested that he keep to the back roads and off highways that accommodated out-of-state Cadillacs.

Josie and Junior presented an amusing scene upon their arrival at the clinic. Junior was nearly a foot shorter than his passenger, and his grimy T-shirt and khaki pants, which he had hiked up almost to his armpits, were in stark contrast to the attire of his rather large passenger. In spite of the hot and humid south Alabama weather, she was swathed in several layers of different-colored garments, all of which surely must have come from a very exclusive "stout shop" located somewhere outside Choctaw County. There were no stout shops in Butler or Pennington.

From my exam room window, I could see the Mutt and Jeff duo, or perhaps it was David and Goliath, struggling with a large rectangular fruit crate lashed with at least a half dozen pairs of old panty hose, stockings, and a conglomeration of blanket pieces and yards of ripped sheets. I assumed the patient was somewhere inside, where the oranges used to be.

As the odd couple strained to haul the crated cat toward the clinic, I hurried to see if I was needed. Standing just outside the front door, I held the screen door wide open as they made their grand entrance, first Josie and then Junior. But seconds later I was suddenly jolted by the backdraft of what I gathered to be Josie's perfume. The stuff reeked, took my breath, and slammed to the back of my cranium while I turned my head and closed my eyes to avoid possible ophthalmic damage. Two seconds later, I was hit with another swell of stench, but this wave was a combination of old sweat and potent billy goat. Junior grinned, as if to say, "I might wash up nex' fall, if I can find a free bar of lye soap." I quickly inhaled a huge breath of outside air and plunged inside to take my punishment. The cat was wailing a loud, pitiful yowl, as though someone were trying to push him out of an airplane door in mid-flight.

The two well-mannered canine patients and their owners waiting their turns were wide-eyed and tilt-headed at all the squalling coming from the crate, and they were equally riveted by Josie and Junior.

When the phone rang, I remembered that I had left Jan alone with my previous patient in the exam room. While she took the call, I quickly retrieved the puppy from her arms and deposited him in a cage in the kennel room. The yowling was getting more intense in the waiting room, and I could hear chunks of the crate being angrily torn out of the makeshift feline carrier as it began to rock around on the linoleum. Now one of the waiting bluetick hounds began baying, and the two-way radio began its staticky way-off messages. It was picking up an atmospheric skip from Dr. Hart in Black River Falls, Wisconsin. In his strange Northern accent, he was asking his wife if there were other farm calls to be made before he returned to the office.

"Honey, it's Mr. W. J. Landry. He wants to know if you can run up there later on this afternoon and treat a bull and several cows that have pinkeye," Jan said loudly, trying to compete with all the honking going on out in the parking lot. Some unruly children left alone in a car were practicing their horn blowing while their mother bellowed at them from a clinic window.

My neighbor, Jerry Thompson, had just walked in the front door with his boxer, and they both greeted every breathing creature there in their loud, booming voices. Jerry knew everybody and was kin to most of them. Now every mouth in the clinic, including those belonging to the dozen pets back in the kennel room, was open and making some kind of racket. Jerry's boxer and the bluetick commenced growling over in the corner, the hair on their backs was standing straight up, and one of the younger pups in the waiting room wet on the floor, much to the embarrassment of his owner. I was dizzy, nauseated, and my brain had almost ceased to function from all the hectic goings-on in the small building. At that moment, I entertained the wild notion of tossing my stethoscope into the corner, walking out the front door, and madly driving to Quebec. All this chaos was brought on by the excessive use of perfume. I now believe some women slosh on ounces of perfume because they know it interferes with normal male brain activity.

All those present agreed that we should go ahead and see about Josie's cat immediately, before he ate the crate. His name was Devil, she said, but she pronounced it "Debal." She declared in a loud voice that Debal's plumbing was stopped up.

Just unlooping all the hose from the crate was a major undertaking, since it was tied with multiple half hitches and granny knots. All of these complicated ties seemed to come together in one massive and unpickable Gordian knot, which we finally cut with a pocket knife after a few minutes of dedicated effort to save the hose for retying a little later. I noticed that I was getting accustomed to the twin odors. Jan had put on a surgical mask, and her face was a light green color.

"How come she's wearin' that mask?" Junior queried.

"Bad allergies," I lied. "It's all this pine pollen in the air."

"Pore thang," someone sympathized.

I said nothing.

While we were trying to get down to the cat, he continued his bloodcurdling screaming, stopping the clamor only long enough to hiss and spit and then try to reach through the deteriorating slats to claw and bite at his tormentors.

Suddenly, Devil's orange-colored nose squeezed through the narrow opening between two slats, quickly followed by his entire head. Except for the frantic look on his face, the scene reminded me of a hatching chick. Once his head was through, I knew escape was imminent. I was frantically grabbing at legs and trying to avoid his filthy snapping teeth when he made good his jailbreak and bolted down the hallway, where he came face to face with the German shepherd that was temporarily tethered to the examination table.

With a quick jump, Devil disappeared into an open cabinet

under the sink. As Josie and I grabbed in vain, we could hear him turning over empty dauber bottles, traipsing through and over syringes and dose guns, and making bottles of calcium gluconate rattle against each other. It sounded as though a small earthquake was taking place beneath the countertop.

"Lord have mercy, Doctuh!" Josie cried. "Ole Debal's gonna break all yo' medicine bottles!"

"Yeah, I know," I mumbled as I rushed to the end cabinet door. Just as I jerked it open, a squalling, furry white mass hurtled past my ear and in an instant was perched on top of the old refrigerator. I knew exactly what was going to happen next.

When Josie and I slowly reached for the terrified animal, he immediately plunged down behind the old Frigidaire refrigerator, squeezed himself inside the mass of screens, wires, and other compressor paraphernalia, and was soon hidden from sight. I assumed he would be incarcerated in there at the very least, or maybe even be fried. I could just see the headlines in the *Choctaw Advocate,* the only newspaper in the county, published every week, rain or shine: BELOVED FELINE LOSES ALL NINE LIVES AT LOCAL VETERINARY HOSPITAL. Then a subtitle would declare PET ELECTROCUTED. VET SHOCKED. Then I'd have to explain exactly what happened to the know-it-alls at the feed store, the barbershop, and even to folks who flagged me down on the road.

"So much for cats being well behaved," I thought to myself. "It's a good thing I decided against that hundred percent feline practice in Birmingham. One wild cat could ruin my reputation as a pretty good cat doctor." I managed a thin smile just thinking about being a cat specialist in the big city. But I was about to change my mind regarding working with the feline species.

"Doctuh John, I kin get him out from behind there," Josie stated. "Y'all just leave me be with him."

With that, I closed the exam room door, leaving the two alone. I finished up with the other patients in the waiting room and in the surgery. All the time I could hear Josie cooing to old Devil in the adjacent room.

"Come on out, sweetie," she begged softly. "Please come to yo' momma. That mean ole man ain't gonna hurt you none."

"Josie, reckon I can help get him out?" I asked, cracking the door.

"No thanks, Doctuh John. I'll git him pretty soon." Now she was lying on the floor and shedding layers of scarves and jackets.

"Well, I've got to go on a large animal call, so I'll just leave you two alone for a while," I said.

What a relief it was to step out into the wide-open spaces and breathe unpolluted fresh air. Heading for the truck, I practiced inhaling and exhaling large lungfuls of the good stuff. But there was something in the Choctaw air that some people found disagreeable when the wind was just right. The huge paper mill over on the Tombigbee River at Naheola, some fifteen miles away in a northeasterly direction, gave off a distinct aroma that reminded me of the small price we were paying in order to live in a growing industrial society, where our citizens could now earn a decent living for their labors. Before the mill came, they were eking out a living off the earth, or driving to the shipyards in Mobile for a week at a time. Being away from family was not an acceptable way of life in Choctaw County. Town visitors poked fun at our sometimes smelly town, but natives simply replied "What smell?" Then they sniffed the air thoroughly and declared, "All I smell is the scent of money!"

I noticed that Junior was asleep at the wheel of his old truck, and I wondered if he was charging Josie by the hour. Perhaps he could make enough from her fare to hose down the malodorous conveyance and slosh a gallon or two of creosote disinfectant all over it. If there was enough creosote left over, the Pennington body odor authority ought to pay him a visit and scrub him down with it.

While I was injecting Mr. W.J.'s pinkeyed cows, he and his hired men went on about my perfume, wanting to know where I obtained the stuff and did I use any particular brand with certain of my high heels or purses. They were busy laughing at the thought of my waltzing down the streets of Butler in high-heeled shoes, turning an ankle every few steps.

"If y'all would listen, I'll explain it to you," I declared.

"Aw, Doc, I think your fragrant aroma says it all. But what is the name of this cologne? I bet it's called Evening in Naheola or maybe Odor d'obnoxious." They all cracked their sides as if the present incident was going to be the last thing to ever laugh at on the planet, and I couldn't help but enjoy the fact that I was providing the material for their hilarity. If it is true that good belly laughs cause one to live longer, that crowd will live to a ripe old age.

After visiting three different corrals at the farm and tending to several "while you're here, Doc" cases, I finally returned to the clinic some two hours later. Jan's car was gone, but Junior's truck was there, now backed in toward the building, with him still asleep inside. I reckoned he had driven up the street for refreshments. I tiptoed up to the exam room window to see what was happening, and there sat Josie in the chair with old Devil asleep in her lap.

When I opened the clinic door, my sensitive nose immediately detected another pungent odor that permeated the interior of the clinic. It was the unmistakable odor of sardines! From my days working in the fields and pastures, and having snacks at country stores, I knew that sardines don't smell too bad while you are consuming them. But if you drop just one of the little morsels on the floorboard of your truck, it will run you out of there later in the day.

Devil loved Possum-brand sardines. They come in a little flat can decorated with the picture of a possum hanging upside down, by his tail, from a tree limb. Peeling the lid back, dousing them liberally with Louisiana hot sauce, and eating them on soda crackers is a pretty fair dirt road treat—when nothing better is available. What had happened here was that when all of Josie's sweet talk failed to bring Devil out from the bowels of the refrigerator, she and Junior had driven up to the IGA grocery store and purchased two cans of sardines. She opened up one can and dropped half of them, one by one, down into the innards of the refrigerator. Then she placed the can containing the remainder of the fish on the floor behind the refrigerator where he could see and sniff the delicacies. She said he was out of there within minutes.

Then, with the help of a surgical mask over my nose, Junior, Josie, a high-school-age helper who thought he wanted to become a vet, and my old faithful army blanket, I finally succeeded in getting Devil sedated and his blocked urinary tract catheterized and flushed. We discussed a change in diet, but I suspected that he would be showing up at the clinic again with the same problem. I might not have cured the cat, but I think I cured the young man of his yen to study veterinary medicine.

The clinic smelled fishy for quite some time after the Devil incident. The odor was eliminated only after the refrigerator was removed from the premises. Apparently, Devil missed a couple of the fish and they just laid there in the inner workings of the appliance and putrefied. Nothing smells as badly as a rank fish — except too much cheap perfume on a female and essence of billy goat smeared on a man. Paper mill emanations are barely noticeable compared to those odors.

I am still very fond of cats, but someone "up there" must have been watching over Jan and me the day we made the decision to become a country vet rather than a feline one.

Eleven

Jan decided that we had a lot in common with Josie Rainey. It seems that we have always had cats popping in and out of our place. They seem to just show up out of the bushes and take up residence without any kind of invitation or application. It may be that people throw them out onto the roadside, thinking that a feline can be resourceful enough to make it on his own, but I believe it is more likely that those persons simply have no compassion for animals and their plight. They never think that a kitten might be attacked by wild dogs or varmints, or hit by a vehicle, or perhaps slowly starve to death because it lacks the necessary hunting skills to survive in the wild. It's a cruel thing to do to a helpless kitten.

I'm sure that we have adopted at least a couple of dozen cats over the years, and we have enjoyed them as members of the family. To name a few, there were O.C. (short for Other Cat), Groucho, Snowball, and J.J., in addition to Go Back, which was the cat we had brought with us to Choctaw County.

Therefore, I wasn't surprised when we added another cat to our household not long after the Devil incident. It was a late Thursday afternoon and I was on my way home from the sale barn when Jan called on the two-way radio.

"James Clark has a cow that's real sick, and he wants you to stop by on the way home from Livingston," she said. "It'll be in the red barn."

It was late afternoon — about "dusk-dark," as some Southerners are fond of saying — when I pulled up in front of the red barn. This is the time of day when you can hear the constant undulating buzzing of the cicadas, or "July flies," from their perches on the sides of the big trees. This is also the time of day when the bats come out of their daylight hiding places and aimlessly flit around in the near dark, almost crashing into inanimate objects but veering away at the last moment because of their highly advanced, built-in radar system. Some of my friends call this "bull bat" time of day, and in the country it is a very peaceful time, when sitting on the front porch with other family and shelling butter beans tends to relieve what we now call "stress."

There was no sign of life at the Clark compound, other than the baying of deer dogs, the occasional bellow of a cow, or the whinny of a horse somewhere down below the barn. All seemed so peaceful. But when I peered into the hall of the barn, I could see the reason for my professional visit. A seven-hundred-pound roan shorthorn heifer was standing with her head held in abnormal horizontal fashion, and directly into a corner of the barn, as she struggled for breath. With the help of the hundred-watt bulb overhead, I could see the pumping of her chest, the open-mouthed breathing and grunting, and the anxious expression of her eyes. She offered no resistance when I touched her chest with my stethoscope.

As could have been predicted, her thoracic cavity was a cacophony of scraping, rasping, wheezing, and popping, indicating severe lung infection and inflammation of the pleura, which is the membrane that lines the chest cavity. Further examination revealed a temperature of 104.5 degrees, moderate dehydration, and no rumen activity. The cow, no doubt recently purchased and moved to the farm, was suffering from a disease called shipping fever, which results in bronchopneumonia. Her prognosis was grave.

The Clarks had no shorthorn cattle in their herd, so I assumed this was a recent herd addition, and I wondered if others had come in with her. If so, they were at risk for the disease, as were the native cattle. I was sure that James had run across a cow deal somewhere that he couldn't refuse, and now he was going to have big trouble. This heifer was at death's door, and I was sure that some of the others were also showing symptoms. Because of the seriousness of the situation, I decided to check around the premises to see if I could find someone of authority.

Today, shipping fever is referred to as bovine respiratory disease, and it is still a very contagious disease, seen frequently in "tourist cattle." These are cattle that have passed through a sale barn, or several sale barns, in a short period of time and have little or no immunity to the viral and bacterial agents that cause it. In addition, they are stressed because of inadequate feeding and watering, and have been hauled around in possum-bellied trailers more than nature intended.

As I walked around the barn, I heard the weak cries of a kitten coming from the corner stall, and then young laughter. Upon investigation, I encountered two young ruffians, about eight or ten years of age, tormenting a tiny gray tabby by poking at him with sticks and squirting him with their water pistols.

"What are y'all boys doin'?" I heard myself saying, repeating the same words in the exact tone of voice as my six-foot-four grammar school principal years ago, when he caught a dozen of us kicking a volleyball soccer style. He paddled our rears with his pine board paddle, the one with the holes bored in it.

I wished for that paddle, and the gumption to use it on the two boys, but instead sent them packing with a few strong words, liberating the frazzled feline from his tormentors. He was wet, his fur was matted, and he appeared to be on the verge of starvation. He couldn't have been more than three weeks old.

At the truck, I dried him with a towel and made a comfortable bed for him on the passenger seat. He was obviously mentally stressed, but he seemed to be in good physical condition except for being skinny. After a few body rubs and soft words, the little fellow was raising his tail cat fashion and trying to purr.

I had noticed a small shotgun house some fifty yards from the barn that I assumed was occupied by one of the Clark timber company hired hands, so I hoofed it up there to see if they could give me any information. Stepping up onto the rickety porch, I detected the pleasant, down-home aroma of country ham, sliced potatoes fried in lard, and cathead biscuits, and I regretted disturbing their supper. Through the open doors, I saw the man of the house arise from his chair and head for the door. I could also see one of the kitten tormentors sneaking quick peeks at me from his table position. I'm sure he thought I was there to report his bad deed to his father. I shot him a mean look, and he jerked his head back and buried it in his biscuits and gravy.

"Sorry to bother you, but have you seen James or Stink around?"

"Naw sir, I saw 'em pull out of the driveway a little while ago. I believe I heard Little buddy say they were goin' to the fish camp tonight," he replied. It wasn't until years later that I found out that wasn't his real name. He was also mature for his age.

"Well, he's got a cow out there in the barn that's real sick and will probably die tonight, and I was wondering if any of the others look sick. Did he just buy those cattle? I don't remember seeing any roan cows here before," I said.

"Yes sir, Stink brought 'em in here a few days ago on a big truck. The rest of 'em are down there in the pasture behind the house," he replied.

"I'm gonna treat this cow, but I don't expect her to live. If you see James, tell him to give me a holler. I'm Dr. McCormack, the vet."

"Yes sir. Ain't you the one what takened that piece of wire out of that bull's innards last fall?"

"Yep, right over there in that barn."

"I'll declare. I didn't know you could cut open a bull like that and him live. I'd sure like one of my boys to learn how to do that," he stated proudly. "What do they have to do to learn how to do that?"

"You just tell 'em that the first thing is to always be respectful of animals. Don't be mean to 'em," I lectured. The boy again craned his neck to peek, but jerked it back when I stared back.

"I'll do that. And I'll tell James you were here as soon as I see they're back from the fish camp."

I knew that might be a while. Ezell's Fish Camp, on the banks of the Tombigbee River and undoubtedly the area's most noted restaurant, was famous for its fried catfish and trimmings. Its decor was appropriately rustic, complete with numerous stuffed deer heads, pictures of giant rattlesnakes, and signed photos of famous and not-so-famous individuals who had been there for the catfish. Mr. Ezell was a good businessman, always looking ahead at consumer demands and figuring out ways to expand his business. He had been one of the first to get into catfish farming in a big way, in order to have a dependable supply for his restaurants and for shipping outside the area. We dined there occasionally, and Tom and Lisa loved to sit out on the porch overlooking the river, hoping that a riverboat would come along and give all the diners several blasts of its powerful horn.

All the talk about catfish and the kitchen smells made me realize that I had not eaten a sit-down meal all day. An insufficient breakfast of coffee and a couple of donuts while on the go had been metabolized long before I arrived at the sale barn around noon. A quick snack of a Dr Pepper and a Moon Pie likewise disappeared by about mid-afternoon. I loved my work with animals and making farm calls at all hours, but when I saw families together in their homes at the dinner hour, I sometimes wished that my job was a little more traditional so that I, too, could regularly sit down with my family and enjoy a normal meal.

The kitten was curled up, fast asleep, in the truck. I gathered a halter and my black bag, then headed back to my bovine patient, who had not moved from her earlier position. She again offered no resistance, and I applied the halter, popped her with the sixteen-gauge needle, and slowly dripped the triple sulfa solution into her jugular vein. What a dilemma! The cow would almost certainly die unless treated, but she was so sick that the strong medicine might also cause her demise. Some twenty minutes later, I was heading home, hoping for the best but expecting the worst for the roan cow.

"Mobile to Base," I said to the two-way.

"Go ahead, Mobile One," replied Jan, seconds later. She was always so official over the radio, as if she were on *Highway Patrol* shows on TV.

"Any calls?" I liked being brief.

"Negative, Mobile One. Come on in. Supper's in the oven."

"I've got a surprise for you, Base. I'm comin' in with it."

"No, John, not another kitten! I'm too busy to bottle-feed another kitten!" How did she know? Of course, she always said that, but she was the one who usually picked them up off the roadside or let people bring strays into the clinic. "I'm sure we can find a home for this one," she would always declare. It was too bad that we didn't have the forethought to open a cat adoption agency!

The next morning, as Jan was feeding the new kitten his warm milk with an eyedropper, James Clark called with a report on the cow. As expected, the news was not good. In fact, it was very bad.

"Doc, I 'spec' you ought to run back up here sometime this mornin'," James drawled. "You left your callin' card on the one in the barn, and she's still kickin', but I'll be dogged if I can figure out how you killed the two lyin' out yonder in the pasture." Even in the face of such an unfortunate occurrence, James maintained his sense of humor and his constant good-natured kidding of his vet. "Calling card" indeed!

A quick postmortem examination of the deceased cattle revealed that they'd both had severe bronchopneumonia, and it was no doubt the cause of their deaths. The twenty-five short-horn cattle had been recently purchased from a neighbor a mile or so up the road, and as expected, they had not been vaccinated against any of the diseases common to cattle in the region. Three dead cows out of the twenty-five were enough to get anyone's attention, especially the man who'd purchased them.

"Stink told me it was risky to bring in cattle with an unknown vaccination history," he declared. "But I thought that was just that FFA talk. I didn't know you needed to vaccinate cows like they were chillun'!"

"Well, if you'd have called me like you should have, I would have verified what your fourteen-year-old son told you," I replied. "Just think about the disease problems you'd have if you sent those children to school without them being vaccinated. I don't see any difference with cattle, do you?"

"Naw sir, Doctor," he said sarcastically. "So just send me a bill if I owe you anything. I don't reckon I need any more of your classroom lectures." A lot of my clients said the same thing.

"But what about the rest of the cattle?" I exclaimed. "You really need to corral them and check for sick ones and vaccinate. You've still got a couple of critical weeks, and you could easily lose several more."

James sat down on a stump, shaking his head and mumbling. "I wish I'd never seen or heard of this bunch of cattle," he announced to all. "This cow deal and this vet deal is gonna cost me plenty before it's all over."

He did lose another couple of cows, plus we spent considerable time and lots of his money treating sick ones. Strangely enough, the first one that I treated survived, but she never did very well, probably because of damage to a large portion of her lung tissue. At one point James declared, "Why don't you just take the ones that are still alive for the bill, Doc? You're the one making all the money off this deal."

"I'd really like to do that, James, but you know how little pasture I have in that small backyard behind the house. By the way, I did remove a sick cat from your barn the other night, so I will deduct the cost of the cat from your statement this month, let's say about four dollars. Do you think that's fair?" For the first time since I had known him, James was silent. I knew he desperately wanted to come back at me with a pronouncement that the cat was a purebred something-or-other and his sire's half brother had won best-of-show at the Selma Association of Cat Fanciers or some other highly regarded feline group, but his heart just wasn't in it. The cow pneumonia deal had temporarily put the quietus on his humorous nature.

The new kitten thrived under Jan's care. After a few days of being fed milk with an eyedropper, he graduated to a doll bottle, then started lapping milk and pablum from a saucer. He grew rapidly and enjoyed life in typical kitten fashion, but he also developed a mean streak, which he exhibited frequently by unexpectedly biting people for no discernible reason. It was a bad habit that would never be broken.

He came close to losing all nine of his lives early in his life, mostly because he was accident-prone. Jerry Thompson's boxer grabbed him by the chest and slung him up onto the carport roof. When she heard the fracas, Jan climbed up a ladder, retrieved him, wrapped him in a blanket, and sped him to the clinic, where our frantic emergency efforts saved him. Either that or he was just too mean to die. That's when we decided to call him Mannix, probably because he was so tough.

It seemed as if Mannix had one health crisis after another. In succession, he broke his tail, was bitten by a cottonmouth moccasin, suffered a dislocated hip, and lacerated a cornea.

Later, he discovered that atop the engine of a recently parked vehicle was a nice warm place to rest and meditate. Jan had no idea that he was in there snoozing right next to the fan belt when she sped down to the IGA grocery store one morning. Upon arrival, however, she quickly realized that the wailing being dispatched from under the hood was that of either a jammed voltage regulator or a deeply troubled cat. Naturally, she assumed it was the injury-prone kitten, but she was hesitant to open the hood because of the probable carnage inside.

Somewhat flustered, Jan flagged down a passing pickup truck for assistance. When they carefully raised the hood, a half-crazed cat missiled out, leaving fur, hide, dust, and smoke scattering in his wake. Mannix swiftly disappeared under a nearby junk car that was parked up on a stack of concrete blocks.

After considerable sweet talk and the offer of a bologna slice, Jan was able to coax the wide-eyed little animal from his hiding place. Another quick trip to the clinic put his minor wounds on the way to recovery. We all considered it a miracle that he survived the fan belt.

After all he had been through, we decided that he must have been jinxed. Therefore, we decided to change his name to Jinx.

In spite of all his injuries and accidents, Jinx grew into adulthood. He was more of a watchdog than any cat I have ever seen, and resented any strangers or strange vehicles coming onto his territory. He would investigate each visitor, sniff the car, leap up onto the hood, and track his muddy footprints over the windshield, roof, and trunk. If a window had been left open, he would pounce onto the seats and check out the interior and sample any vittles. Crackers were his special snack. When he found them inside a car, he would rip open the package, take a small bite out of several crackers, then crush the leavings and scatter them over as much of the carpet area as possible, so that cleaning would be more difficult.

I was always amazed at his ability to detect the sound of my truck from a distance when I came home late at night. He would usually meet me at the driveway, his one good eye mirroring the headlights of my truck. Jinx was as faithful as a good dog.

Jinx lived with us for twenty-two years before his body parts finally wore out. The muscles in his legs had gradually atrophied to the point where they were little more than skin and bones. His teeth had become only a stubby memory, which made mealtime such a challenge that he was served only cuisine of mushlike consistency. The time had come and we all knew it.

We put his grave out back, with a large stone at its head. He was a rock! We all learned some valuable lessons from old Jinx, just as I did from an old mule many years ago. Loyalty, consistency, perseverance, and mental toughness, among other things. We might not always admit it, but we can and do learn so much from our animal colleagues.

Working with the animal kingdom gives a veterinarian a constant opportunity to see life and death up close and personal. Sometimes we struggle with a difficult obstetrical case and rejoice with the owner when a newborn calf finally inhales for the first time. Then later we watch in wonder as he stands unassisted and finally nurses his mama as she proudly cleans him with her rough tongue. Perhaps an hour later we are humanely putting an old dog to sleep and giving the grieving owners as much support as possible. In the case of the animals on the Clark farm, the cows expired unexpectedly while a scrawny kitten on the verge of death was saved and lived a long life. Watching nature at work, and sometimes interfering or assisting, certainly keeps us all humble.

Twelve

⟿ "How can such a puny little dog survive with something that nasty in his throat?" I said to myself as I examined the huge, inflamed left tonsil. "No wonder he's been in here so many times for so many ailments." But it was mostly for coughing, gagging, and scooting around on his rear end.

The patient was a typical sickly Chihuahua named Bully whose mama kept the road hot traveling from their home to my clinic. Almost every week she presented him for treatment of the "coughing and gagging syndrome." Now I was trying to end that problem once and for all by removing his rotten tonsils.

Today tonsillectomies seem to have fallen into bad repute as "unnecessary surgery" among many human physicians. Likewise, small animal veterinarians don't seem to perform them nearly as frequently as they did three decades ago. Back then, I found that removing Bully's diseased tonsils improved the quality of life of the owner as well as that of the sickly Chihuahua. For example, one of my earlier and more frequent patients in Choctaw County was "Tiguh" Toone, from Picayune, whose visits were closely akin to an armed conflict. But after he was relieved of his tonsils he enjoyed good health and my entire outlook on life improved dramatically.

Actually, a tonsillectomy was not a surgical procedure that I enjoyed doing, because the patients were invariably small, unruly, sickly, and overly pampered. Just getting the little dogs anesthetized was an ordeal of the first order, because of their immense dislike of anyone who tried to look inside their mouths or stick a needle into their wriggling behinds. Once a patient was asleep, the surgical procedure was not especially difficult, except for working in such tight oral quarters and being exposed to the almost unbearable halitosis caused by a lack of dental hygiene. The complication that I feared the most was hemorrhage from the severed tonsil, so I was meticulous about controlling any bleeding. Also, from a social bond aspect, their mamas were more protective of their little canine darlings than they would have been of human children, and the day of the surgery was almost as stressful for me as it was for them. Some mamas waited impatiently in the waiting room during the surgery, pacing, wringing their hands, and sobbing while I struggled and sweated with the beloved patient. Others went home to pace, wring their hands, and sob, but kept in touch by dialing the animal clinic at ten- to twenty-minute intervals for bulletins on the status of their precious pets. Surgery on the president of the United States would have been child's play for the tonsil removal and family information update system at our clinic. Of course, after the surgery I could drive out to a farm call and the safety of vaccinating a large herd of wild cattle, and leave Jan or Mrs. Lee, our Friday receptionist, to handle the family, but I felt a little guilty about their having to bear the brunt of a thousand questions and find tissues for tears. Jan has no peer when it comes to dealing with clients under stress, because she is sincere, courteous, and has a way of putting anxious people at ease that I have always appreciated and envied. But after this trying time for everybody concerned, the end result of a healthier pet made it all worthwhile.

I poked as many fingers as possible into the gaping mouth of the sleeping Chihuahua, trying to view and then snare the remaining, obviously diseased, tonsil in his pharynx, when my peripheral vision detected a pickup truck similar to mine slowly pull up to the surgery room window, rev up the engine, and slowly inch forward until the front bumper tapped the concrete wall of the clinic. Then the driver mashed on the horn for at least five seconds.

"Who the heck is that?" I yelled, momentarily pausing in mid-snare to point an icy stare at the person whose vehicle seemed to be considering razing my clinic. "Some people just have no appreciation for the property of others."

"Oh, it's just Happy Dupree," declared Mrs. Lee. It was Friday, and Jan was doing her civic duties or maybe enjoying a rare game of bridge with her friends. "He's just messin' with you, like always. You know that fool ain't right."

When a citizen of the Deep South declares that someone "ain't right," it can mean that he's a few grains of wheat shy of a bushel or that he's totally dependent on others for daily life. But what they usually mean is that the individual is goofy, acts like a clown or buffoon, and is continually doing abnormal things, such as running his truck into the side of his friend's building. It was for sure that Happy Dupree was a fun-loving jokester.

I shook a forcepped fist at him through the window as he disembarked from his truck and shuffled toward the front door. While I seated the snare around the second tonsil to my satisfaction and sheared it off, I could hear the small talk at the reception area and fake outrage at the amount of his latest vet bill as he scribbled out a check for a large portion of it. Happy had a bad habit, in my opinion, of just "paying a little along" on his bills and never paying any of them in full. I expected he would be clomping into the surgical arena presently and that a friendly argument would soon follow. I was not disappointed. After all, Loren, Clatis, Harry Moore, and my other friends did the same thing — because the "consultation" they freely gave during the construction of the building made them feel as if the clinic was theirs. And, contrary to what I might have said to them about their free range in the facility, I was delighted that the local citizens came by to say hello and inquire into the goings-on there.

"How 'bout it, Happy. What you doin', boy?" I asked.

"Aw, just slummin'," he replied. "Thought I'd come by here and pay a little on that fool bill somebody sent me from this joint

the other day. Seems like I'm always being asked to make a payment on this place. It's ridiculous!"

"Yeah, that bill was ridiculous," I apologized. "It was about
half what it ought to have been. Workin' cows in that old rotten
catch pen, gettin' my feet stomped, nearly gettin' gored by old
cull cows, sorry help and —" I looked up and noticed Happy
staring intently, almost trancelike, at my patient.

"What are you looking at?" I asked.

"John, did you know that dog layin' there is dead?" he
stated, his gaze still fixed on the closed eyes of the dog. He
hadn't heard a word of my carefully worded insult.

"What's wrong with you, Happy? You ever seen a dead dog
breathe?" I said sarcastically, just as the little Chihuahua took a
slow, deep breath. Had the patient's mama been there, I'm sure
she would have been on the floor by then, out cold from such
outrageous conversation.

"Well, he shore looked dead awhile ago," he replied. "Why
are you messin' around in his mouth like that?"

"Taking out his tonsils. Look at that rotten tonsil there in the
basin." He stared briefly at the unsightly specimen, then turned
away in disgust.

"You took that mess out of that dog right there?"

"Yep, this dog right here." There wasn't hide nor hair of
another dog within sight.

"You're jokin'. Not a tonsillectomy on a dog! I never heard of
such!"

"Oh yeah," I allowed. "I do it all the time. These little dogs
come in here with the sore throat, coughing, and gagging just like
kids. But when we get those tonsils out of there they don't have
any more problems."

"How do you know they got the sore throat?"

"Because I'm a professional, and I've been highly trained to
recognize disease symptoms in animals. People from as far away
as Picayune and Demopolis drive here for this operation." I
knew that would set him off.

"You're well trained all right. Trained on how to charge folks.
I'll bet you charge a big fee for taking out tonsils, don't you?"

"Naw, not much, just fifty dollars."

"FIFTY DOLLARS!" he screamed. "You mean to tell me that folks are willin' to drive all that distance and pay that?" He stood there shaking his head back and forth. "You ought to be ashamed, takin' folks' hard-earned money like that! You wouldn't catch me throwin' money away like that."

"What do you suggest I do, Dr. Dupree? Take a limb to 'em and run 'em off when they come in the door asking for help?" I asked as I peered down into my patient's pharynx. "And may I remind you that you were the one who encouraged me to expand my small animal practice, and how people with pets will do more for their animals than farmers will for their livestock. Remember, you told me to always wear a nice jacket and have my stethoscope around my neck just so, and to kiss the dogs when they come in for shots. You were the one!"

"Aw, Doc, you beat all. Seems to me like you just gone crazy with that pencil!"

"Shh! Shh!" I ordered. "I need complete quiet while I'm doing this delicate surgery!" Happy had seen all he could stand and was quickly back out harassing Mrs. Lee, and probably picking up some cow medicine or maybe writing another check for the balance of his bill. Miracles sometimes do happen!

"Cows and hogs out there in the country dyin', and he's in here, fiddlin' with some rich woman's lapdog," he fumed, loud enough for me to hear.

"Get on out of here, Happy," Mrs. Lee scolded. "You talk too much. That lapdog is just as important to those folks as your cows are to you!" She had been a neighbor of his and she had his number.

I heard the front door slam, then saw him crawl into his truck and hit the starter. He looked at me and shook his head as if he loathed what I was doing. But when he backed up and turned to the right, he stuck his head out the window and yelled, "BRING YO' POLE AND TOMMY, AND WE'LL GO FISHIN'!" Then he was off, an impish grin creeping across his lips. I grinned, too, when I remembered taking Tom with me on a call to Happy's farm, and after the work we went to the pond with our fishing poles. Happy was so insistent that Tom catch a fish that he did everything but dive into the water and put a fish on his hook. Beneath all that gruffness and those surly rough edges, there was a heart big as a watermelon, known only by those who were to be counted as his very close friends.

Not long after the Happy-and-tonsil incident, I was making a couple of farm calls in the south end when Mrs. Lee called me on the two-way radio.

"Dr. John, Happy Dupree just called and wants you to come by the house as quick as you can. He had heard that you were going to be in his vicinity today, and said it was an emergency but wouldn't let on about what it was." That was strange, because he was usually very explicit about what was going on with the sick cow in question. But I knew if he said it was an emergency, it truly was. I would waste no time in getting there.

"OK, I'm just leaving the Brewer place, so I'll whip north and should be at his farm in ten to fifteen minutes," I declared.

When I wheeled into his driveway and skidded to a stop behind his parked truck, Happy came scurrying out the back door carrying something wrapped in a blanket. As he bounded my way, he would occasionally throw a worried look down into the wrinkled blanket. When truckside, he frantically uncovered a panting, wild-eyed, slobbering terrier dog.

"Dr. John, this is Glenda's little dog, and it's in a bad way," he said sheepishly. "Glenda's off at 4-H camp this week, you know, and when I got home from the hay field at dinnertime, this little ole dog was on the verge of a conniption. She won't eat or drink or even let her puppies nurse. I just know she got into some of that rat poison out there on the porch!"

"Puppies? Did you say puppies?"

"Yeah, she had four of 'em several days ago. Oh, man, I'd hate to have to bottle-feed those little things. Reckon you can save her?"

"Uh huh," I said to myself. "She's got eclampsia, and a little slow IV calcium will put her right as rain in a few minutes. But I'm gonna give Happy a dose of his own medicine first."

Glenda's dog was suffering from an acute calcium deficiency

brought on by a sudden demand for milk for her newborns. The cause of the condition is the same in all the species, but the symptoms vary. In the canine, the signs include a high fever, a wild-eyed look, rapid and openmouthed panting, and a jumpy, nervous demeanor. Sometimes the early symptoms are mild or even undetectable to the casual observer, but an astute owner will always know that something is wrong. Eclampsia should always be suspected in a sick, heavy-milk-producing, small dog that has recently delivered puppies.

"I don't know, Happy," I said slowly, removing my stethoscope from my ears, then taking another long read from the thermometer. "This little dog is running a high fever and is seriously ill. We really ought to do some blood work, maybe send her to one of those fancy clinics in Meridian for some X rays, and put her in intensive care. That is, if she means that much to you and your family."

"Well, uh, yeah, Doc," he stammered. "Actually, it's Glenda's dog, you understand, so I..."

"Yeah, but we've got to do something fast, 'cause I'm afraid she's beginning to fade on us. We can't wait much longer."

"How much is all that gonna run?" he asked weakly.

"Probably about fifty dollars, maybe more. You know it costs to do all those tests and work up the case. But we'll hold it down as much as possible," I promised.

"I'm not too keen about goin' all that way to Meridian. What about you just carrying her back up to your place and do whatever you can do there. Just try to save 'er. Glenda's little ole heart would break if this dog was to die, especially if it was on account of me." Beads of sweat the size of field peas were popping out on his forehead and slowly zigzagging downward and then disappearing into the forest of his bushy eyebrows. I knew then the shoe was on the other foot for a change. Perhaps before I was through he would better understand the feelings of other people for their animal companions.

"Before we do that, let's go back up on the screen porch and give her a shot or two in the leg vein here, just to see if it might give her a little relief," I suggested. "Reckon you can restrain her for me and hold her left front leg real still?" I recalled a similar scenario from the previous year, when I made my first social-business call to meet Carney Sam Jenkins. There in his shop, where he ran his taxidermy business as well as his home-made veterinary practice, was a dog not unlike the present one. Both dogs were new mothers and both were owned by young children. I remembered how sad the little girl was when she thought she had seen her pet for the last time, and how elated she was some time later when she returned to find the dog much better and on her way to recovery.

Just as before, I hustled to my vehicle for needle, syringe, a little cotton and alcohol, and some calcium solution. A few minutes later Happy was holding the leg just as I wanted, and I carefully made a venipuncture, then slowly injected the solution into the patient's bloodstream. Happy was quiet as a mouse, but I could hear his accelerated breathing and feel an occasional droplet of his forehead sweat drip onto the back of my syringe-holding hand. I knew he was closely watching every move that both the dog and I were making.

"Now let's put her back with her puppies and in ten minutes we'll see if she'll drink some fresh water," I ordered, after easing the needle out of the vein and massaging the spot lightly. While he busied himself with the puppy box, over in the corner of the porch, I took the syringe and needle back to the truck and busied myself there for a few minutes, just waiting for the recommended ten minutes to elapse. I dropped by the well house, washed my hands, then stopped by the pen where Happy kept his passel of deerhounds and exchanged pleasantries with them. Finally, I sauntered back toward the house and stepped up onto the porch, where Happy was dropping pans, drawing water, and bumping into chairs, yet neither of us uttered a word for an embarrassing period of time. Finally, he broke the silence with an astute observation.

"She looks a lot more like herself, Doc. Not nearly so nervous," he suggested. "What do you think?"

"Why don't you give her a cupful of that good well water, Happy, and let's see if her tongue works," I suggested. He was just waiting for the order, and instantly placed a pan in front of our patient. She started lapping and soon had consumed all the water and was licking around the edges, searching for more.

"Well, I declare, I think she's a lot better," I opined. "It's like she's not the same dog."

"Does that mean she won't need all them high-priced X rays and tests now?" he asked.

"No, I don't think she'll need that now," I answered. "Look, Happy, I was just trying to make a point with you. You remember when you came up to the clinic a while back and I was doing that tonsillectomy? You really gave me a hard time about that, and you made fun of the elderly lady who doesn't have anybody else in the world but that dog. I think I have just proved that even a rough old hardhead like you has some feeling for a helpless creature, even if it's a lapdog."

"You're right, I reckon. You know I was just kiddin' you about that tonsil deal. But please don't tell anybody that I agreed to spend fifty dollars on a dog that won't hunt anything but a biscuit."

When people accept the privilege and responsibility of owning a living creature, whether it is a companion, beast of burden, working animal, recreational animal, or potential food source, they are also accountable for the maintenance of that animal's health. Too many individuals abuse that privilege, and the end result is often poor performance and needless suffering. Even though my friend Happy Dupree bumped his gums a lot about his veterinarian's wasting time doctoring on lapdogs, when the situation was reversed he wanted his family's pet taken care of right then.

People must treat animals with the respect they deserve, not just because they are live creatures but also for the contributions they make to our lives. They may provide us with food or watch over our property, as well as give us their love and companionship. They're more than livestock — they are an emotional investment that requires constant maintenance to keep up the return. Those people who don't tend to the needs of their animals shouldn't be allowed to own them.

Thirteen

⮑ In addition to testing cattle for brucellosis, I was spending considerable time "working cattle," which refers to putting the herd through the squeeze chute and carrying out such adventurous jobs as vaccinating, deworming, castrating, dehorning, checking for pregnancy, and any other procedure the owners desired while the herd was corralled. This job wasn't done simply for the excitement and pleasure of the community, it was done in order to prevent disease, increase productivity, preserve comfort and safety, and in many instances determine if certain of the bovine individuals needed to be culled and sent to town. Cows that are not producing a calf every year, those who are disciplinary problems, or aged ones whose teeth are old and worn down are all candidates for removal.

The timing of many of these procedures depended upon the season and management of the breeding of the herd. If, for instance, the calves were born in the late winter and early spring, the vaccinations were best given in the late spring, while the pregnancy exams were done in the fall at about weaning time. Herds that calved in the fall would obviously be on a different schedule. It was more difficult to schedule a time for herds where the farmers allowed the bull to run with the cows year-round, since there would be calves of all sizes on any given day of the year. It is simply less stressful on the calf, farmer, and veterinarian if the calves are "worked" when they weigh two hundred pounds rather than five hundred pounds.

Many farmers solicit the assistance of their neighbors on "herd-working" days, since it is a lot more convenient to have two or three workers chuteside, plus two or three in the back putting the cattle down the chute. This statement is made assuming that a corral is, in fact, standing and sturdy enough to sustain the struggles of a group of animals who are not willing participants in this entire operation. It also assumes that the humans present have at least a basic knowledge of what to do, where to stand, when to yell, and how to wave a stick at the right time.

All but one of the workers or spectators who help to castrate the calves should be immune from fainting. Some may wonder why in the world it is necessary to have a fainter present. It's because working cattle tends to get very routine and boring to all present, except for the veterinarian and the animals, so the adventure of watching and waiting for the fainter to do his thing breaks the monotony and keeps the bored ones from daydreaming. If an individual wants everything programmed perfectly, all neat and tidy, then he should go into another line of work, such as piloting a jetliner or performing heart surgery.

Joe Bob (Sinking) Jenkins raised fainting to an art, and his collapsing episodes could be timed almost to the second. He collapsed 100 percent of the time approximately thirty seconds after he observed anyone touching any unusual object hanging from the hind end of a cow. He fell out 75 percent of the time when observing a swine castration, and about 50 percent of the time when he saw the same procedure being performed on a bull. He was in constant demand because the locals just loved to watch him in action.

There will always be "drop-ins" (DIs), usually two at a time, who are passing by on the gravel road and see the activity going on at the corral. DIs usually don't have regular day jobs since they are retired or disabled—sometimes their most strenuous daily activity is driving to town to pick up their spouses, who put in long hours at the Vanity Fair ladies' undergarment factory.

The number of DIs at any given cattle working is directly

proportional to the quality and quantity of refreshments available. For instance, I have found that Louisiana cattle workings have more DIs per happening than anywhere else in the United States because proper refreshments are the number-one consideration there.

In addition to the DIs, there should always be a know-it-all (KIA), like Safford the Yapper, on site. The KIA has seen it all, at least five times, and will always dispute the pronouncements of anybody there, whether it is the King of England or a world-renowned specialist on working cattle. Many KIAs are part-time store sitters.

"I wish y'all would looka here!" someone could declare. "This is an albino black Angus heifer with horns growing out of her brisket, plus her tail is growing out of her last rib."

"Yap, I've seen several of those. Saw one in Russia years ago. 'Course, she's not a true albino, she's what I call a pseudo albino. The reason for this phenomenon is..." Then a long dissertation on albinoism begins. That's when earplugs are handy to have.

Carney Sam Jenkins was the resident KIA in Choctaw County. Even though he had never been to Russia or Louisiana, he always knew a better way to do every item of work, criticized the construction of the corral, talked constantly, and was always able to make himself heard above the yapping of the dog.

There should be a minimum of two dogs, preferably curs, patrolling the corral and chute area at any veterinary procedure. Dog One is the designated "horn dog." It is his responsibility to quickly retrieve horns as they are detached from the dehornees. What he does with the horns is strictly up to the dog, as long as he either eats them on the spot or buries them in the pasture for lean horn-eating times in the future. Horns from young calves are still somewhat soft and edible for dogs with good teeth. Adult cow horns are bony hard but are good for gnawing and cleaning teeth. A good horn dog will eat horns until both veterinarian and owner are concerned about his well-being.

"Buck, you look like you swallowed a watermelon! Why don't you bury some now, boy?" a concerned voice says. But Buck grins a dog grin and licks his lips while peering down the chute in hopes of seeing his next snack. But eventually the horn-burial ceremony begins. I am always amazed at how quickly a top horn dog can grab a horn off the ground, run some distance away, dig a hole, deposit the horn, cover it up, and return for another, all without the spectators realizing what is happening.

I have seen owners severely chastise horn dogs when they become so bloated they begin to "white eye" on the job. But even a world champion horn dog can't do away with two hundred horns in a short period of time, so when they begin to pile up in front of the chute, the poor dog should be cut a little slack.

Dog Number Two is present only for the purposes of aggravation. That is to say, he harasses the bovines by snapping at them through the fence, but aggravates the humans to a greater extent by constantly being underfoot and yapping at the wrong end of the animal. This causes a constant flow of threatening hullabaloo from the crew.

"Go t' house, Rastus!" someone constantly screams, throwing clods, rocks, and surplus horns at the totally brainless cur. After a missile whistles dangerously close to his head, a typical aggravation dog will blink his eyes rapidly a few times, obviously awaiting the arrival of additional projectiles, then tuck his tail between his legs, lower his head in shame, and take about five slinking steps toward the house. But when he hears the commotion of the next victim being clanged shut in the squeeze chute, he stops, turns, and looks back toward the corral, licks his lips, grins, and then allows stupidity to override his common sense. In spite of knowing that he will soon be stoned again, he plunges back into his single-minded ritual of barking and biting at the cattle through the sides of the chute boards until someone yells "Go t' house, Rastus!" and the cycle is repeated.

Either dog could pull double duty in an optional third category, the chase dog. His or her duties consist of chasing after, or even trying to outrun, nonfamily-owned vehicles that move into or out of the farm premises, but especially the veterinarian's truck.

Probably the champion of all the truck chasers was a dog named Luckie, who resided at the Hillsman farm. He was a half-collie, half-greyhound creature whose short hair and long and lean build made him an ideal candidate for racing with a busy veterinarian's truck as it left the farm for the next call. Even though Luckie was the designated horn dog, I never knew him to gorge himself to the point of not being able to run, at least in his prime. Our usual race began after all the cattle had been worked and all the equipment stored in the truck. As I washed my boots, I began the prerace encouragement and friendly taunting, while Luckie became more excited with each phrase that I uttered.

"You ready, boy? I'm gonna beat you to the road today, Luckie! Let's go!" I'd say. He would whirl around, bark, his long red tongue flopping and slinging droplets of saliva into the air as his eyes followed every move that I made. Finally, I would hop into the truck, slowly back out of the big barn's hallway, and with a heavy slap on the side of the door, we'd be off.

The S-shaped quarter-mile gravel driveway from the barn to the county crushed-rock-and-tar road was bordered by an alfalfa field on the right and a fescue pasture on the left. If my truck and I had gotten a head start and the fescue on the left wasn't too high, Luckie would dart under the fence at the curve to the left, then cross in front of the speeding truck to the right side of the road shoulder, where he would let it all out for the next two hundred yards. Then, where the driveway curved to the right, he would again go under the fence and into the alfalfa for thirty yards or so before he emerged from under the wire for the short jaunt to the paved road, where both dog and truck would skid to a stop. The trick then was for me to fool him into thinking I was going right but go left instead, or vice versa.

After a series of races between just the two of us, a new dog came on the scene. Fluffy was a small tan shepherd of some degree, and as her name implied, was mostly a mass of dog hair and fuzz. Early on in her career she had suffered fractures of several pelvic bones, and I had often marveled at how well six weeks of confinement and Mother Nature had knitted the bones back together. Once her recovery was complete she decided to run with her faster associate, but she needed some trick to keep him from completely running away from her. It wasn't long before she discovered that if she latched onto Luckie's collar with her teeth at the outset of a race, it would not only slow him down but also help her along. Frequently Luckie could shake away from her grasp, but even then his fast pace was slowed somewhat, because he was constantly looking back, trying to verify Fluffy's position and to see if he was in danger of being caught.

On one of his last races, I faked a left turn at the road, which fooled him into going that way at about thirty miles an hour for about fifty yards until he discovered the ruse. By the time he discovered his mistake, I was going the other way and seconds later had turned back left into the driveway that led to the broiler houses. But Luckie cut across the hay field and joined me, whereupon we raced neck and neck for half the length of the first three-hundred-foot-long house. As we approached the large feed bins on the left side of the driveway, it occurred to me that Luckie was spending too much time looking back over his shoulder at Fluffy and not paying any attention to the bins. But I assumed he knew all the obstacles that were in his path, and I had my own obstacles to contend with, trying to avoid the junk that bordered the right edge of the roadway and the potholes in the wheel paths.

BONGGG! Without looking I knew the sickening sound was that of a speeding dog skull colliding with a piece of industrial-grade angle iron that was anchored in concrete below and sturdied by an empty tin bin above. As experts of dog–grain bin accidents well know, the addition of several hundred bushels of corn or soybeans to the bin will cause a more dangerous-sounding *thud* or *splat* when crashed into by a dog. I was thankful that the bin was empty that day.

As I jumped from the truck, I saw that Fluffy had passed her knocked-senseless colleague and was bursting past the end of the first broiler house, entirely unaware that the race had been called because of unconsciousness. When I turned my attention toward Luckie, I realized he had lived up to his name. He was only staggering, shaking his head, licking his lips, and whining, the obvious signs of canine angle ironitis. Upon examination, there were no bloody lacerations or extra knots on his head, although his eyes were glazed over and they appeared to be crossed.

Unfortunately, Luckie never had the desire to perform a full-fledged race again. He would sometimes make a halfhearted token effort when I left the big barn, but then fall behind at the curve and eventually stop and stare as I drove out of sight. Neither did Fluffy seem to possess the heart to race trucks alone. She was just an aggravation racer.

~

Even though the owners of the livestock are usually on hand during the work, I consider their presence optional. Actually, having the owner present often requires a longer period of time because of his constant questions and reciting of each animal's pedigree.

"Doc, is that a red spot on that heifer's back? She's my best one! She's out of old Three-Teat and Ferd is her sire. What's that on her ear, a knot? Is that cow crippled? She's my best one! Check the tail on that steer, Doc, it just don't hang right." Such constant pronouncements and questions threaten to drive me to the truck for a mouth gag and horse leg tape. I believe once the owner has gone through exactly what he wants done, his comments should be limited to whining and complaining about why vaccine, dewormers, and the veterinarian's time are so expensive.

Appointments for herd work are frequently set up days, weeks, and sometimes months ahead, in order to accommodate planting or harvesting time, weaning dates, and in Alabama, the college football schedule. Anyone within the borders of the state suspected of working cattle during the Alabama-Auburn football game would be ostracized or perhaps charged with a misdemeanor. Of course, the transgression couldn't be proven because any possible witnesses would all be glued to their radios and televisions.

Then there was the problem of rainy weather. Since the appointment was made so far in advance there was always the possibility that a rainy spell had turned the uncovered corral into a sea of mud. If rain interrupted work for very long, it messed up everything, including the desire to get back out there when it slacked up. Sometimes the off time led to daydreaming, which is a dangerous pastime for hardworking people.

One warm morning we were in Mr. Jimmy Throckmorton's barn hall, just sitting there on bales of the previous year's coastal bermuda hay, waiting for a hard shower to stop. We were about halfway through the vaccinating and other routine herd work.

Carney Sam Jenkins, resident KIA and great philosopher, occupied the entire bale to my left. He needed extra room when he sat because he usually brought out his razor-sharp Sears and Roebuck pocketknife and whittled while he rested. He was a wild and unpredictable whittler, his knife frequently slipping as he carved, often landing on the floor or occasionally in a nearby neighbor's thigh muscle. He was also an incautious tobacco chewer who drooled excessively and frequently spattered nearby companions when he expectorated — and he did expectorate frequently and voluminously.

I shared a bale with Possum Miller, a young farmer who spent too much time playing golf. If he wasn't playing, he was thinking about it. I occasionally teed it up with him, but I couldn't handle his uncontrollable temper, which caused him to throw clubs during fits of anger, sometimes high up in bushy oak trees or deep in the kudzu-covered woods. Several small trees on the golf course had succumbed to attacks from Possum's bent-up clubs. However, he was good at working cattle and often showed up to help when I was in his area.

The owner of the herd, Mr. Jimmy Throckmorton, wasn't sitting. Instead, he was nervously pacing back and forth in front of the door, fretting and fuming over the time lost to the rain.

"I don't have time for this!" he bellowed. "I got hay on the ground, a funeral to go to, a pig to cook for that paper mill crowd. I just don't need this!"

Carney Sam stopped his whittling, leaned forward, and evacuated his oral cavity, sending forth a torrent of vile extract into a puddle of water just outside the open door.

"Aw, quit yo' trompin', Squire," slobbered Carney, wallowing the chaw around in his mouth. "Enjoy this nice rain that the Master has sent us. We need this shower." As usual, his common sense and steady demeanor showed in the brief statements that he uttered.

Mr. Jimmy was known to his close friends by several nicknames. Squire, Counselor, Judge, and Professor were all used when he was addressed. The reason for all these titles was the fact that he apparently knew some law. Some thought he had been off to a big law school up in the Northeast somewhere, while others suspected he had taken a vague two-week correspondence course he saw advertised in the back of a comic book. But the fact was, he and Carney both possessed a lot of common sense, and they were both behind-the-scenes advisors and supporters of various politicians and causes.

The rain continued to assault the tin roof of the barn, interrupted only by occasional spine-tingling claps of thunder. It appeared we had worked the last bovine of the day. During a lull in the rainstorm, I asked a daydreaming question.

"What would y'all do if all of a sudden you had a million dollars?"

"Man, I'd go out to California and play golf at all those fancy courses I see on TV," Possum declared. "Then I'd fly across the big water, rent me a car, and play all those courses in Scotland."

"Aw, Possum, you'd get killed over there," warned Jimmy. "They tell me that bunch over there all drive on the wrong side of the road."

"Well, I'd hire me a chauffeur then," answered Possum. "I'd be over there a month or more."

"Don't forget you'll have to come home in time to pick your corn and dig sweet 'taters," I suggested.

"Oh yeah, that's right. But I'd get me a full-time hired man and he'd do that."

"What would you do, Carney?"

"I reckon I'd get me a brand-new red pulpwood truck from Clatis Tew down at the Chevrolet place, rip off both doors, and hang a big Poulan bow chain saw from the back standard. Then, I'd take a club and dent up the hood a right smart so it would resemble all the other pulpwood trucks runnin' the roads around here, and then I'd go out in the woods and cut some paperwood."

"You'd cut paperwood!" screamed Possum. "That's the hardest work there is, except for workin' in tobacco, cleaning out henhouses, and minin' coal!"

"You don't understand," replied Carney after another prodigious spit. "I'd cut wood when I wanted to and quit whenever I got good an' ready. Why, it might take me a month or more to cut a cord. Wouldn't that be a fine way to live?"

"What about you, Mr. Jimmy?"

"I'd build me the finest catch pen, with a roof, lights, and a cold drink machine that didn't take money. The Dr Pepper man would come out here and fill it full of cold drinks for my friends every few days," Jimmy said. "Then I'd get shed of these piney woods, line back cows, and get ahold of some fine purebred Black Anguish stock from out west."

"Black Angus," I interrupted.

"OK, whatever they are," he answered. "Then I'd build me a fine home up on that ridge yonder. I'd sit out on the porch and watch 'em graze this green Choctaw grass and make money. I just might run for the state legislature, too. Couldn't do any worse than what's over there now."

"Doc, what'd you do?"

"What are you askin' him for?" sneered Carney. "He hasn't been here but a year and he's already one of the richest men in the county. He rakes in a pile of money every week up at that sale barn, he works on all them rich women's lapdogs, and he vaccinates thousands of dogs for rabies all over three counties. He's got a gold mine, I'm tellin' you. That's why they opened up that other bank in town!"

"Don't pay any attention to him. He's gotten into some poison and it addled what little brains he's got," I said. "I'll tell you what I'd do. I'd use most of it to pay off my debts, and then I'd build my wife a nice home. Then if I had any left I'd pay some outfit up north to publish the book I'd write about all the crazy characters and liars that I run into every day in my job."

"Liars? Anybody we know?" asked Possum. "Or are you talkin' about that south Marengo crowd?"

"I reckon that people are pretty much the same wherever you go," I replied.

"Hey, boys, it's slackin' up," said a suddenly happy Uncle Jimmy. "Let's finish up these calves so we can get on with our other work."

We did finish the calf work sloshing around in the mud, but not with the same enthusiasm as before the shower. Somehow the wild dreams of big money, trips to Scotland, the power of politics, and new pulpwood trucks interfered with the work at hand.

There's a good lesson to be learned from dreaming too big and at the wrong time. Sometimes, when you come back down to earth, it makes the routine chores seem terribly stale and undistinguished. Especially when the rain is falling and mud is four buckles deep on your five-buckle overshoes.

Fourteen

~~ "Doc, I know it's your day of rest and all, but could you come down here?" the Sunday afternoon caller requested. "Got a little problem with a calf." Since many of my callers just assumed I knew who they were by the sound of their voices, they didn't take two seconds to identify themselves. They immediately went into the reason for the call, leaving me stalling and straining my ear to catch a hint of some speech imprint to frantically run though the name files in my brain before I had to ask and be embarrassed.

The only thing more aggravating than trying to figure out the identity of a caller is to have the caller taunt you while you are trying to do it. Occasionally I grow weary of the guessing game and tell the caller what I really think.

"Bet you don't know who this is, do you, Doc?" The caller laughs.

"Sounds a lot like Joey Jackass to me," I reply curtly.

"Well, you don't have to be such a smart aleck," the unknown and faraway voice asserts, probably through pursed lips. Then I feel bad because I have violated the be-courteous-to-everybody rule that is most important to anyone in the service business.

"You still there, Doc?"

"Uh, yeah, I'm still here." And still searching, searching.

"Doc, it's the Meathead. He's bad sick!" The voice was sounding urgent.

Now I knew! It was Waldo King, local timber cruiser, animal lover, landholder, a good client, and a great friend. He always sounded urgent over the phone, but this day he seemed more urgent than usual.

"What you reckon it is?" I asked.

"Well, he and those others we weaned last week knocked the fence down yesterday and got into the lot where Kathy is feeding those steers out. They got into the feed bin and gorged out on corn and cottonseed meal. Jessie and Dilmus are ailin', too, but Meathead's sprawled out on the ground, moanin' and in a bad way. Kathy's gone to Mobile to see her mama, and she'll skin me and you both if we let anything happen to Meathead." Suddenly it was a "we" problem, but I'd had nothing to do with it.

It was a simple problem caused by Meathead's gluttonous appetite, which had caused rumen overload and acidosis, but there was no simple treatment. If his human contemporaries had overconsumed in a similar manner, they would have simply chewed up a few antacid tablets, but because of Meathead's vast four-stomach arrangement, he needed a hundred or more of the same tablets, plus intravenous fluids and an all-hay diet when his appetite returned.

The Waldo-and-Kathy duo had become an excellent account for the practice because they believed in taking care of the health of their animals. They tried to prevent health problems by timely vaccinations and parasite control, but when one of their pets or livestock seemed to be ill or was injured, one of them was on the phone to the vet pronto. I was even called out of a church service on one occasion to attend an obstetrical case on their farm. That calf was named Pond Bank because he was delivered while I was standing waist-deep in the edge of their pond.

Kathy was the herdsperson, taking care of the fifty head of crossbred cattle, four brood sows, three dogs, and one cat. Their herd was unusual in that all the cattle and swine were named. In addition to Meathead, there was Trixie, Deer Face, Little Stupid,

Johnette, and a host of other bovines with names relating to their appearance, deportment, or weather conditions at birth. Some even carried the names of persons seen passing by on the country road in the hours immediately surrounding the blessed birth, or of helpful neighbors who showed up during the birthing process to assist Kathy with her worried hand wringing. Kathy was always flustered when one of her animal mothers was in labor, but as soon as the new arrival touched the ground she immediately took leave of her fidgety behavior and took charge of neonatal affairs.

In her spare time, Kathy played softball, taught a Sunday school class, worked a big garden, and looked after Waldo. But she should have been a veterinary nurse. She possessed patience, persistence, a gentle touch, and that intangible something that seemed to work healing magic on sick or weak calves or pigs. She was able to save critically ill animals time and again, when others would give them up as a lost cause.

Meathead was a prime example of her efforts. His birthing had been a very slow, difficult process, and I had been called to assist. When he finally made his backwards entry into the cold, cruel world, he appeared lifeless, but after clearing the mucus from his throat and shaking him upside down, then rubbing him briskly, Kathy got him to start gasping for breath and pumping his sides with great effort. Calves born backwards have a greater risk of drowning or respiratory problems because they frequently try to breathe before they clear the pelvic canal of their mothers, which results in their inhaling uterine fluid.

"Let me have 'im!" Kathy suddenly ordered, pushing aside all the amateurs. "I'll get 'im to breathing." I was sure that he wouldn't survive.

As I turned my attention back to the mother cow, I could hear Kathy talking to the little calf in soothing and comforting tones as she massaged his chest and legs. She used clean towels instead of straw for calf rubdowns. She stated with authority that straw was just too rough on a newborn's sensitive skin. "How would you like your naked skin rubbed down with straw? Huh?" she asked when some bystander pooh-poohed her towel massage. The questioner would turn red and hang his head in embarrassment while kicking rocks and clods.

A few minutes later she had the little calf sitting up, and even though he had some difficulty breathing, things were looking much better. Now the cow was looking down at her new offspring with much pride, making little sniffing, mooing, and grunting noises, and finally starting her determined tongue-massaging action all over the calf's body.

"If y'all will get out of my way, I'll milk some colostrum out of this cow and get it into this little dude," she announced with great authority.

And so it went. She fed the little calf several times a day with a bottle until he was strong enough to be helped up and allowed to nurse the natural way. After a week of good nursing and encouragement, he could get up unassisted, nurse, and even explore the barn.

The name Meathead came from Waldo. When I met him on the road a couple of weeks after the blessed event, we stopped and conversed briefly.

"He's the dumbest calf I ever saw, Doc," he allowed. "He acts screwy, like he sometimes tries to find the teat on the wrong end of the cow, or he gets on the wrong side of the fence and then can't get back. Why, he's just a regular Meathead!"

"You reckon he's crazy?"

"Naw, he ain't got enough sense to be crazy!" he replied.

It turned out to be a very appropriate handle. When we vaccinated in the spring, Meathead got a foot hung up and then turned upside down in the squeeze chute, resulting in our wasting valuable time getting him upright. When we ear-tagged him, he managed to mangle up the ear by scraping it on a pine tree. Then it got infected and had to be lanced and drained, which created scar tissue that made the damaged ear droop considerably lower than the good one. His appearance, as well as his behavior, prevented his being selected as a prospective 4-H club calf.

Once an early summer storm blew up out of the southwest, and he and two of his associates were under a big oak when it was struck by lightning. His associates were killed instantly, but somehow he escaped with only twenty minutes of unconsciousness. When I arrived on the scene and sloshed a large open bottle of ammonia around his nose, he started to shake his head and thrash around. Minutes later he was standing, looking his regular goofy self. Waldo allowed that the lightning probably relieved him of what little sense there was inside his cranium to start with.

So now Meathead was laid out because he had allowed his gluttonous appetite for sweet feed to override his self-control. That seemed like a fitting end to his mistake-ridden life.

The recovery rate for my treatment of cattle that overload their rumens with corn has not been stellar, and I suspect that other veterinarians have similar records. My first two cases of rumen overload in Choctaw County were at Mr. Kent Farris's place, where the cows had gotten into the mash fermenting for his homemade liquor, and my fifty percent recovery rate there was just about average. I'm still looking for that sure cure for this ailment.

Meathead was inside the barn lot, not thirty feet from the spot where he had been born. He was sprawled out on the ground like a giant blob, but with his eyes closed cow fashion. His nose was rigidly poked down into the dirt, and without that support he would have surely collapsed over on his side. After poking, pushing, and thumping on his side a few times, I realized that Waldo was jabbering, wanting to help.

"What you gon' do, Doc? How bad off is he? Can we git 'im well before Kathy gits home? You need a bucket of water? Do I need to go git hep? Watch out where you step, Doc!"

"Just calm down and listen to me, Waldo! Just listen!" I shouted. "We've got to pass this tube down him and give him some oil to move all that stuff out. Then we'll give him a bunch of IV fluids and antibiotics. Then we'll start him on some rumen culture to get his stomach back to working again. And no, he won't be well by the time Kathy gets home. It's gonna be several days, if he makes it at all." But Waldo refused to hear any part of my last two sentences.

"Just hang on, old boy, Doc's gonna fix you up, by granny," I heard him mutter as I headed for the truck for an armload of medicine.

Ten minutes later, as the fluids were pouring into Meathead's jugular vein, I offered my prognosis.

"I wouldn't be surprised if you might not have old Meathead to kick around any more by this time tomorrow," I said. "He can't get up or even hold his head off the ground. His stomach is like slop, and he's real dehydrated. Just too many things going against him."

"I sure hope you're wrong, Doc. I don't know how Kathy'll take it since he's sort of her favorite."

The next day Meathead was somewhat better. He wasn't comatose anymore and he sniffed and nibbled on a little grass hay. I was encouraged by his progress and also glad to know that Kathy would be home that evening. If we could just keep him going until she returned, I'd feel a lot better, because I thought he might perk up even more when he heard her voice and felt her touch.

The next day when I stopped by on my rounds, the first thing I saw was Kathy, dressed in coveralls and a camouflage hat. She didn't resemble Florence Nightingale in her appearance, but she sure did in the way she worked her nursing magic on Meathead. He was actually standing with his head in a plastic bucket she was holding.

"Kathy, I hope that's not grain you're feeding him. He can't take it yet," I cautioned.

"Now, Doc, you know me better than that. This is just some warm water with strawberry Jell-O and electrolytes in it. He's thirsty!" she declared. "He's drank nearly a quart this morning. He's gonna get his rumen culture at eleven and then at noon I'm gonna see if he'll eat some of this good alfalfa hay that I got from down the road."

"Well, I'm glad you got home when you did, to nurse him back to health."

"Me, too!" she said. "You and Waldo would have fiddled around and let this yearling die!" I wondered why we hadn't been given an iota of credit for all the hard work we had done before she returned from her gallivanting.

"By the way, did you come prepared to operate on Bertha today, or did Waldo forget to ask you about it?" she questioned. Bertha was the head sow at the farm.

"My scalpel's always ready, whenever you are," I replied. I didn't have a clue what she was talking about, since Waldo had obviously forgotten to inform me about the problem. "Where's the patient?"

"In the lot, of course. Where do you think she is, in the kitchen?"

"Well, nothing I see at this place surprises me anymore. Cows named after vets and preachers, dog funerals out under the pines..."

When Kathy's old pets passed away, she gave them a decent burial not far from the house in a special place at the edge of the woods. On a couple of occasions I had been summoned to put pets to sleep and assist in their burial. When I arrived, a grave had been meticulously opened and a quantity of roofing tin and a pile of pine straw were nearby. The beloved and faithful pet was laid in a nice box that was lined with his favorite blanket or fireside sleeping mat, then carefully placed in the grave and surrounded by the pine straw. Next, the tin was placed atop the straw and coffin, and dirt was piled on top of that. When the physical chore was over, I was asked to say a few words about the deceased. I had not officiated at many animal funerals, but because of my numerous trips to the King farm and household, I had gotten to know all the inhabitants quite well and could recall many pleasant memories of every pet, which made it quite an honor to preside at their last rites.

Shortly we were joined by Waldo at the hog lot fence, and Kathy was pointing out the problem with Bertha's face. I signaled to Waldo to keep quiet, so that Kathy wouldn't go into her usual diatribe about the forgetfulness of the male species. There was a small raw mass, probably a glorified porcine wart, protruding some two or three inches from the left corner of Bertha's mouth.

"Yeah, Waldo talked to me about this problem while you were off gallivanting all over the country," I lied. "We can fix that, although I don't know why. It's not as if the finest plastic surgeon in Hollywood could make her look any better." Waldo winked and giggled. Kathy picked up a corncob and faked a throw to my head.

"Yeah, but what is it?" she replied.

"Probably a benign fibropapilloma, but it could be a basal cell carcinoma. I won't know until I do the histopath," I replied, dead serious. Again, a feminine hand quickly reached down for two more corncobs and made another feint toward my head. I ducked, because a hard-thrown cob to the side of the head can do some damage.

"There you go again, Doc, usin' them big words," she warned. "If you ain't careful you're gonna say something like that to some of that Toxey fillin' station crowd one of these days, and they're gonna think you're cussin' 'em. Then the fur's gonna fly! And I wasn't gallivantin'. Now, can you speak English? Is it cancer, or what?"

"I spec' it's 'what,'" I said snidely. The corncobs left on the ground were out of reach by this time, so a pursed-lipped Kathy simply glared my way in disgust, obviously displeased over my diagnosis of "what."

I enjoyed looking at the faces of my friends when I laid some pathology jargon on them. Most wanted a succinct diagnosis in plain Alabama English, with no fancy or erudite phrases. But I didn't want to lose all my medical vocabulary, which was necessary for writing up reports or consulting over the phone with one of my learned, and white-smocked, professors.

Kathy was worried that the mass might be malignant, but she was more concerned about Bertha's appearance, since her headquarters and lounging area were right next to a heavily traveled gravel road. Several helpful but curious neighbors had stopped by the house and inquired about the affliction.

"What's that funny-lookin' thing on yo' hog's mouth?" they asked.

"That ain't no hog, brother, that's Bertha King!" Waldo

replied, "And that's just a wind on her lip. Doc's gonna fix it when we get through layin' by corn. He's gonna give her a face-lift operation!"

A wind on an animal is like a knot on a tree. A wind can be an abscess, a benign tumor, or just a hard unidentifiable mass on the side of an animal, but it is not a scientific term happily embraced by medical vocabularists.

Kathy decided she didn't want to be involved with Bertha's surgery, which was just as well with me. I knew she wouldn't like all the racket that was just getting ready to break loose. We nose-snared Bertha in the usual hog-catching way, which resulted in the expected steady sow scream. I'm sure it was heard five miles downwind. Quiet immediately descended upon the lot, however, once the intravenous sodium pentobarbital did its job. There were no problems with the surgery, and there were no complications. The difficulty arose when I returned a couple of weeks later to remove the sutures. As I confidently strode into Bertha's accommodations, I heard and then saw her charging toward me, making those "oof, oof" noises with her chomping and slobbering oral cavity. I felt a scary chill ascend my entire spinal cord, and I scrambled, in a panic, up to the top of a self-feeder as she snapped and sniffed down below at the scent of a well-remembered intruder. Waldo was hiding behind a fifty-five-gallon drum, snickering at my unfortunate fate, while I examined the fruits of my surgical handiwork from my lofty perch.

The scar on her face was beautiful. Actually, there was no visible scar at all. The only things that could be seen were the white sutures. I had left the ends long for easy retrieval, and they were sticking out the side of her mouth, giving the appearance that she had been trying to grow a one-sided, white, stubby-bristled mustache.

"What a great job!" I congratulated myself as I sat uncomfortably frozen on the pointed top of the feeder. "Waldo, get that hog away from over here!" I yelled.

"Doc, that ain't no hog, that's Bertha!" he corrected in between spasms of laughter. "And she remembers what you did to her the other day."

Eventually, a few ears of corn from the crib coaxed her away from my general vicinity, so I scurried down and sprinted to the truck. From there, I loudly instructed both Bertha and Waldo on what they could do with the sutures and drove away in a huff, leaving Waldo doubled over in a barely audible but continuous cackle.

Meathead also survived and did well. When I last saw him, he was trying to butt his associates away from three feed troughs so he could continue his gluttonous ways. He surely didn't show any adverse signs of his previous overindulgence.

Veterinarians aren't usually thought of as cosmetic surgeons, but my colleagues and I routinely perform cosmetic dehornings on certain calves, trim ears on some breeds of dogs, and have been known to descent skunks, even though the procedure is frowned upon by the veterinary profession. But I have done only one face-lift on an ugly sow. It was not especially exciting, but it is comforting to know that if porcine face-lifts ever become popular, I may be able to cash in on the skills I perfected on Bertha King.

Fifteen

⌒ I have never felt that I possessed adequate knowledge of the equine species or their owners to consider myself an "equine veterinarian," even though my veterinary school training was thorough and state-of-the-art. I had learned that just knowing about medicine and surgery was not nearly enough. In order to get a sick horse treated or a healthy one dewormed, vaccinated, and the teeth floated, a veterinarian must have a working knowledge of various restraint procedures — as well as a little "horse sense" about which animals require restraint.

Not only do horses and people share high intelligence and a low threshold for pain, they also share a variety of personality traits. Some are congenial, easygoing types that respond to external stimuli in a patient, uncomplaining manner, while others are nasty and tend to come unglued at the slightest provocation. But the difference between the two species is in their predictability. If an equine patient attempted to kick down the barn and maim every other breathing being at last year's annual preventative health "horse-o-ree," then that horse can be counted on for a repeat performance in the following years. I believe that the human species is a little more unpredictable.

In addition, "horse folks" are different from "cow folks" and "dog folks." To be in the presence of horse enthusiasts for the first time is an eye-opening but confusing experience. While cattlemen discuss and complain about the current downward trend of cattle prices, horse owners reverently recite pedigrees as if they were passages from the works of Homer or Shakespeare. And while pet owners rave about the intelligence and loyalty of their dog or cat, equine devotees talk about show ribbons, the various treatments for colic and which kind of truck pulls a horse trailer with more authority.

"Well, I've got a colt out of Merry Belly by FourGo who was standing at Possum Trot before he was gelded. I'm sure you heard about them forgetting to oil him before he was vanned to Alabama and of course he foundered. Now he's got chronic laminitis, which has rotated both fore third phalanxes. The farrier correctively trimmed him and put on bar shoes, but by that time he had Bute-induced gastritis, which was obviously that vet's fault. He don't know the first thing about horses." It's hard for people who are out of the equine loop to comprehend the above jargon without the use of a glossary of equine terms and several minutes of careful thought. All except the part about the vet not knowing anything, of course.

I was studying my equine textbooks frequently, carefully reading and rereading the chapters by Gibbons, Vaughan, Hoffman, Wheat, Guard, and other famous equine specialists, in an effort to become familiar with the different types of lamenesses and other problems that I was seeing and to learn how to diagnose and treat them just by conducting a good physical examination of the patient. But I was finding that a difficult part of practicing equine medicine and surgery was learning how to predict the outcome of a treatment. It was obvious that experience was the best teacher of that skill.

My becoming a "horseman" was taking much longer than expected. A visit to check on James Bryant's horse brought that message home loud and clear.

"Dr. McCormack, I need you to come up here and check out a sick mare," James said. "She acts like she's choked." I always dreaded getting choke cases, because they were so difficult to deal with. This condition occurs occasionally when a greedy horse gobbles his food down too quickly and a double-handful-sized mass of dry feed clogs the four- to five-foot-long esophagus. To make matters even worse, the choked portion can be far down in the thoracic area, which creates an even bigger nightmare for both horse and the veterinarian. A large doughy mass can't be pushed down or pulled back up without considerable risk of further injuring an already inflamed and perhaps gangrenous esophageal lining. Many chokes, even when relieved, leave the patients with some scar tissue that could predispose them to similar episodes in the future.

Mr. Bryant's farm was located in southern Sumter County, just across the Choctaw County line. I made frequent visits to work with his cows, but it was my first trip to attend a horse. The twenty-minute trip allowed me time to list all the different possible diagnoses in my mind.

"Maybe she just choked on an apple or pear," I said to myself. But that wasn't very likely since it was way too early for apple and pear season. "Maybe she's had strangles and the nerves in her throat have been damaged," I mused. Strangles is a troublesome and very contagious respiratory disease of horses that frequently is complicated by the formation of abscesses in the lymph glands of the neck. Then I thought of botulism, an uncommon disease in most areas, which causes muscle paralysis. I wished I had obtained a better history over the phone, which might have made the trip less fretful. I vowed to ask more questions of future callers.

When I turned in at the short driveway and made my way beside the nice brick house, I saw the mare standing near an outbuilding between the house and barn. A young foal was at her side, moving back and forth, nuzzling the mare's udder. From my windshield examination, it was readily apparent that the mare felt poorly. Her head was down, her body was rigid, and I noticed that her tail wasn't making the back-and-forth movements it should have been making, especially during fly season. Even when James came off the back porch, my gaze stayed riveted on the ill horse, looking for any sign that would precipitate a diagnosis. But no lights were being snapped on in my upstairs. After exchanging pleasantries with James, I asked him for some background on the mare.

"Well, she's an eight- or ten-year-old quarter mare, and this is her second foal she's had since she's been on this place. She's never been sick before that I know of," he declared. "I noticed her this morning trying to drink out of the horse trough, but I could tell that she wasn't getting anything down because there weren't any ripples going down the side of her neck. Then she'd stick half her face down in the water, trying to drink that way, but when she moved away from the trough, water would just pour out of her mouth. I've never seen anything like that. Plus, Doc, she just doesn't look right out of the eyes." An observant stockman notices little things like that, as well as unusual behavior, appetite changes, and an animal's being at the wrong place in the pasture at a certain time of day. "A neighbor had a mare acting just like this one a while back, and she was choked on something."

"What's her name?" I asked, rubbing her neck.

"We call her Fannie," he answered. "I don't know why, but she's kinda special to us."

I soon became engrossed in the routine of my examination. Her temperature was up some three degrees, but her pulse and respiration were only slightly elevated. She felt hot and sweaty, and I stethoscoped a strange thumping sound in her chest. "She must have the hiccups," I thought to myself, even though I had never heard of a horse having such an irritating malady. With my brow wrinkled and both eyes squinted, I backed off and stared at the patient while considering the hiccup possibility. The mare also had her brow furrowed and her eyes squinted, as if she, too, was in deep thought. She was drooling and seemed to be making throat noises, as if trying to swallow. Even though it didn't exactly fit the pattern, I had convinced myself that choke was the most likely diagnosis.

"She looks anxious," James volunteered. He hit it right on the head. She did look anxious and very worried about something. As an afterthought, I went back to the mare's side and spoke a few soft words before palpating her udder for any evidence of mastitis or edema. "Fannie's sure got the milk, hasn't she?" I said.

"Yeah, she milks like a cow. It's about more than one foal can handle," James answered.

"Well, let's pass this tube down her throat and see if she's choked," I suggested.

With James holding the patient's head and speaking to her in soothing tones, I started the eight-foot-long, three-quarter-inch-diameter tube up through her nose and down into her pharynx. But the tube kept trying to go into the trachea because of her refusal or inability to swallow. Finally, after several attempts and repeated rotating of the tube, it eased down into the thoracic esophagus, where I detected a small amount of resistance, but then the tube seemed to slip right into the stomach, just as it was supposed to do.

"Did she unchoke, Doc?" James asked as I retracted the tube.

"It felt as though there was something down near the stomach, but I think it moved on out," I replied.

"Good, good," he replied. "I kinda like this old mare, even though she's just a hay burner. Isn't that right, old girl?" he said, giving the mare a few love pats on the neck and looking into her anxious eyes. I might have convinced James Bryant that things were back to normal, but I hadn't convinced myself. He promised to call me the following day with a report.

On the way home, I kept going over and over all the symptoms I had seen, because I knew I was missing something. I knew that I was going to figure it out and it was going to be something very simple. And I was sure that it was going to be something other than choke, because choked animals don't unchoke that easily, and they don't have the hiccups. I thought about calling one of my veterinary school professors and relating the situation to him, but I was afraid of being ridiculed on the phone, as well as in the next faculty meeting.

"My fellow veterinarians," he would probably say to his stiff-necked associates around the giant testing table, "do you remember a recent graduate by the name of McCorkle, or maybe it's McCormack?" Most would shake their heads negatively. "The boy called me this morning with the most asinine question about a choked horse."

"I think I do remember him," another full professor would reply. "He was a very poor horseman, and he favored cattle and hunting dogs. We should have held him back and required that he spend at least another year in the equine clinic with Dr. Vaughan." I swallowed hard and blanched out at the suggestion of wrapping horses' legs and frantically dodging flying hooves for another 365 days. No, I wouldn't be calling the university for consultation.

Arriving at the clinic, I drove around back, entered through the kennel room, and beelined it to my textbooks, still piled on the floor in the surgery room. Maybe I could do some quick reading before Jan discovered that I had slipped in the back door. A quick look through my latest edition of *Equine Medicine and Surgery* yielded no clues, and neither did Frank's *Large Animal Surgery*. Finally, as a last resort, I picked up an antique, dog-eared, coverless book that had been published in the 1800s by a Dr. Williams, flipped to the back, and slid my forefinger down the musty pages that were crumbling away at the edges, scanning the alphabetical index for the promise of a word or phrase that described what I had just seen twenty minutes before. Near the bottom of one of the pages I saw "Spasm of the diaphragm." Could this be the cause of the mare's "hiccups"?

Little things mean a lot to veterinarians, especially when things aren't going well with our patients. So with the excitement of a graduate student on the brink of a scientific breakthrough, I hurriedly flipped back toward the front of the book until the paragraph describing problems of the diaphragm appeared. My eyes devoured the old phrases and well-written sentences with the enthusiasm of a first-week veterinary student. About halfway down the page was the one-line gem that I was hungrily seeking.

"That's it!" I cried. I slammed the book shut and ran for the truck, all the while berating myself for being so stupid.

"What an idiot!" I ranted. "She has a young foal, lots of milk, anxious expression, flared nostrils, everything the book says. I must be the worst horse doctor in the entire state of Alabama!

Thank goodness I didn't call Auburn and ask for help. I would have been the laughingstock of the state association.

Even though it is impossible to be exposed to every animal disease or pathological condition while in veterinary school, except in textbooks, I was still distressed with my failure to diagnose such a simple disease in Mr. Bryant's mare. Somehow I had missed seeing this condition before, but I should have been able to use my common sense and figure it out. I spun my tires getting around the building, only to encounter several cars parked out front and Jan standing in the front door.

"Honey, I didn't know you were here until I heard the back door slam. You've got people here. Where are you going?" I have always wished that my mind worked as fast as Jan's. She can cover more ground in a short paragraph than anyone I know.

"Of course, I'll be right in. I was going back to check on James Bryant's mare," I answered.

Two hours later the dogs, cats, and birds had been treated, and I was telling Jan about Fannie, and how I was sure I had made the diagnosis from an eighty-year-old textbook.

"How about calling up there to see if the mare is any better," I asked. But I knew what the answer was going to be.

"No, she's no better, maybe even a little worse. I'd appreciate it if he could run back up and take another look at her," would be the reply.

Minutes later I was darting up Highway 17 with the pedal to the metal, bent over the steering wheel in deep driving concentration. Small children playing in their swept-clean yards paused in their games when they heard the whine of my engine and the whistle of my two-way radio antenna slicing through the wind. I blew the horn in long bursts when the locals driving up from side roads dared to even look as if they wanted to pull out in front of me, then rocked their conveyances with wind gusts and thousands of grains of sand from the swath I was cutting through the atmosphere. Then I heard Jan's call on the radio.

"Go ahead, Base," I said into the microphone.

"John, I have Mrs. Bryant on the phone, and she said the mare is not any better. She thinks her condition has gotten worse and she wants to know could you come back up there and recheck her. Mr. Bryant doesn't think she's choked now." That made two of us!

"Tell her to hang up the phone and look for a cloud of dust!" I declared, repeating the phrase that I had heard Dr. Foreman, my former employer, use on many occasions.

"Dr. McCormack, I appreciate you coming back up here. Fannie looks worse to me," James declared as I stepped out of the truck.

"I think I know what her problem is now, James," I said. "Let's give her five hundred cc's of this calcium and see if it won't straighten her out."

Shortly, the dark brown solution, called Cal-Dextro No. 2, was glugging slowly through a two-inch, sixteen-gauge needle into her left jugular vein. She stood quietly, except for an occasional whinny to her foal, as though she knew there was a good reason for all the probing, poking, and palpating. The foal was in continual motion, switching his short tail, shaking his head, but never straying far from her side. I knew in just days the Bryants were going to revel in the sight of the young colt bolting through the pasture and cavorting around as if he was the happiest being on the farm.

We made small talk as the calcium-and-dextrose solution slowly dripped into Fannie's vein. Sometimes the owner and veterinarian ease the tension surrounding a situation by conversing about other more pleasant subjects. So, as Mr. Bryant kicked at dirt and discussed the status of the wild turkey population in south Sumter County, I nodded in agreement while aimlessly examining Fannie's neck skin with one hand and holding the calcium bottle aloft with the other. It's probably a subconscious mechanism the brain initiates to prevent thinking about the possibility of a treatment failure and all the unsatisfactory things that might go wrong. But ultimately, the facts of the case must be faced and a prognosis offered by the person who owns the stethoscope and uses the needle. Many clients are not comfortable with inquiring about whether their sick horse is going to live or die. Instead, they ask a question or two about some future event that involves the patient.

"Do you think her illness will interfere with her getting back in foal?" Mr. Bryant inquired. "I was thinking about breeding her back right away." Naturally, I was just as evasive with my answer.

"I don't anticipate that being a problem, but I think you should wait a few days to see how she responds to this treatment. And remember, if you haul her up to the north end of the county or even a few miles down to Choctaw, that will be stressful for her and it might cause a relapse." I felt sure those were true statements, but I had not answered his question with the yes or no answer that he had asked for.

Then he asked for my recommendations for Fannie's diet for the next few days, as well as for the entire six-month-or-so period when she would be nursing the foal. Several other pertinent questions followed before he got around to the big one.

"You do think she's gonna make it, don't you?" he asked, almost apologetically.

By that time, fifteen minutes' worth of calcium had slowly dripped into the mare, and I could already notice a positive difference in her attitude. Her respiratory rate had decreased, the "hiccupping" had almost stopped, and she didn't have the anxious facial expression of before. In fact, as the minutes ticked off, I noticed that I was beginning to take on a little of the self-confidence that I had observed in those big-time, famous equine veterinarians who always wore suits and drove big cars on their rounds.

"Oh, yes sir, I believe she's going to be just fine. I think some adjustments in her ration might be in order, and I'll put that down on paper momentarily," I replied. As the last of the medicine disappeared down the tube, I removed the needle and massaged the site, probably just as those Kentucky horse vets would have done. Then I washed up my gear and stowed it in the truck while James led Fannie around the yard and up to the water trough.

"I think she's a lot better, Doc. And look ahere, she's drinking water!" James exclaimed.

"Yes sir, I believe you're right," I said matter-of-factly.

"I believe I could get into this equine thing," I thought to myself. "'Course, I'd need a nicer vehicle, maybe a Cadillac, some nice clothes, and a string tie with a horse on it." I grinned just thinking about being so attired, then driving right up to the arena at all the area horse shows and making a grand entrance. I'd probably even have an assistant, or at least a flunky to carry my black bag, open gates, and hold the horses while I made astute uncanny diagnoses to the owners and all the spectators regarding the health problems of the patient—as long as I had my antique textbooks nearby, of course. But the voice of my present client brought me back to reality.

"Doc, I've got about twenty-five calves that need to be vaccinated for the Bang's disease. Reckon when you can get to it?"

After a piece of pecan pie on the porch, I made notes on dietary suggestions, and then we checked our calendars and arranged a date for the vaccinations. As I scribbled the appointment down in my little day book, I felt as if my status had dropped a little, from noted equine specialist to plain old cow vet.

Before leaving, I looked in on Fannie, who was grazing contentedly on a grassy spot in front of the barn, her tail swishing briskly back and forth. Occasionally she would stomp one front foot at a troublesome horsefly. The hiccups were gone, her nostrils normal, and her eyes clear. It was an amazing transformation in just an hour.

"Dr. John, I thank you for what you did," Mr. Bryant said as he handed me a check. "I think you know more about horses than any vet I've ever seen."

As equine enthusiasts have probably already figured out, Fannie was suffering from eclampsia, a metabolic disease of mares that have recently foaled. The old book had told me that "spasm of the diaphragm, characterized by a rhythmic thumping of the chest wall, is a classic sign of eclampsia in the postparturient mare." It is essentially the same disease that affected

Happy Dupree's little dog when she had her puppies. It is brought on by a sudden decrease in the amount of calcium in the blood. As the udder fills, the calcium-rich milk pulls the calcium from the blood, and in some animals the symptoms of eclampsia develop. The basic calcium-deficient condition is seen occasionally in other animals, especially in the dairy cow, but it is called parturient paresis, or milk fever, in that species. Cows are affected much more quickly and more severely, usually being found down, and will die if not treated quickly.

The standard treatment is to slowly inject a quantity of calcium gluconate intravenously, which results in dramatic improvement. Some of my Choctaw County cattle-owning clients called it "the Lazarus medicine" after they had seen a comatose downer cow arise and walk in less than an hour after the calcium injection. I always enjoyed observing the open-mouthed look on an observing neighbor's face when the "miracle" occurred. It also made me feel that I had done something to help not only the cow but the family as well.

A minute later, after a handshake, two smiles, and two good-bye waves, I was on my way south in high spirits, reviewing the Fannie case and filing the entire scenario away somewhere in the recesses of my cranium. Whether or not I would someday become a famous equine doctor, at that time I vowed to never again miss a diagnosis because I didn't look at the patient, the circumstances surrounding the patient, and use some common horse sense. My colleague Dr. Dilmus Blackmon said it best.

"You miss more by not looking than by not knowing!"

Sixteen

It seemed as if our equine case load had picked up following my "miraculous cure" of Mr. James Bryant's mare, Fannie. Even though I had made no overt claim as to my "brilliant" diagnostic work or "competent" treatment of the mare's eclampsia, these adjectives were being frequently tossed around in daily discussions of Fannie's case and other current events at country stores in the north Choctaw and south Sumter County area. According to the rumors that I heard in Chappell's barbershop and the co-op feed store, equine health care and the perceived proficiency of "that vet down at Butler" dominated the conversation for several days after my visits to the Bryant farm. All sorts of information about the case, some of which was highly inaccurate, as could be expected, had been flowing freely as the store sitters, their apprentices, and regular customers reviewed and critiqued the incident.

"I heard the vet didn't have the right kind of medicine so he had to go to Meridian and borrow some from Dr. Till over there," one man had reportedly stated.

"Naw, I think what actually happened was this," an older man with more sitter seniority had supposedly said. "It was such a rare disease, he went back to his office and called the best race-track horse doctor up in Kentucky and consulted with him just to be sure he was right about his diagnosis and treatment. I heard that race horse feller told him that what he was doin' was right as rain, and if he was down here he'd treat that mare exactly the same way. And that ain't all!"

"What else?" an apprentice asked, leaning forward on his nail keg with wild-eyed anticipation.

"He offered Dr. John a job on the spot. Told him he'd double whatever he was makin' here if he'd just come up there and do nothin' but thoroughbred horse work."

"What'd our vet say?" another apprentice asked. (I really did like the "our" vet part.)

"I'm not sure what he said, but I did hear over at Joe Ward's store yesterday that his wife makes deposits every day in both Butler banks. Somebody saw his truck parked over at the Sweetwater bank one day last week. So it's obvious he's makin' plenty right here in Choctaw and there ain't no need to move way up north somewhere where folks talk funny and it's always cold. You see him flyin' up and down these roads every day, sometimes more than once."

"You got t'at right! I can't understand why anybody would want to live anywhere but here, do y'all?" All heads nodded in agreement, as they, too, pondered the plight of those who lived elsewhere.

"He makes enough every Thursday at the sale barn in Livingston to live high on the hog," declared a cattleman. "I see him every week testing all those cows and vaccinating a bunch of hogs. Last week some lady came driving up there with a dog for him to doctor on, and folks are always bringing calving cows and cut-up horses to him there at the barn."

I don't know how folks can get their information so crossways, confused, and erroneous, but I have found that to be the case in more places than west Alabama. But as I heard of the things that happened about the horse, I just smiled and let them carry on. The best public relations in the world for a country vet is word-of-mouth, and especially country store prattle.

Therefore, I didn't know whether the increased caseload was due to my perceived equine expertise or perhaps to the nice summer weather that was causing horse owners to ride their horses more frequently and pay more attention to their health needs. Jan, ever the pragmatist, said it was because I was the only vet in the area since the semiretirement of Carney Sam Jenkins, local homemade veterinarian and trusted sage. Actually he had not retired, he was simply being more selective in seeing patients and was referring all the surgical cases, fractures, and most of the horse work over to our clinic. I felt as though we were getting a lot of calls because of word-of-mouth, but I was sure that Jan was correct.

The next Sunday afternoon, my main man Loren and I were standing in the pro shop talking with Mr. Idrain Doggett, the manager, getting ready to play a golf match with our resident professionals, Billy Davis and "Titanic" Thompson. Nobody could beat those two, so we had been hitting practice balls in the early mornings for several weeks in anticipation of the great challenge ahead of us.

"Idrain, somebody will probably call in here asking for me to come look at a horse. But don't come out on the course to get me unless it's an emergency, because if we don't complete all eighteen holes, the bet is off," I requested. "This is a big match, and my main man and I have our games in top shape. I just know today's the day we're gonna finally work those guys over."

"They've been out here every day practicing and plottin'," he warned.

"We have, too, but it's been early in the morning. We figured they'd find out, but we don't really care," I said boastfully. "While I'm here, you better let me have a sleeve of those hundred-compression black Titleist balls."

"Well, I think they already know, 'cause I heard them refer to y'all as the 'dew sweepers,'" Mr. Doggett whispered, leaning over the counter. "But, Doc, you probably ought not be using a ball with that high a compression rating. If you hit it a little off center, it's like hitting a steel ball with a fireplace poker. That ball's made for better players, like Davis and Thompson."

I just stared at him momentarily, wondering if his opinion of my golfing ability would rub off on my finely honed swing. But from the blank look on his face, he never realized that his remark might have had such a psychological effect on my game. The ego and spirit of golfers can be bruised quite easily.

"That's OK, I aim to hit 'em hard today," I vowed, while trying to shake his bruise off my psyche. "Remember now, unless it's an emergency, just tell 'em I'll call when I get in. If it's something simple, like a wart on a pony's nose or a horse that's been blind for a month, that can wait."

"I understand. I hope you and Loren whup 'em," he whispered, again leaning over the counter and looking around to be sure no one was aware of his favoritism. "But regardless of the outcome, the main thing is to just do the best you can." I wished he hadn't said that!

For ten and a half holes all went according to our plan. On each hole my driving was superb, thanks to our recent practice, which had grooved my swing, and the new high-compression balls, which were soaring high and long in Sam Snead fashion. Loren was "putting on a clinic" with his putter, knocking balls into the hole with the skill of a Master's tournament champion. Billy and Ti were grim-faced and silent, except for occasional mutterings.

"The fool's unconscious," I heard Billy mumble when I uncorked a three-hundred-yard drive. "And my knee hurts. Maybe that's why I can't putt."

"Now Loren's gone crazy," Ti wheezed just seconds after a twenty-footer rattled the bottom of the cup for an eagle three. "My gallbladder's killin' me, and I can't get around on none of my drives." It is right amusing how aches and pains seem to develop in a golfer's body when his opponent is wearing him out!

"Billy, the only chance we got is to hope that Wild Eddy Neely shows up drunk again and drives that old piece of junk truck of his up on the eleventh green and takes Doc off to doctor on a cow." We enjoyed a chuckle about that incident, which had occurred a few months before.

Things were going so well that I knew that nothing could ruin our long-awaited day in the sun. For the first time in my golfing life, every time the club head made contact with the ball it was sweet-spot perfect, and our runaway mastery of our opponents was building our self-esteem to unbelievable heights. It was getting very difficult for Loren and I to maintain our gentlemanly on-course demeanor and contain our glee. The months of being constantly beaten and humbled by supposedly better players had taken their toll on our confidence, but today was our day and nothing could stop us now. My mind was so caught up in concentrating on how I was going to manage the next shot or play the next hole, I was in another world, having no conscious thought of what type of animal tragedy or plague might be lurking out in the fields and pastures of the real world.

But as we were putting on the eleventh green, I was awakened from my hypnotic trance by the sound of a golf cart snapping downed limbs and twigs as it crashed through the pokeweeds in the rough between the eleventh and twelfth fairways. It was Mr. Doggett, and he was zeroing in on our foursome.

"Oh no, not again," I moaned. "I told Idrain not to come over here with a message for me!"

"Naw, you said for him not to come over here unless it was an emergency!" Billy exclaimed.

"Y'all know what hole this is, don't you?" asked Loren.

"Yeah, it's the Wild Eddy Neely hole," I said. "That means bad luck."

"Mr. Titanic, Idrain has just saved our hides!" declared Billy. Now our opponents were all smiles, and happily dancing jigs, while Loren and I stood stone-still on the green with stern and depressed looks on our faces. Finally, we turned toward the arriving cart to hear the obvious news.

"Doc, I hate to do this, but a feller over at Mount Sterling just called and wants you to come over there right away and put a yearling horse to sleep." There was a brief silence while the four of us reviewed the words we had just heard, trying to find a hidden meaning somewhere in the message. Our foes had started walking toward their cart, removing their gloves and conversing about their good fortune. After all, the deal wasn't done until we finished eighteen holes.

"Put a horse to sleep. That is what you said, right?" I looked back toward the tee and saw the next foursome happily heading for their drives. Their laughter told me they were at least a million miles away from even the thought of a horse call.

"Yep, that's right."

"Did he say anything else?"

"Oh yeah, he's got a horse that ran a tree limb three foot up into his belly. I think he wants you to look at him while you are out there."

"Is this a joke, Idrain? This sounds like some of Dave Barr Tutt's foolishness."

Dave Barr was another semipro golfer who was always joking around with his so-called friends.

"No, Doc, I'm tellin' the truth. The man said he saw the horse run past a pine tree that had a sharp limb sticking straight out, and the horse ran slap into it. He saw the limb, bark and all, disappear up under the hide and then break off."

"Is the horse down?"

"No, he just ran off into the woods!"

Loren had lit a cigarette and was practicing his putting stroke on the back edge of the green, but upon hearing Mr. Doggett's drawling and rustic description of the unfortunate placement of the foreign body, he collapsed to his knees in a spasm of giggles. The other two followed suit, and soon the cacophony of cackling was reverberating throughout the pine tree–lined fairway. Obviously, it was no laughing matter, but the entire scenario was more than my associates could handle.

"FORE! GET OFF THE GREEN!" It was an irate member of the group a hundred yards back in the fairway who had cupped his hands around his mouth and was yelling about our dawdling on the green. They were anxiously standing with hands on hips, glaring at the high jinks going on up ahead.

"Let's get out of here before we get drilled," I yelled.

"That might be a good idea, Main Man," declared Loren, wiping away tears with his golf towel. "At least it would get us out of our misery." He continued his chuckling as both carts wheeled around and scattered toward the clubhouse, each finding a different route homeward. We could see Billy and Ti smiling and laughing at their good luck and directing their cart toward the area of the course that was used for hitting practice balls.

"You know that's the last chance we'll ever get to whip 'em, don't you, Loren? We'll never play that good again, and they'll never forget it."

"Main Man, it's just like opening up a business. You got to try, and if it fails, folks will say, 'Well, he almost didn't go bankrupt.'" I filed that little "Lorenism" away inside my cranium for future reference. I like people who have gumption enough to try to make something from nothing.

The horse call was only five minutes from the golf course, and thanks to Mr. Doggett, the owner, his wife, and at least a dozen children of school-going age were out in the front yard waiting for the vet. The adults and older children were sitting in a few chairs and on upside-down zinc buckets, while the younger ones were scuffling, wrestling, chasing each other around the yard, and frolicking with two mangy cur dogs. The scattering of watermelon rinds and an almost empty pitcher of lemonade served notice of what had been going on in the yard the past hour or two. I smiled at the peaceful family scene; that and the apparent seriousness of the tree limb trauma to the family's horse had eased, but not erased, my irritation at being called away from my one and probably only moment of glory in the field of sports.

After salutations all around, I asked the obvious question. "Where's the horse?"

"The boys are out in the woods looking for the one what's got the stick stuck in her side. But while they're lookin', I'd like for you to kill this colt for me."

"Why? Is something bad wrong?" It is a common occurrence for a veterinarian to receive a request to humanely destroy a horse. But the patient is usually old, suffering from terminal disease, or the victim of some severe and irreparable trauma. To purposely end the life of a pet, horse, or other farm animal is not a pleasant chore, but it is a fact of veterinary life when all parties involved agree that it is time for the suffering to stop. I feel it is the duty of veterinarians to assist their clients in making such a difficult decision and to do what they can to make the process as painless as possible. But this was the first request that I had received to euthanatize what seemed to be a perfectly good horse.

"Naw sir, I'm just aggravated with him 'cause he won't let me put a halter on his head. He's head shy, ear shy, and a fool," he answered, pointing toward a bay yearling in the barn lot. The colt had his head over the fence, his ears straight up, trying to figure out the identity of the intruder. The gentleman didn't seem to be a hothead or cruel person, but I could feel the hair beginning to stand up on the nape of my neck. I took a deep breath and spoke.

"Let me explain to you that I don't go around just putting healthy animals to sleep without there being a good reason," I stated. I could feel my lips purse, an unwanted habit I had developed over the past few years when my temper began to rise. "Do you reckon there's something wrong with his ears? Have you looked?"

"No, I can't catch him. He'll eat out of my hand, but when I move my hand up the side of his face, he throws his head up, whirls around, and kicks at me. I ain't gonna put up with that."

"Yes sir, I understand that. Why don't you get a bucket of sweet feed and let me see what I can do. What's his name?"

"He don't have a name, so I just call him Fool."

"That's a first," I thought to myself.

I removed my lariat, halter, twitch, and black bag from the truck and placed everything but the thirty-foot rope just on the outside of the barn lot fence. Moments later the colt was eating from my hand, just as the owner had predicted. But when I rubbed his nose with my left hand, he began jerking his head up and snorting. I understood his message loud and clear. I sat the feed bucket down on the ground and walked away as if disinterested.

"Don't mess with me or I'll pop you!" he seemed to be saying in equinese.

"Do you mind if I throw a rope on him?" I asked. "He's gonna carry on a little bit."

"No sir, I don't mind," replied the owner.

"Then why don't y'all step outside the lot while I get him caught, because he's not gonna be in favor of what I've gotta do." The lot cleared as if a bomb threat had been announced.

When the colt raised his head out of the feed bucket the third time, I flung the loop on his neck. As expected, an uproar commenced. In typical bucking horse fashion, he jumped, kicked, squealed, even ejected short melodious bursts of gas, while I firmly held on to my end of the rope, in spite of being semi-dragged around the lot. The dogs became interested and soon got involved in the fracas by barking and trying to nip the colt's heels or any other convenient place.

"You dogs git! Go t' house, Duke! Git out from here, Lobo!" someone yelled. Then I saw a couple of the older children rake several rocks up from the ground with their fingers and whistle them toward the dogs. Unfortunately, they flailed a handful in the general direction of the lot and one stung the side of my leg. My loud "YOW" and a quick backward dance to avoid the next barrage of missiles helped to disperse the dogs. I refused to rub the tingling spot on my leg just to show them how tough I was.

"Dang, Billy Joe, you hit the man!" the father scolded. "Can't you aim no better'n 'nat?" The dogs had retreated to the outside perimeter of the fence but were now peering over the bottom board, nervously licking their lips and whining, obviously craving just one more snap at the roped horse's legs.

Surprisingly, once the dogs were out of the way, the horse soon calmed down enough for me to locate a well-rooted post, around which I made two loops with my end of the rope. A couple of minutes later, as the entire family pulled on the rope and I waved my arms behind the patient, we had him snubbed up tightly to the post.

I decided to conduct my ear examination from the other side of the fence, so I hopped over the fence and applied the twitch to the end of his nose. A twitch, when applied properly, seems to cause some "mild discomfort" to the nose, which takes the horse's mind off the other things you are doing to him and encourages his cooperation. So with one hand working the twitch back and forth in an entertaining manner, I reached for his left ear with the other hand while kicking out at one of the dogs who was determined to taste horse flesh one more time. The colt squealed, shook, and anxiously eyed me as I grasped the swollen cartilaginous portion of the outer ear and opened it up with my fingers. To my surprise, it was loaded with dozens of ticks and a lot of dry, crusted blood. I should have known that was the problem, because the same affliction frequently befalls the canine species. I remembered seeing a dog in so much pain it required general anesthesia to extract the one tick that was causing all the torment.

"Here's his problem. There must be a dozen or more ticks in here," I declared, peering down into the opening. Every head strained over the fence to see. I snatched off one of the large, blood-engorged arthropods with my forceps and held it up for viewing.

"See his legs wiggling. He's got eight of 'em," I declared, practicing my teaching routine. I enjoyed seeing young people being intrigued by the wonders of biology.

"Uhh, gross!" whined the ones not so inclined, as they made ugly faces and quickly retreated from the show-and-tell session. But the one or two who liked such discoveries hung on the fence, wanting more.

"Let's give him a little of this tranquilizer here, then we'll get these varmints out of there. I'll bet he'll feel a lot better, don't you?" All agreed except for Dad, who said nothing, but just stood there with a hangdog look, no doubt feeling guilty over his euthanasia plans.

It took only five minutes or so to remove the ticks, clean and medicate the ears, and give antibiotic and tetanus antitoxin injections. The tranquilizer had done its job so well that when I released the patient he remained in the same spot, his eyes almost closed and his mouth drooling.

In the meantime, the older children had located the other patient a small distance from the barn, so in order to maintain a quieter working environment, I suggested that we lock the dogs in the corncrib. I had no desire to be stoned again. Then I drove the truck a hundred yards out behind the barn as the children brought a couple of buckets of water. As I maneuvered between pine stumps and sweet gum trees, I thought about how common it was to be called upon to treat animals suffering from "foreign bodyitis." I recalled numerous fishhook swallowings, needles and bones in throats, and rubber bands around puppy necks. Dogs were always swallowing rubber balls, corncobs, rocks, and even wads of junk from overturned garbage cans. Cattle frequently swallowed long pieces of wire, which sometimes penetrated the wall of the second stomach and found its way to the exterior. But horses usually seemed to encounter nails in feet and wooden objects that penetrated into the body.

The boys had caught the gentle old gray mare and haltered her, but she refused to budge, instead preferring to stay in the relative comfort of a grove of young pines. I approached her quietly, uttering soothing phrases and rubbing my hands over her body, not trying to look at the injury until I decided how she would react to a strange person. As I rubbed her back half, her almost white hair came off in great handfuls, which caused me to wonder about her general health and whether she'd been dewormed lately. Horses in the summer and fall should be slick with a healthy hair coat. Then my eyes traveled toward the front half of her body and I was startled by the sight I saw.

Just up from the point of her shoulder was a jagged laceration some four inches in diameter, and protruding from the opening was a sharp, snaggy, three-inch-diameter chunk of wood, obviously a tree limb of some kind. There was some blood around the laceration proper, and several long clotted rivulets streaked all the way down to her left front foot. Considering the serious nature of the unusual trauma, she had lost a relatively small amount of blood. Further examination revealed the outline of a large cylindrical object just under the skin that traversed backwards and seemingly ended at the point of the hip, some three feet from the opening. I had heard older, more seasoned veterinarians relate stories about equines having foreign objects penetrate unbelievable places on their bodies, but that was usually "happy hour" talk, and I was skeptical as to its validity. Now I realized they had possibly been telling the truth.

The few family members who had dared to come out and see the wounded mare were all talking at once, but I heard little of the chatter as I concentrated on the problem at hand, much as I had been concentrating on my golf shots an hour before. Finally, I stepped back and listened to the witnesses to the accident.

"Ain't much to tell," the oldest boy said. "She was loping along like she always does, and just got a little too close to that limb sticking out from that pine tree back there. I saw her run into it and heard a snap, then she sort of staggered, stopped, looked around, and bit at her side a few times. Then she limped on out in the woods. I still didn't believe the limb had jobbed in her side, but then I noticed it was gone from the tree and I couldn't find it lying anywhere on the ground." His wide-eyed siblings were nodding in agreement. I'm sure my eyes were the widest ones there.

In addition to the hopefully simple task of removing the wood from the horse, there was the large concern of postextraction infection. There was no telling how much pine bark and horse hair had been buried in the muscles and connective tissue along the route of invasion. There was a great deal of pine bark at the entrance wound, so I was hopeful that the stick had been "debarked" as it went in. I tentatively tugged on the exposed wood and tried to move it back and forth, which caused the mare to fidget a bit, but it was so tightly lodged it barely wiggled. Even though I didn't know the location of the buried end, I surmised that if it had penetrated the abdominal cavity and on into the viscera, the patient would have been in shock, or perhaps already dead. Therefore, I was going to work on the assumption that the end was buried deep in the heavy muscles of the front part of the thigh or perhaps in the region of the pelvic bone. This was one of those times when I wished for the advice and consultation of one of those more experienced colleagues. But I was in the woods and had to make my own decision, whether right or wrong.

Even though the mare was quiet and cooperative, I injected

her with a strong dose of tranquilizer before proceeding further. Then I shaved, scrubbed, and injected a local anesthetic into the area where I thought the end of the limb was buried. I knew that I was going to need an opening anyway on that end for through-and-through flushing and treatment with antibiotics during the convalescent period. My plan was to locate the deep end of the limb, push it back toward the point of first penetration, then ask a competent family member to grasp the exposed part and extract it with my fetal extractor, which was a six-foot metal rod onto which had been attached a winch and cable. On the opposite end was a Y-shaped device, called the breech spanner, that was placed on a cow's rear parts when removing a large fetus. In this case, I would place the breech spanner just in front of the horse's shoulders, secure the cable to the exposed wood, and then have a helper ratchet it out while I pushed from the other end.

Retrieving the needed equipment and drugs from the truck, I smiled at my common sense and dirt-road ingenuity, and wondered if my equine specialist colleagues in Kentucky dressed in their smart Italian suits and driving their Cadillacs would have come up with such a plan. Then I almost laughed out loud when I thought about my relating the story someday to a group of young, green practitioners at a future "happy hour" event. I knew what they would be saying to each other later, after I had hobbled off to bed.

"Does that old fool expect us to believe that garbage? He's so old and out-of-date, and his memory is gone, too," one would say. The others would shake their heads sadly.

Still smiling, but not giggling anymore, I attacked my shaving and scrubbing with vigor while explaining exactly what I was going to do, as if the crowd were fourth-year veterinary students sitting around an amphitheater, their hands and chins eagerly placed on the guardrail in front of them, their ears straining to catch every word and voice inflection. At this stage, most veterinary students are just beginning to realize that all the answers to every animal health problem can't be taught or gleaned from textbooks. Book knowledge alone isn't enough; it must be combined with creative solutions when never-before-heard-of conditions arise.

Ten minutes later, I had created a six-inch incision just in front of the hipbone, incising down through muscles until I could feel the wooden object. Luckily, it had buried itself in a large muscle mass, and with a little tugging, I found that it was freely movable. I applied the twitch to the mare's nose and explained how to manipulate the fetal extractor. Presently we were easing the object from its resting place by the pull-and-push technique and I could clearly see the lump disappearing, like a kitten moving under a rug. I carefully pushed the stick forward, and when the last of it plopped out, my sleeved hand and entire arm had disappeared under the skin of the horse and the tips of my fingers were exiting the wound. Had the general public seen this revolting sight, they would have surely run screaming into the woods, or perhaps the more creative ones would have suggested making a horror movie based on the scene. Nevertheless, digital examination revealed no apparent major damage, and I commenced my flushing routine by inserting a large stomach tube and pumping copious amounts of weak iodined water back and forth through the massive wound. Later, I treated the wound with antibiotics, then injected the mare with the usual antibiotics and tetanus vaccine. When released, the patient stiffly walked off a few steps, looked around and nuzzled the site of the injury, then put her head to the ground and pinched off several mouthfuls of grass. We shook our heads, all wondering the same thing.

"How do animals do it? She's just been through a major procedure that would have laid a man flat out for weeks, but here she is acting as if nothing has happened."

I returned to the farm to treat the mare on an almost-daily basis for the next week or ten days, and periodically thereafter until the wound healed. As expected, infection set in early on, in spite of all the antibiotics and the good care that she received. You can't stick a dirty, sap-covered chunk of wood into the body of a horse and not expect some infection, no matter how thoroughly you treat it. It took a couple of months for complete recovery, and she was left with a nasty scar and a slight limp in her left rear leg. We all thought that was a small price to pay for a good recovery from such a serious wound.

"The Fool" was sold to a horse-loving neighbor a short time later, and she named him Sweetie Pie. Later, when I was called to administer routine vaccines and dewormers to Sweetie Pie, his owner questioned me about the wrinkle along the edge of his left ear. But I avoided a truthful answer about its origin; she would have been appalled if she had known that I had once been called to do away with such a Sweetie Pie.

As the practice grew, the percentage of time spent and income from horse work continued to rise. Some of the calls were from large barns in adjoining counties that were devoted to boarding large numbers of horses, and those were exhausting days filled with tube deworming, vaccinating, and rasping down the sharp teeth of dozens of horses. Such hard work and long hours left little time for such recreational pursuits as playing golf. Loren was also busy with his practice of pharmacy, deer hunting in the fall, turkey hunting in the spring, and bass fishing the rest of the time. My greatest regret is that we were never able to defeat Billy and Ti on the golf course. But that regret is salved by the knowledge that I am a pretty low handicapper when it comes to removing ticks and sticks from the bodies of suffering horses. After all, removing those foreign bodies is strangely akin to hitting a golf ball out of deep woods between two saplings and fading it nicely onto the green some two hundred yards away.

Seventeen

Visiting the supermarket in Butler was a trying experience for me, so I avoided it if possible. But sometimes Jan asked me to make a quick stop at Charlie Hale's IGA on the way home from the clinic for one or two items. Her instructions as to where those items would be found in the store often weren't very clear to an amateur shopper, but they were quite specific as to brand, price, or size.

It wasn't the time it took to search the thousands of shelves on the endless aisles that made me avoid the store, but it was the fact that I could always count on running into clients who would follow me around, wanting to talk nonstop about their pets or livestock. The conversation was not limited to health matters, but might cover the latest tricks Rover had learned or how the cows tore down the pasture fence and helped themselves to the neighbor's corn patch. I usually enjoyed such conversation, but not in the grocery store and not when it took an hour to figure out exactly which jug of detergent or bleach Jan wanted. Besides, it was quite embarrassing to be conducting a question-and-answer session on dysentery while fidgeting in front of the delicatessen, which was actually nothing more than the bologna section of the meat cooler. We didn't have a real deli in Choctaw County.

I've always thought it was odd how animal owners seem to talk the loudest when they are publicly discussing any ailment relating to bowels, reproductive function, or the death of one of their animals. I just stand there red-faced, hands buried in the front pockets of my blue coveralls, my nervous feet quietly shuffling in "aw shucks" fashion, while nonanimal-owning shoppers stop, stare, and listen intently from the end of the row as they make the turn by the broom and mop bin. Yet when they are going on about what a marvelous recovery their pet has made because of the great skill and compassion of the local veterinarian, they use a voice no louder than a whisper.

It was a busy Friday evening at the store and I was in a rush to get home with the cheese Jan had asked for, so with my Funk's G Hybrid seed corn cap pulled low over my forehead, I slunk through the sparse crowd at the first checkout counter without so much as a head nod to the ladies there, then made a hard left at the soap section, shortcutting my way to the dairy section. Unfortunately, a perfectly coiffured, blue-haired lady with a Chihuahua in her shopping cart appeared in my peripheral vision as she made the turn from the adjacent aisle just a couple of seconds behind me. I felt a cold chill when I realized the dog had been a recent and reluctant patient at the clinic. But it was too late to hide.

"What's the name? What's the name?" I whispered to myself. I had become so frustrated with my inability to remember names. Sometimes it seemed the harder I tried the higher the mental block was raised.

"Precious! That's it! And she's Mrs. Brown. Mrs. Bozo Brown!" I was congratulating myself when the yell came.

"Oh, Doctor!" she cooed. "I was just thinking about you. I hate to bother you while you are getting your Clorox, but my Precious has that cough and sore throat again. Do you think you could just feel her forehead and see if you think she's feverish? I just know she is." I have always wondered how Mrs. Brown and other Chihuahua owners could tell for sure that their pets had sore throats without even looking down in there. I reckoned it was because of the way the patient licked his lips or swallowed in a gulping fashion. I had often wished for a thirty-minute refresher course on canine sore throats and three and a half hours on new techniques of humanely restraining the little creatures.

"Why of course," I said, surrendering to the mild inconvenience and gingerly reaching for the pet's head. But the instant reaction wiped the smile off my face.

"Grrr! Yap! Yap! Yap! Grrr!" snarled the ill-mannered pup as I hurriedly removed my hand from the grocery cart and its snapping contents. Teeth were still clicking and saliva was flying as I buried my valuable right hand deep in my back pocket.

Even though she didn't have a pitchfork, horns, or a pointed tail, the dog was a known demon in the community. She was always attacking much larger dogs and trying to chomp on the ankles of visitors to the Brown home. I recalled the fear I experienced when she had shown up at the clinic for treatment of the chronic throat condition or for routine exams. On more than one occasion I had tried to get rid of her by referring her to a colleague in Meridian.

"Dr. McDaniel over at the Red Hill community in Mississippi is one of the finest veterinarians I've ever seen on these serious throat problems," I had bragged. "He's been off at all those educational short courses on coughing dogs, and he specializes in just the type of problems that Precious has. He's a regular ear, nose, and throat man!"

But he referred Precious back to me, along with a glowing report of my professional ability with small dogs and how lucky Mrs. Brown was to have such a caring and brilliant vet in her town. I could just envision the sorry rascal giggling in the kennel room, knowing that he had beaten me at my own game.

"Precious!" she cried out. "Shame on you. Don't try to attack the nice doctor, he's just trying to help!" I had heard that just-uttered phrase so many times, it made me wonder if it was part of the Chihuahua owner's creed.

As expected, other shoppers were slowly beginning to peek around the corner of the aisle to see the brewing fracas. Clerks had ceased stocking the shelves and stood frozen with cans of pork and beans and okra poised in midair, hoping to see someone get dog bit. I was becoming red-faced with embarrassment as I stood waiting for Mrs. Brown to finish her lecture to Precious, who had slunk so low in the shopping cart that she was almost hidden among the packages of pitted prunes and bunches of turnip greens. But I could see her licking her lips in shame and those sad eyes looking pitifully upward as she wallowed around in the groceries, her tail tucked as far between her hind legs as it would go.

Mrs. Brown continued her lecture to the freakish-looking dog, reciting the Golden rule, quoting biblical scripture, and then she went into fine detail about how hard I had studied in veterinary school just to be able to cure sick dogs. Perhaps she was right, but I would have preferred working with a large cow at that moment.

"Maybe if you just held her in your arms she wouldn't be so frightened," the lady suggested as she picked up the pooch and quickly thrust her into the front of my coveralls.

"Man alive!" I said to myself. "How do I get myself into these situations? And with all these people looking and pointing." The aisle was stacking up with people, all of whom had been in a large rush just moments before but were now enjoying the strange performance on row six.

The good news was that Precious, although trembling and dribbling something wet into my right pocket, was now behaving much better than before. She didn't try to bite now as I cautiously rubbed her head with my left fist.

"She does feel a little warm to me," I declared. "I suspect she has a degree or two of fever."

"I knew it! I just knew it!" Mrs. Brown loudly informed the large crowd. "She's running a fever!" Suddenly, I was struck with an idea.

"Perhaps I should write you a prescription," I suggested, fumbling through my pockets. "I think I have a piece of paper somewhere here in my coveralls. Then you can go by the drugstore and get the pharmacist to fill it for you."

"A prescription? I didn't know you wrote prescriptions for

dogs," someone exclaimed over by the oven cleaner products. Several others shook their heads in disbelief.

"Oh, yes, cats too," I replied, trying to smile.

"How about bulls and horses?" asked the comedian.

"All the time," I answered. "Just use a bigger sheet of paper."

I shifted Precious to my left hand and went to a half-empty shelf, where I commenced scribbling a hard-to-read sulfa drug order on the back of a counter check. Some people seem to expect getting a prescription that is impossible to be read, even by the most experienced pharmacist.

"Why, this is written on the back of a check," exclaimed Mrs. Brown when I handed her the document. "Will it be good?"

"Certainly! If the druggist has any problem with it, tell him to call me." I made a mental note to put a few prescription blanks in my billfold for use at the grocery store.

As the crowd slowly dispersed and Mrs. Brown put the prescription away in her purse, I heard the booming voice of Happy Dupree, self-proclaimed consultant to my veterinary practice and fishing buddy.

"Aw shoot," I mumbled to myself. "If Happy sees me holding this dog in my arms, he'll hassle me about it till the cows come home." But he had spied the commotion and was wheeling my way.

"What in the world, Dr. John? What are you doin' with that overgrown rat?" he boomed.

"Hey there, Happy," I said, smiling but with teeth clenched. "This is Precious Brown, Mrs. Brown's little Chihuahua. Isn't she cute?"

"That's a dog?" he asked, looking stunned.

"I'll have you know, sir, that my Precious is more like a human than a dog. She sleeps on my bed and I love her more than you can imagine," Mrs. Brown said, gathering the patient from my grasp, then smothering her beloved one in her bosom and raining kisses atop her doggy head.

"Well, you must not care too much for it if you let this guy doctor on it," Happy retorted. "He killed my best cow just the other day."

Mrs. Brown looked somewhat taken aback as she placed Precious back in the cart. But she recovered quickly.

"I'll call you tomorrow if there's no improvement," she said to me with a smile. Then she turned to Happy and looked him square in the eye.

"Sir, you are a coarse clod!" she boldly announced. She jerked a can of Sani-Flush from the shelf and fled.

For a few seconds there was silence, except for the sounds of choked laughter being emitted from my throat. Happy watched the lady walk away and shook his head slowly from side to side.

"Listen, Happy, you ought to be a little more diplomatic with pet owners. They don't like folks calling their dogs rats," I cautioned.

"Maybe you ought to quit catering to all these women with their lapdogs," he said. "Then you'd have more time to hunt and fish."

"Aw shut up, Happy!" I groaned as we parted ways.

A minute later, while pondering the great cheese decision, I heard the squeak of a cart and the clomping of hard-heeled engineers boots approaching the milk section. I recognized the boots as those of Carney Sam Jenkins, the legendary homemade veterinarian of Choctaw County.

"Howdy, Doc," he almost yelled, reaching for a gallon of Borden's. "Miz Doc got 'chu shoppin' too?"

"Yeah, you know how it is. I hate coming up here, because somebody always wants to talk about their sick dog. But she's got her hands full with the kids and all, so I try to help when I can. By the way, how's your neighbor's milk cow?"

Too late, it dawned on me that he shouldn't have been buying milk and that I should have kept my mouth shut about the cow. After all, the black Jersey was the community milk cow. I had treated her for mountain laurel poisoning a few days before.

"Aw, Doc, she DIED!" he answered, his voice echoing throughout the store as if he were wired to the public address system. There was instant silence, except for the hum of the coolers and the whine of the butcher's band saw as it whizzed through a chilled carcass.

"OH YEAH, she DIED, graveyard DEAD, not five minutes after you left," he restated. "I sure wish you had treated her for the HOLLERTAIL like I wanted you to do! Now I gotta buy this here high-priced, weak, blue john milk." Many older citizens who were accustomed to drinking the unpasteurized and unhomogenized milk produced by the family cow referred to processed store-bought milk as "blue john" because of its lower fat content and almost blue appearance.

Just as before, shoppers stopped pushing their carts and were staring in our direction. Some seemed shocked about the expired cow, whom they obviously thought had been treated improperly, since Carney Sam had said so.

"This happens to me every time I come in this blame store," I thought to myself as I looked around for an escape route. Aunt Sissy Bailey was on down the way at the egg place, opening cartons and checking for cracked eggs. I didn't want to go that way, since her old dog had just died of kidney failure in the clinic. Back up the other way, I could see other clients working their way toward the dairy case; many of them were moving their lips, no doubt already practicing the questions they were going to ask their pet's doctor. Each time Carney Sam verbalized a loud "DEAD," however, they would stop momentarily in their tracks, their mouths open and heads tilted, as if reconsidering their decision to confer with the killer vet.

"Maybe I can go out the back way here," I thought as I looked at the narrow opening between the cottage cheese and a display of canned hams. But the instant I made a move in that direction, Theodore Miller, the part-time butcher, made a move to cut me off. He was wiping his greasy hands on a once-white apron as he blocked my escape route.

"Doc, about that hoss of mine," he commenced. "She still ain't doin' jus' right. I wonder — "

He was cut off in mid-sentence as a higher authority apparently interceded on my behalf. The lights flickered once, then twice, then glorious darkness fell upon the huge store. Then there was silence, except for a few startled mini-screams and carts bumping into canned goods.

"I got a light," I blurted out, pulling a penlight from a coverall pocket. "Which way is the fuse box?"

"Way over to the left, Doc," offered Theodore. Actually, everybody called him Taydoe, a southern way of saying Theodore.

"Hot dog, I can escape out the back way," I mumbled, abandoning my shopping cart as we hustled by the chitterlings and tripe section.

"Where's the rear door, Taydoe?" I asked, stumbling over crates of strawberries and sacks of onions. "I gotta get back to the clinic pronto!"

"Straight on back, Doc."

"Here, you take this light, Taydoe, I'll see you later," I replied when I saw daylight through the cracks.

"Yeah, you go ahead, Doc, 'cause I know you need to see about the lights at the clinic. But this old hoss, she..."

By then, I had jumped over a pile of boxes, avoided several sacks of potatoes, and sideswiped a large bale of brown paper bags. I burst through the back door and leapt off the dock and was soon jogging around the building, across in front of the building, and toward my always ready and faithful truck.

"Whew! What a blessing," I whispered, looking toward the heavens. "Somebody is looking after me." But as I sprinted by the front door, one of the cashiers cut me off. She was holding a small box with holes punched in its side.

"I was hoping your wife, or maybe even you, would come in today," she said. "Would you look at this kitten for me?" She retrieved a small, white kitten about two months old that was covered with dirt, fleas, and dry fur.

"Your wife is real good with kittens, even though she's not a vet. Maybe you can tell me what's wrong with this one." It didn't bother me that she preferred Jan's feline skills over mine.

"Sure. Powder her real good with flea powder, give her a can of sardines in oil, and bring her by my office Monday morning."

"Gotcha, Doc. Much obliged until you're better paid."

Driving off, I could barely make out the figures of shoppers as they all congregated in the front of the store. Some even pointed at the turncoat vet as he sped away. I felt like a jerk for leaving the scene, but I didn't have time right then for hours of seminars on pet care and equine herd health — I'd had just about enough.

"Did you forget the cheese, honey?" Jan asked when I walked in the back door.

"Uh, naw, they were out."

"Out! What do you mean out? No store in America is out of cheese!" she replied. "I needed that for our supper!"

"Look, let's just put the kids in the car and go down to the Dairy Queen. Terri called the clinic this morning and said she had stuffed bell peppers on the menu today. Maybe the crowd will have cleared out by the time we get there."

Several minutes later we made our entrance into the small restaurant. We exchanged pleasantries with Terri, one of the owners, and one table occupied by out-of-towners. It appeared our timing was good for a relaxing meal. Presently, Terri was at tableside, taking our order in between short stories about her "Hungarian terrier" she called Toefew, so-named because he was missing two toes.

"Tom and Lisa, I bet you both want a big hamburger and french fries, right? And Cokes? Dr. John, I know you want the stuffed bell peppers and two milks," she chattered. "Oh, did you hear that Toefew treed a possum in the neighbor's yard the other night? I was mortified! You want collards or grits with your chicken, Jan? Then the next day he comes up with a gigantic rat! Do either of you recall offhand when his rabies shot is due?"

"I think it's June," declared Jan.

"That's what I thought, because I remember it was hot weather and —"

"I don't remember, Terri, but I know I'm starved. Could you bring me one of those milks right away, and a pone of that corn bread?"

"OK, but there's something else I want to get your advice on when I get back," she said as she pranced off. I just looked at Jan and shrugged my shoulders. It seemed as if we couldn't even relax and eat a leisurely meal out without having to talk about business.

Several minutes later, I heard the front door open behind me and the sound of footsteps heading in our direction. Then Jan smiled and spoke to someone occupying the booth to my rear. An arm suddenly appeared over my left shoulder.

"Thanks for the use of your penlight, Doc. The power came back on about a minute or so after you left." It was Taydoe, the butcher from the grocery store. Presently, he was trying to squeeze into the booth beside Lisa and me.

"Doc, I'm worried about my old mare. She just ain't plum right. You got any idea what ails 'er?"

Lisa and Tom looked up at Taydoe as if he had lost his mind. Jan and I simply looked at each other and smiled.

It is nice that owners respect their veterinarian enough to ask for advice about their animals, even if the consultation is away from the usual workplace setting. Sometimes, however, it is even nicer to visit the supermarket or the Dairy Queen without having to hear about a deceased cow or a dog with indigestion.

Some of my more businesslike colleagues claim they never do exams on their small animal patients or write prescriptions on scrap paper in the Clorox department of the grocery store. I assume they rarely visit stores frequented by their clients or perhaps they wear a fake nose and glasses, or maybe they just tell them "Give him a children's aspirin and call me in the morning!"

Eighteen

~ "Dr. John, it's our Sadie!" the excited and obviously distressed female caller exclaimed. "How soon can you get up here?" After the second sentence I recognized the voice as that of Di Hay, the feminine half of Hay Dairy Farm. She and her husband, Buck, owned and operated a small dairy farm in the county to the north.

"Uh, what's wrong, Di? Got a cow down?" I knew it was an emergency, not only because of Di's anxiety level but also because of the time of day the call came in. It was right at dusk, and it was Wednesday evening. That was the night for many of the meetings in town, from board meetings and choir practice to the city council get-together at the city hall. I had become an occasional member of the church choir because we had been forced to sit in the front pew one Sunday morning when we arrived late for the eleven o'clock service. Preacher Hastings had apparently detected my loud bass voice when we sang "Onward, Christian Soldiers" and "Standing on the Promises," and he mentioned after church that he'd be most appreciative if I showed up for choir practice on Wednesday nights. It's always been hard for me to tell a preacher no.

I also needed to attend the city council meeting, not as an elected official but as an appointed member of the utilities board. The town owned and operated the water and natural gas distri-

183

bution systems, as well as the garbage pickup and sewage systems. The council members were always wanting reports from each of those departments, perhaps because of some crisis or a complaint from a constituent. When I became a member of the group, I was assigned to work with the sewage department, which came as no surprise to me.

It seemed especially difficult for me to attend those Wednesday night meetings of community duty. It seemed like that was the most popular night for animal emergencies. At the city council meeting just the week before we had been in deep discussion of an aroma problem with the sewage lagoon when we heard a commotion outside the conference chamber. When the man nearest the door arose to investigate, he discovered a frantic lady and her mild-mannered husband searching for Dr. McCormack. Seconds later the rather large but obviously corseted lady strode briskly into the meeting, her meek husband in tow, holding a large supermarket paper bag. I noticed the bag had been rolled down several turns from the top.

"Oh, Dr. McCormack," she sniffed, "thank goodness I found you! We have suffered a horrendous tragedy." The city fathers stopped their important deliberations and peered anxiously at the out-of-town couple. "My husband slammed the car door on my little Chihuahua's tail, and AMPUTATED it! Oh, boo-hoo-hoo!" she cried. "Mr. Pup has suffered so much." Upon the accentuation of the word *amputate,* each councilman who wasn't already on his feet immediately sprang to them as if the attorney general in charge of prosecuting corrupt elected officials for the state of Alabama had just raided the assembly room.

"Oh, I'm so sorry," I sympathized. Now each official present was standing with his jaw dropped, his eyes finally focusing on the paper bag. "Did you bring Mr. Pup?"

"No, but I brought the tail," she said sadly but proudly. "Open the sack, Buford!" The man did as commanded. He noisily unrolled the sack and held the top open for viewing. I was the first viewer, since I was arguably the foremost animal health expert in the room and therefore felt that I had earned the privilege. Sure enough, there at the bottom of the bag in a small puddle of blood was two inches of perfect Chihuahua tail. I looked up at the pitiful man, and his woeful eyes told me that at that moment he would have given a large sum of money to have been in Iceland or any other faraway place. Someplace where they didn't have lapdogs and henpecking of husbands was illegal.

Each of my associates also peered into the bag and tried to make some appropriate comment about the tragedy and how the little fella must have suffered. I wasn't sure whether they were sincere or were just practicing sympathetic slogans for the upcoming election. Then I quickly guided the lady and gentleman out the door and onto the sidewalk, because I was sure that dog tail jokes and the ensuing giggling were about to commence inside.

"Where do you folks live?" I asked.

"We live in Why Not, a little community just over the Mississippi line," declared the lady. I like towns with funny names. Although Lick Skillet, Skinnem, TyTy, and Wolfskin are among my favorites, Why Not is the one I enjoy hearing the most.

"Why don't you go on home, get your little dog, and bring him back over here to my clinic. We'll see what we can do," I stated. I didn't know how I was going to tell the lady that tail reattachment was not my specialty.

Back inside City Hall, the council was trying to conduct important town business, but the general mirth was making that difficult. Occasionally, a guffaw rang out for no apparent reason. When someone complained about "the govmint" requiring the city to certify some asinine procedure, the meeting came to a halt when the mayor said, "That's like the tail wagging the dog!" The resultant hilarity, wiping of eyes with hankies, and further attempts at jokes made serious business impossible. Finally, the mayor banged his gavel on the table.

"We'll just cut this short," he announced to another round of laughter. "This is the end."

"I'm sorry this group made my client's dog the butt of a joke," I declared. More chuckling permeated the semidarkness as I walked out the door.

An hour later, I was cleaning Mr. Pup's tail stump and

putting in several sutures. Once I explained the situation of blood flow obstruction and resultant gangrene, the lady was not hard to convince of the futility of trying to reattach a two-inch piece of dog tail. Then she apologized for coming to City Hall and interrupting an important meeting.

"But I was just so upset and nervous!" she exclaimed. "I just don't know why I didn't bring Mr. Pup along the first time."

"Yes, ma'am, I understand," I replied. I shook hands with the man, offered a few words of aftercare instruction, and watched them disappear into the night. I heard later that the gentleman passed away not long after our encounter, and I secretly wondered if he had been nagged to death for the tail amputation tragedy.

~

Di was calling this Wednesday evening about a very ill Holstein calf named Sadie. She was the result of a planned mating of two high-scoring parents whose hard-to-read pedigrees made them valuable not only as breeders of fine future show ring examples of the Holstein breed but as high-producing milkers as well. Sadie was only a few days old but had been stricken with the scours, a deadly form of diarrhea usually caused by the *E. coli* bacteria.

"She's down and in pretty bad shape," Di declared. "We wouldn't even treat her if she didn't have the potential to be such a fine addition to the herd."

Affected young calves have some degree of diarrhea, depending upon their individual immunity level, the degree of exposure to the bacteria, and its virulence. Shortly after birth and within a few hours thereafter, the bovine baby must consume a large meal of its mother's colostrum, which is her antibody-rich first milk. Since a calf is born totally lacking in disease-resisting antibodies, it will not survive without that first milk. To add another kicker to this complicated process, the intestines of the newborn calf have only a few hours in which to absorb the large antibody molecules.

The symptoms of *E. coli* infection are diarrhea and dehydration due to the loss of body fluids and electrolytes. Many calves have only a light infection, to which their normal immune defenses react properly, and they are back to normal in a few days. A more severely infected calf may need antibiotics and large amounts of oral fluids. Once dehydration reaches the 7 to 10 percent range, most victims are down and out, their eyes sunken, their body temperatures subnormal, and they are near death. They need intravenous replacement of fluid and electrolytes if they are to survive.

Unfortunately, the owner of the sick calf and the veterinarian are faced with a dilemma. Even though both parties are well aware of the need for a large quantity of intravenous fluids over a period of several hours, there are a number of reasons why this course of treatment may not be selected. First, the economics of livestock production usually dictate the treatment regimen. Many livestock owners simply cannot afford the vet costs of inserting an intravenous catheter, the road time and professional time involved, and the expense of the fluids and other drugs. Actually, the value of the calf is often so low that the needed treatment costs more than the animal is presently worth. This fact of life is probably the most difficult part of being a veterinarian. We see sick animals every day for which there is a known and effective treatment, but we are unable to save the animal because of economic considerations. Our food producers in this country are paid very little for their products, and they must watch expenditures very carefully.

I asked Di Hay the usual question about the sick calf.

"Have you treated her?"

"Yep. I used some of those scour pills that we got from you and dosed her with some of your kangaroo juice mixture several hours ago, but she's crashed since then," she replied. Good old kangaroo juice is a simple and inexpensive homemade concoction of salt, soda, and syrup mixed in a gallon milk jug with tap water, and is given by mouth. If it doesn't make 'em hop up and scoot off across the field, then IV fluids are needed.

"OK, I'm on my way. Hang up the phone and watch for a

cloud of dust!" I exclaimed. Help was on the way, so tie up the dogs and open the gate!

I asked Jan to call City Hall and leave word that I would again be absent from the council meeting and that I would give my report on the stinky sewage problem the next week. Actually, the problem had almost been eliminated, thanks to consultation with a high-priced "odor consultant" in Mobile. It was a simple oxygen–carbon dioxide ratio problem, but I wanted to present my research in front of the group and make it sound a lot more complex than it really was. That's what the consultant had done in order to justify his astronomical fee.

Tom accompanied me on this trip and hit me with his usual barrage of sick animal questions. I tried to answer them in five-year-old language, while pretending to be a world-famous scours consultant who continually flew all around the country, dropping in on dairy farms like Superman, making pronounce-ments and recommendations, then flying off to the next opera-tion. It seemed to me that if an odor engineer could make a living that way, then a scours veterinarian could, too. Perhaps I'd have to become a "specialist" in some other obscure area of veterinary medicine, such as moonshine indigestion in woods cows or fox-hound dentistry. It was fun to daydream about the future and wonder just what Jan and I and the kids might be doing by the year 2000.

Just as a consultant might do, I reviewed with Tom all the causes of calf diarrhea, the treatments, and preventative mea-sures. If he was bored by the lecture, he didn't let on. I found myself wondering if he might decide to study veterinary medi-cine and maybe come back home and take over my practice. I had seen other sons from veterinary families who did that, and I always thought that would be a satisfying way to ease out of a hectic veterinary practice. Instead of working seven days a week and being on duty twenty-four hours a day, cut back to three days a week and take the emergency duty every now and then. We'd see whether Tom wanted that type of hard life later on, when he was old enough to really help out around the clinic and on calls. At five, he was interested in anything his dad was doing.

We found the little calf lying flat out on a layer of hay in a stock trailer adjacent to the Hays' calf barn. As expected, her eyes were sunken, her hair roughened, and her rear end dirty and matted. She wasn't moving except for the slow up and down breathing of her rib cage. After I checked and found a weak eye wink reflex, I slung down the thermometer and asked Tom to take her temperature.

"It's so nasty, Daddy. And it stinks!" he declared.

"Well, it's got to be done, Tom, so get yourself a handful of hay and wipe it off. You can do it." A minute later he had raked the dried manure and debris off the calf's rear end and had the thermometer inserted in the proper place. When I pinched the skin of the neck to assess the state of dehydration, it failed to drop back to its normal position. When I stethoscoped the chest, I found her lungs were clear but the heart was weak.

"That's long enough on the thermometer, Tom," I said. "Let's see what it says."

I held the thermometer at eye level, slowly rotating it back and forth until the silver streak was clearly visible in the late afternoon twilight.

"This says ninety-four degrees, Tom. That's so low, maybe we ought to do it again."

As before, he gathered a small wad of bermuda hay, wiped off the thermometer, and replaced it. I was glad he didn't use his pants as a thermometer wiping towel. Minutes later, we obtained the same reading.

I heard Buck's tractor racing down the lane, then watched as he maneuvered a hay rake into a spot next to the trailer. Shortly, he was standing over the critically ill calf and I noticed he smelled of grease and fresh-cut alfalfa, just like a dairyman should smell in the summertime.

"See you finally brought somebody up here who knows what he's doing." He grinned, nodded toward Tom, who was feeling the calf's ears and looking at her gums. I thought that was a good sign of a future vet student.

"I think we're gonna need everybody we can get on this one," I suggested. "She's bad off."

"I know that! Why do you think I called you up here at sup-pertime? I've been in the hay field all day, trying to get this hay cut and put up before that rain comes in here this weekend. I'm starved to death!"

"Why don't you go on to the house and eat while Tom and I try some heroics on this patient. I do want you to know that I misplaced my magic wand last week, so don't expect too much."

"Just do what you can, Doc, 'cause she's a special calf. I'm just sick about letting her get in this shape, but Di and I have just been so busy. Her momma's been in the hospital, and one of my milkers got in a fight over in Cuba and he's in the hoosegow. I just can't see to everything."

I can't imagine how a dairy farmer gets all his chores done! Out of bed at four A.M. to milk the cows, then clean up the milk-ing parlor, treat the sick ones, feed the milking herd, the dry cows, the bred heifers, the open heifers, the weanlings, and then give the baby calves their milk. In between all that, he has to check all the equipment and see what's broken down and figure out how to get it repaired quickly. Work at a dairy farm never stops.

I was glad that Buck had vamoosed because I thought it would be easier getting the job done if he wasn't there asking lots of questions while I was struggling to get a catheter into the jugu-lar vein. The vein was collapsed, and I was sure that the proce-dure was going to require making an incision down through the skin, right on top of the vein.

While Tom made two trips back to the truck for two gallons of electrolyte solution, I rigged up the IV tubing, then shaved and scrubbed a spot on the left side of Sadie's neck for the catheter. After a couple of tries, the catheter was threaded down the vein, the jugs hung from the side of the trailer, and the fluid was softly gurgling into our patient.

Sadie had hardly moved during the entire examination process, except for a soft, almost imperceptible whispered moo when I stuck her with the catheter needle on the second try. In addition to her electrolyte loss and imbalance, she was in a state of toxic shock, the result of endotoxins being absorbed from the *E. coli* bacteria.

"What do you think, Tom?"

"I don't think so," he replied. I was amazed at his perception of the situation, but he had been exposed to a lot more sick animals and the real world of veterinary medicine than most preschool children. He had ridden with me on a number of calls in the past year, and had watched as I treated and performed cesareans and other surgeries on many dogs and cats at the house and clinic. In fact, he might have known too much for his own good and that of his kindergarten group. His teacher had mentioned on a couple of occasions that it might be better if Tom weren't quite so descriptive about where a large animal vet had to put his hand and arm, and that delivering puppies was a subject that should be covered a little later in the preschool curriculum.

Tom and I went by the house on the way out. We found Buck at the kitchen table holding a half-eaten cheese sandwich in one hand and the telephone in the other. Spread out over the table in front of him were Holstein association registration papers that he constantly touched and moved around while he talked with the classifier over the phone. No doubt he was getting ready for a visit from an official of the purebred association. Di was at the other end of the table writing checks. There was a generous pile of bills in front of her.

"One of those checks mine?" I asked, sticking out my hand. Apparently it was not a good time to ask for money, since she did not appear to be amused. I'm also usually pretty somber when I'm writing checks, and I don't have the responsibility of raising feed for a hundred or more hungry Holstein rumens or worrying about whether my top calf is going to make it through an acute illness.

"Di, you or Buck need to check the fluid level on the calf at the barn," I said.

"When?"

"After the ten o'clock news," I suggested. "Slow the fluid

down to a drop a second and then you'll have to change to the second jug about milking time in the morning. Then I'll be by here about noon tomorrow on my way to the sale barn and see what the situation is like." This wasn't the first time the duo had been designated intravenous fluid therapy technicians.

Buck waved and whispered a thanks as Tom and I headed for the door. Di came along to see us out and asked Tom questions about his future interest in the world of animal health. But he was sort of lawyerlike in his answer. Sort of evasive and noncommittal. Could it be that he would become an attorney? He had obviously inherited Jan's gift for gab!

"Next time you bring Lisa along, Tommy," suggested Di. "Y'all can play with our girls on the swing set. I'm sorry they weren't here tonight, but they are spending the night with their aunt."

"Lisa's too young to go on calls. She cut her leg and had to go see Dr. Paul," he said excitedly.

"Cut her leg?"

"Yes, ma'am, right here." He pulled his right pant leg up above his knee and pointed out the approximate position where barbed wire had slashed a two-inch gash on his sister's thigh. "Dr. Paul used a big needle and thread to sew it up." I had been severely rebuked by the doctor and Jan for allowing such an accident to occur. But I had been treating a cantankerous mule while Tom and Lisa were projecting around with the client's children.

"Dr. John, I'm sorry we weren't there to help with Sadie tonight, but we're so far behind with our work, plus we've gotten pretty attached to her, and I didn't want to be there when you stuck that big needle in her neck," she apologized. "She's not gonna make it, is she?"

"All I can tell you is that she's mighty sick. I've seen others like her survive, but most don't. Let's get all this fluid dripped into her and we'll see," I said, trying to be as evasive as attorney Tom.

It was noon the next day when I stopped by the farm and beelined it to the trailer. The first thing I noticed was the open rear door. There was an empty gallon jug lying on the floor, and the other jug and its intravenous apparatus were hanging from the side of the trailer. But there was no sign of Sadie. I assumed the grim reaper had paid a late night visit to the farm and made off with her. But there were no telltale drag marks through the hay in the trailer or on the ground outside indicating that she had been dragged off to the bovine cemetery. Next, I checked inside the calf barn but found only twenty-five or more of her pals who assumed it was snack time and immediately let loose with a chorus of juvenile "moosic." But there was no Sadie.

No one seemed to be around. I assumed Buck and the hired man were in a hay field somewhere, and then I remembered having seen Di's dirty car at the beauty parlor when I came through town. Or maybe Buck was there getting his hair styled and Di was in the field getting the alfalfa baled! He did have a standing appointment with the hairdresser there every Wednesday. Perhaps he had rescheduled it that week because of his haying activities.

As I turned out the driveway and headed for the sale barn, I tried to cheer myself up by picturing old Buck at the beauty parlor, sitting quietly in a long line of fine ladies, all with the biggest portion of their heads jammed up in those absurd-looking beehive hair dryers and their fingers flipping through the pages of *Good Housekeeping* and *Mademoiselle.* All except those getting pedicures, of course, who were assigned gossip duty.

It's hard to hear the latest gossip with your head stuck up inside a roaring mechanical device. Therefore, the regulars had become quite proficient at lip reading and drawing their rumor conclusions from innuendo and the bits and pieces of information they could hear. Someone who wasn't an expert at lip reading spent a lot of time pushing the hair dryer up and away from her good ear in order to hear better. Of course, this meant that their hair dried slower and that's the reason why novice beauty parlor devotees often spent twice as long under the dryer as did the more seasoned veterans. Buck had told me all about beauty parlor protocol one day while I was pregnancy checking his cows.

I knew our veterinarian/dairyman bond of friendship and

respect was solid and deep because I was the only one he would allow to pick on him about his weekly excursion to the coiffure palace. But I still thought it was odd that such a practical, down-to-earth, and bucolic individual would make this event his one hour or so of recreation for the week. Perhaps he enjoyed it as much as I enjoyed kidding him and being amused about it. Right now, however, my thoughts were on Sadie.

"I shouldn't be so disappointed," I said to myself. "That little calf really had only two chances to survive, slim and none." But it's hard to accept that a treatment has failed and that the patient has died. I thought about her occasionally the remainder of the day while working at the sale barn.

"Doc, this is Buck Hay," Buck said when he called late that night. Even though I knew his voice quite well, he always identified himself. I often wished that all my clients had been that courteous, and wouldn't leave me racking my brains for a clue to the unknown caller on the other end of the line. "You doin' good tonight?" His voice sounded happy. Could it be that the call would contain good news?"

"I'm good. What about the calf?" I blurted. "I came by about noon today but couldn't find anybody or the calf, so I assumed she died."

"Naw, she lived, Doc!" he exclaimed. "When I checked her at midnight, I was surprised to find her sitting up. At milking time this morning she was standing, and I changed jugs just like you said, and about mid-morning she jerked out your catheter and line and walked out of the trailer. When I came around the barn on the tractor, she was standing in the driveway. 'Course, she wasn't very steady, but it looked like she was wanting to go to the house. So I just picked her up and tractored her down there and put her in that dog pen."

"I can't believe it!" I exclaimed. "Have you fed her anything?"'

"Yep, she sucked down a couple of quarts of kangaroo juice then, again when I got home from my hair appointment, then later this afternoon and tonight, plus she took a small amount of milk tonight. It beats all I've ever seen!"

I thought so, too! But it was good news to hear. Sadie continued her recovery in grand style, and grew into advanced calfhood without further health complications, although she was smaller than her contemporaries. Di spoiled the calf unashamedly, and she soon became a constant topic of conversation. Di and Buck thought her IQ was probably up near genius range; she pouted when things didn't go her way and reacted to a vaccination by standing away from her associates with her lower lip pooched out, just like a child.

The Hay duo were very grateful to their veterinarian for what he had done for their beloved Sadie. A few weeks later Buck called to inform me of something nice he had arranged for me.

"Doc, you have probably heard of Mr. LeRoi, the fella that does my hair. I told him about what a good vet you are and all the trouble you have with your curly hair. He said that he isn't taking any new clients, but as a special favǒr to me he would take you as a special client. Your initial scalp evaluation and hair management course of action will be on me. What do you think of that?"

"Uh, uh, I don't know what to say," I stammered. What did he mean, "all the trouble you have with your curly hair"?

"It's not much, but it's our way of thanking you for saving Sadie's life," he said.

"Let me think about it, Buck. You know how busy I am," I declared.

"That's the good part, Doc. He said he'd set you up on Thursdays about ten o'clock, and you can run by there on your way to the sale barn." He seemed so pleased with himself, I found it difficult to refuse the offer.

"I thought my hair looked fine. What's wrong with it?"

"Oh, Doc, it's always so disheveled and in a constant state of disorder. It just doesn't look very professional, and it does need to be worked with by a professional stylist," he argued. "You'd be surprised what Mr. LeRoi can do for your appearance." I was seeing an entire new side of Buck Hay!

"For right now, I believe I'll pass on it. I'm just too busy to take the extra time every week. Plus, I like the stylist I have now. I'd really miss them and all the people I see there."

"Who do you use?"

"Chappell and Myatt, down here in town."

"Doc, they're just barbers!" He spit out the word *barbers* as if just saying it caused a bitter taste in his mouth. "They don't know the first thing about how to style a head of hair."

Even though I was a constant guest on the Hay farm, somehow I avoided the fate of being the only other man in the Choctaw County area who had his hair fixed by a professional hairdresser. I cannot imagine the embarrassment and laughter that would have been caused by my walking into the sale barn auction ring with a perfectly set permanent. Perhaps that would have worked if I had taken that job at that fancy small animal clinic in Memphis. Besides, the beauty parlor might have been a good source of local gossip, but it had nothing on Chappell and Myatt.

Nineteen

~ The early fall timing of our planned clinic grand opening was perfect. People were happy that the long hot summer was nearly over, the smell of football games was in the air, and harvest time was near. Jan had decided that Wednesday was the best day of the week for the celebration, and so she, the world's greatest chairperson of such events, made the announcement via phone calls and posters set up inside and outside of the clinic. I informed Chappell and Myatt at the barbershop, knowing for certain that this would be a priority news item for their second-to-none free news dissemination service. We also put up notices at the Co-op Feed Store, Doggett's Hardware, both banks, and the FFA building at the Choctaw County High School. That just about covered all the bases.

Not only was the seasonal timing great, but the weather was perfect for our big day. The Meridian TV weatherman had promised "no rain" and eighty degrees for the east Mississippi–west Alabama region, and from the appearance of the morning sky, his prediction was on target. I was worrying about rain, since the gravel man had been ailing and our parking area was still bare ground or grass.

Even though I arrived early to clean, feed, water, and treat the patients, several clients, friends, and other well-wishers dropped by on their way to work, jokingly demanding their punch and cookies.

"Got a couple of Moon Pies and RC colas out in the truck you can have, but you'll have to wait until about eight-thirty for Jan's cookies and punch," I explained. "Didn't y'all read that sign out there that said 'Open House Ten till Two'? I'm still feeding Purina dry to the crowd in the back."

Jan and Lisa arrived promptly at eight-thirty with the rear of the station wagon loaded down with chips, dips, and other goodies of all kinds and an assortment of nice receptacles for holding all the snacks.

"These sure are pretty trays. Where did they come from?" I asked, hauling in an armful.

"John, you know very well they were wedding presents. We've used them a number of times," Jan replied, expertly arranging trays at just the right angles on the card tables.

"I've never seen them before in my life," I said. "But they sure are nice."

There was muttering from the combination punch bowl–microscope area, where she was creating a concoction from several juices and soft drinks. From the muttering, I gathered that I had indeed seen the trays before, and then there was something said about my not paying attention to anything but the veterinary business. I didn't have time to decipher the "woman talk" she engaged in because a car came to a sliding stop just in front of the door. A woman jumped out of the driver's seat and hit the door running.

"You Dr. McCormack?" she puffed.

"Yes, ma'am."

"My dog just got hit by a car," she exclaimed, wringing her hands, but staring at the table of sweets over by the screw worm spray shelf.

"OK, let's look."

On a blanket in the back of the car sat a sad-faced hundred-pound yearling German shepherd, his right rear leg extending off the seat at a strange angle to the rest of his body, which was generously blotched with a combination of mud and abrasions.

"What's his name?"

"King. And I'm Julie Page."

"I'm glad to meet you. When did this happen?" I asked, making a tentative move toward his head and calling his name. His eyes warily followed my hand, a signal that clearly told me that he didn't want anybody messing with him, especially a stranger, and I'd better back off. My hands and fingers were already abundantly scarred from dog bites, and I was getting to the stage in my practice life that I disliked being bitten. It wasn't so much the burning pain of the bite, or the threat of rabies, but being temporarily one-handed made it difficult to pass a stomach tube on a horse or handle a difficult bovine obstetrical case.

"He's been missing two days and we've searched high and low for him. This morning one of the neighbors found him on her porch."

"He doesn't appear to be in shock, does he? Let me get a muzzle on him and then we'll see if we can figure out a way to haul him inside," I said.

"Oh, he can walk, but that bad leg dangles. You think it's broken up high?"

The femur is the most commonly broken bone in dogs, especially from their encounters with automobiles. It seemed that fractured femurs came in spurts in every practice where I had worked. Maybe a week would pass without one, but then we might see three in one day. Carney Sam Jenkins, the great disseminator of dirt road common sense and theories new to my ears, speculated one day about why fractured femurs came in clusters.

"It's the sign of the moon, I'm tellin' ye'," he had vowed back in the winter, while holding his daily whittling and spitting seminar around the potbellied stove at Miss Ruby's store. "You check your almanac and you'll see that broke legs show up more when the moon is full."

"Why?" asked one of the apprentice store sitters.

"It's because of the gravity of the moon. You see, something tells dogs to go roamin' around when there's a full moon, and some way or 'nother there's an attraction between a dog and a car at that time. Doc, you can explain it better than I can, you got all that education." Six pairs of eyes immediately turned away from their hero and toward the young vet for his version of the moon theory.

"Now wait a minute, Carney, that's your tale and I'd rather you'd finish it. I'm not sure I can add any more to what you've already said. Besides, I gotta go, Mr. W.J.'s looking for me up at the Norman Lewis place ten minutes ago." I grabbed my Moon Pie and ran out the door, filing his moon-and-femur theory away in my brain for further consideration and study at a later date — a much later date.

King hobbled into the examination room without much difficulty, except for the guests who were arriving for the celebration. They were all obvious pet lovers, and as they peered sympathetically at the broken-legged dog slowly making his way into the hospital, I could just imagine what they were thinking.

"That poor animal. I wonder what they'll do for him. I'm glad it's not my dog!"

"Y'all having a party?" Julie asked as I put the muzzle on our patient. She didn't seem nearly as nervous as before, and I hoped it was because she was now confident that we were going to take good care of King.

"Yes, ma'am, you may have noticed the sign out front. We're celebrating the grand opening of our clinic. King is our first official patient." I knelt and gently palpated King's thigh for a couple of minutes while she congratulated King on being the first patient.

"Here's what we have," I declared. "He has a mid-shaft fracture of the femur, just as you thought, and he needs to have a steel pin inserted in that bone for it to heal properly. All these abrasions don't seem to amount to much."

"Can you do that?"

"Yes, but I want you to understand that we're just a country clinic, and I don't have an X-ray machine yet. So if you have any concern about that I'll be glad to refer you to one of the pet hospitals in Meridian." We simply couldn't afford the expense of an X-ray unit at that time.

"No, I'd rather you'd do it, if you feel comfortable with it. Stink Clark up on Highway Seventeen told me that you took a long piece of wire out of his sick bull's stomach last fall and that he's in the pasture now acting like nothing was ever wrong with him," she stated. "If it's all right with you I'll get on back up to the store."

I promised to call her after the surgery was completed.

Good old Stink! He and his family had been responsible for many sick animal referrals, both large and small, to our clinic. I was finding out that word-of-mouth was by far the best advertising a vet could have.

"Jan, come in here a second," I yelled. She was over at the large animal pharmaceutical shelves, showing two older couples some of the large sulfa boluses that we gave cows suffering from pneumonia. As expected, the guests were aghast at the size of the pills and were making the usual kill-or-cure jokes about the medicine.

"Where's Lisa?"

"She's out in the waiting room coloring and playing with her dolls." We had assigned one corner of the waiting room as the toy corner, not only for Tom and Lisa but also for the children of our clients. It helped to entertain them, and it kept them out of the sometime unpleasantness of the exam and surgery rooms.

"What time are the kids supposed to get here?"

"Mrs. Minsloff said about ten-thirty or eleven. Why?"

"I've got to pin this dog's leg, so I think I'll start on it now. That way I'll be finished before they get here. It might be interesting for them to see a dog anesthetized and with sutures and a leg splint in place."

"You know I can't take folks on tours, help you, and answer the phone, too," she declared.

"If you'll just help me get him down, I can take care of the rest by myself." Like most solo practitioners, I had done early morning and late night surgeries alone for so long that I had become accustomed to it. But it did require thinking ahead to get the necessary suture material, blades, packs, and four-by-four sponges opened in advance. When observing my MD colleagues

performing surgery, I was surprised at the crowd of assistant surgeons, nurses, technicians, and flunkies milling around the surgical arena, seemingly bumping into each other looking for
something to do. I found myself wishing for just one of those
assistants.

An hour and a half later, and just as I placed the last suture
in King's ten-inch thigh incision, the bus and the short motorcade
of mothers from the kindergarten drove into the parking area. I
could see Tom standing opposite the driver, as if he were a tour
guide, pointing to the clinic and talking away, no doubt lecturing
to his associates about the status of veterinary medicine in
Choctaw County and how he had been instrumental in the
supervision of the clinic's construction. I just hoped that he
wasn't describing how puppies were born again. All he needed
was a microphone and he would have been in five-year-old hog
heaven.

The kids were soon lined up buddy style, two by two, and
were marching behind Mrs. Minsloff across the parking area. Her
no-nonsense cadence reminded me of a paratrooper drill
sergeant's. Three mothers who had been pressed into chaperon
duty for the one-hour outing at the vet clinic brought up the rear.
From behind my closed surgery door I heard Jan greet them at
the open front door and then usher them into the waiting room
for a pretour welcome and orientation. It was no wonder that
Tom loved to talk. He was just doing what came natural because
of the talking gene he had inherited from his mother. Just two
more years and Lisa Bug would be doing the same thing.

"How many of you boys and girls have pets at home?" I
heard Jan say. Now she was getting into the meat of her tour-
guide rhetoric. As expected, every child there shouted "I DO!"
and it sounded as though every one of them was jumping up and
down with the pronouncement.

"OK, that's good! Now we are...Did you want to say something, young man?" Apparently someone had raised his hand.

"Yes, ma'am. My dog died," he said sadly. Veterinarians can
hear the word *die* very clearly, no matter how much hearing loss
they have. I just hoped the unfortunate dog hadn't passed on in

my clinic, and if so, I hoped he wouldn't announce that fact to all his friends and the few adults there sipping punch. I decided to act.

"Nurse Jan, bring the boys and girls in here so I can show them what I'm doing," I shouted, opening the door. Soon they were shuffling down the shiny new tile of the hallway and quietly filing into the ten-by-ten room, which contained the soundly sleeping dog atop the stainless-steel table. Tom was holding the hand of his friend Pat Sue with one hand and gesturing with the other as he informed the others about the location of the tape, cotton, syringes, and other supplies. He was a proud little man, and it made me very happy, but I interrupted to explain what I was doing.

"This pretty dog broke his leg and I had to fix it. See, I made an incision right here" — pointing to the sutures — "and put a steel rod in his leg bone so it will heal better. Now I'm putting a splint on his leg for support." I was trying to talk in my best preschool voice.

"Is that dog dead?" It was the same voice that had said "dead" before.

"No, he's sound asleep. Did you see him breathe just then?" Most agreed that they had seen the dog take a deep breath.

Then the questions began to come. Some wanted to know more details about the dog on the table and was the patient in pain, while others wanted to talk about their cats back home. Some told about having seen me on their farms and how I had treated a large animal there. Others related long, drawn-out, disjointed but happy tales that made no sense.

"My dog died," repeated the voice.

"That's too bad," I replied. I was going to change the subject, but Tom spoke first.

"What happened to him?" asked Tom. I cringed at the thought of what might be coming. I was just sure that he was going to say that his beloved pet had died right here in this very clinic because the vet didn't know the first thing about doctoring sick dogs, and he knew that was so 'cause his daddy had said so.

"He got out in the road and a paperwood truck knocked the

tar out of him. Killed him deader 'n a hammer," he declared. "Daddy said — " Mrs. Minsloff mercifully cut him off before any more of the gory details were broadcast.

"Why don't we go on and see more of this wonderful hospital for pets?" she said, gathering her charges and hustling them to the next station. I was relieved as they exited the room. Dealing with a group of kindergartners is hard work — and stressful, too!

While Jan showed the children the rest of the clinic, I finished up with King's splint and managed to get him carried back to a large cage. I called Julie and discussed what I had done, and we talked about the long convalescent period and how she should handle King when he went home in a few days.

Our grand opening was a great success. Several people brought their pets in for shots, skin ailments, and elective surgery, and many called and offered their congratulations. We were so proud of our clinic and all the support of our friends in the community. Jan and I were floating on cloud nine.

Twenty

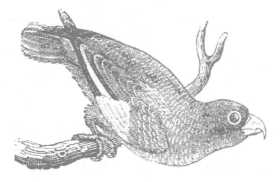

About three P.M. that same day, I made a quick large animal call to dehorn, vaccinate, and castrate a few wild calves a mile north of the clinic. I enjoyed being outside for an hour, even if working the wild calves put me in a low-grade fist-clenching mood. When I arrived back at the office there was a big Cadillac parked out front.

"John, this is Mrs. Foster. Her parakeet is sick," Jan said as I walked in the front door. I usually came in the back, but the station wagon was parked in my way. "And we're heading home now that you're here." I hugged the kids goodbye and waved at them out the window.

"You have a nice family, Doctor," the lady said.

"Yes, ma'am, I do. I'm a lucky man."

"Well, Buster here is the only family I have," she said sadly. "And he's mighty sick." I felt sorry for the well-dressed lady, who was obviously quite wealthy but was still lonely.

"He's a pretty little bird," I allowed as the elderly lady placed the cage on the exam table.

The little fellow was an iridescent mixed green color, though his feathers were ruffled and askew. He was sitting quietly in the bottom of the cage with his head hanging low and staring at the cage floor, as though suffering a terrific headache. It was obvious he needed medical attention.

"Yes sir, Doctor, Buster's been doing poorly for the last couple of days," Mrs. Foster reported. "He's not his usual chirping and vibrant self. He just sits there acting as if he's cold all the time."

"Well, let's see what we can do about that," I suggested as I opened the cage door and reached inside.

I quickly captured the feathery creature in my meaty right fist and was extracting him from his home when my attention was temporarily drawn to the loud noise of two dogs disagreeing in the kennel area.

"Heah, you dogs!" I stated rather emphatically. "Quieten down in there! Sit!"

Immediate silence prevailed. It's amazing sometimes how intimidating a loud voice can be.

I had almost forgotten about the little bird in my right hand until I felt his beak weakly flop onto my forefinger. At first I thought maybe he was experiencing a "falling out" spell, but upon instant reflection of the avian medicine courses I had recently taken in veterinary school, nothing registered regarding fainting poultry. At that moment, I was pretty sure that I had just bought into the bird business.

"What's wrong with Buster, Doctor?" the poor lady asked. But she already knew. Her eyes had widened and her mouth was gaped open in apparent shock. I realized my face was frozen with the same look of restrained panic.

"Uh, I believe he's passed out," I stammered. "Let me see if I can give him artificial respiration."

I quickly laid Buster out on the cold exam table and made a heroic effort to revive him. But birds do not respond well to CPR efforts, and it is hard to administer to such a wee animal. I valiantly tried mouth-to-beak resuscitation, chest massage, and loud talk. None of that worked, nor did placing him in the deep freeze for three seconds, which sometimes initiates respiratory action. He was dead.

"I'm afraid Buster had a massive heart attack, ma'am. Unfortunately, it was fatal. I suspect that he died of shock."

"Oh no!" cried the lady, "poor little Buster. He never hurt anybody. Ooh, ooh!"

She was sobbing now as she cradled the little bird in her hands. Her heart was breaking.

For the first time in my life I started looking around for some strong rope and a chair, since I was considering hanging myself from the rafters. My gaze fell upon the scalpels on the counter, and I wondered if it would be more expedient to just slash my wrists. I'd never felt so rotten in my entire life.

"I am so sorry about Buster," I apologized, "but sometimes these little birds go into shock and die of fright when they are stressed. Perhaps we can find another somewhere over in Meridian."

"No, I just wish you had been a little more gentle with him. You deal with big animals most of the time and you are just too rough on little birds," she lectured between sobs and tears.

"And another thing," she continued. "If you are going to work with people's beloved pets you should wear some nice slacks, a tie, and a white jacket. You must look like a doctor!"

What could I say? I really had not been that rough with him, other than yelling at the dogs. That loud racket probably had done him in. And my appearance could have been improved. I looked down at my big, rough hands. They were callused and stained with black tattoo ink from the previous large animal call, were cracked, cut, and chapped from rough farm work. They surely didn't appear to be "bird healing" hands.

"Mrs. Foster, I am sorry about this, and you are exactly right," I apologized. "Obviously, I can't bring Buster back, but if you would allow me, I would like to drive over to the pet store and get you another little bird. That would make me feel a lot better, and in time I'm sure you will learn to love Buster's replacement," I said. "This is a big day for us here at the clinic, and I'd hate to let it end without trying to make amends."

"Well, I know it really wasn't your fault, because he was sick and all, and I had read in my bird book that these things do happen when a little bird is stressed. But I don't know whether I ever want another bird or not. I'll have to think about it," she said softly.

"Would you like to give it some thought? Why don't you think about it for a couple of days, and then I'll call and we'll discuss it again. In the meantime, I'll see if I can locate his replacement."

She refused my offer to bury Buster for her, deciding to take him home and put him out in her flower garden. I escorted her to the car, then directed her safely out into the road.

Within an hour, I had changed my appearance and was on my way to another farm to dehorn more cattle, this time full-grown, rough-looking, piney woods cows. I was still shaken from the bird incident, and I knew that it would stay with me forever. But I vowed from then on to be more gentle with my patients and do something about my hands and working apparel. Happy Dupree, my client, buddy, and so-called career advisor, had already preached me that sermon.

It was my first call to the Circle D Brahma Ranch, and I noticed the cowboys sitting on the corral all had the look of escapees from the mean farm. None of the three had shaved in days, and they all wore scowls that would have stopped Superman in his tracks. They looked at me in disgust as they jawed their great chews of tobacco.

"Another green vetnerry!" the ugliest one mumbled between spits. "Got on pretty white coveralls and little white tennis shoes. And look at them lily-white hands!" I knew better than to wear white coveralls, but I was so upset about the bird and what the lady had said about my attire, I suppose I wasn't thinking straight. And my hands weren't really that clean. I had just scrubbed them repeatedly with Comet scouring powder. But it was too late to turn tail and run back to town.

"Doc, you gonna play tennis or dehorn cows?" a toothless wonder questioned amid laughter, snickering, and continued voluminous spitting.

"Look, one of y'all just come up here and catch heads for me and I'll get those horns removed. Don't worry about what I look like."

Within a minute we had a cow caught, its nose tonged and pulled around to the side. The cow was one of a small group of aged cows whose horns were long, showed lots of concentric rings, and were the consistency of antique granite. After injecting novocaine to anesthetize each horn's base, I gently lifted the heavy Keystone dehorners and placed them meticulously over the horn, making sure the cut would include a ring of hair all the way around the base of the horn. Then I slowly tried to pull the handles together. The cow stomped in the chute and tried to sling the dehorners off as I strained, squinted my eyes shut, and gritted my teeth, but the horn remained intact.

"Looka here, Doc," the head cowboy yelled. "You're just too easy and gentle. You act like this is one of your little lapdogs or a sick canary. You got to go at this hard and kind of vicious like. Here, lemme show you how we do this back home in Texas!"

With that, he elbowed me aside, grabbed the two handles, and with a karate-type yell, snatched the two handles together. The immediate result was a lightninglike crack, followed by loud struggling in the rickety metal chute and the wild geysering of blood from a severed artery.

"That's how it's done, young feller!" the pleased cowboy uttered as he rendered the air greenish-brown with a sudden flush of well-used juicy tobacco debris.

There was certainly nothing gentle about the way he'd removed the horn from that cow. As I gently clamped off the bleeding artery, my self-appointed instructor continued his critique of my technique and appearance.

"Doc, I reckon you don't do much cow work, do you, 'cause yo' hands are so pretty and clean. And if you're gonna go out on farms and git amongst the stock, you oughta wear some work clothes and boots. Them whites make you look like some kind of intern or somethin'."

"Yeah, that's right," echoed another member of the crew. "And don't do like one vet did and come out here with a tie on. A tie! I can't believe it!"

Veterinarians engaged in mixed practices often have a tough time making all their clients happy with their appearance, wardrobe selection, and the condition of their hands. Also, it's kind of hard to work all day with a herd of wild and unruly Brahma cattle, then come back to the clinic and hurriedly readjust to handling fragile birds and kittens.

I was continuing to learn the art of veterinary practice, although quite painfully at times. The day of our clinic's grand opening I learned to dress for the occasion and found it was acceptable to use plenty of lotion on my hands, just as long as the cowboy crowd didn't find out about it. I also learned to always ask a parakeet owner to hold her little bird while I examined it from a safe distance.

Two days after the passing of little Buster, my phone call to Mrs. Foster found her in much better spirits than I had expected. She had decided that she would indeed like to have another bird. A quick trip to Meridian produced a little green fellow that very closely matched the late Buster. Mrs. Foster and I became waving and speaking friends, but she always took her avian health problems to an out-of-town veterinarian.

Twenty-one

⌒ One of my first farm calls had been to Happy Dupree's farm for the purpose of putting a group of fifty or so calves through the working chute for the usual vaccinations and so forth. As is the case with all tough and independent livestock owners, I'm sure Happy was leery about the veterinary skills of the young greenhorn practitioner who had been recommended to him by the county agent. I also wondered whether I could do the job according to his specifications.

All went well for the first thirty calves. But while I was crouched down behind a wild yearling heifer removing an extra teat, the beast somehow extracted her head from the rickety head-holding device and came stomping back over my helpless carcass. Amid the chaos and commotion of the moment, I could hear Happy's loud booming voice exploding in an uncontrollable fit of laughter. I didn't know what to think of someone who was directing his guffawing at me, especially when he didn't know the extent of my stomp wounds. That's when I learned that everyone laughs when the vet gets hurt.

Nevertheless, I hopped up, spat some of the dirt and debris out of my mouth, scraped some of the mud and manure off my coveralls, brushed myself off, and called for the next patient — all the while trying to ignore the burning sensations that had been produced by the churning action of the heifer's hooves.

"Any feller who gets stepped on that bad and jumps right up and keeps goin' can't be all bad," he announced later in between chuckles. I took that as a compliment.

The incident signaled an odd beginning of a fine new friendship. Not only did I become his farm veterinarian after that, but he also sort of adopted me, since all his sons were daughters and they didn't share his enthusiasm for hunting, fishing, and other pleasurable outdoor pursuits. Few people have the good fortune to have a real friend like Happy Dupree.

"I got some calves to vaccinate," he'd say when he phoned in. "And bring yo' line. We'll hook a few bluegills after we fix up the calves."

If I didn't bring my line, he'd fuss and fume, and go on about how a good vet would always have at least one fishing rig stowed away somewhere in his truck. "You have such a great opportunity to go fishing every day, because you're all over three counties. I wish I had the chances you have. Nearly every farm you visit has a pond or lake." On one hand he was telling me how to run my business, and minutes later he seemed to think I should be fishing all the time.

In September, he called one night to talk about the upcoming deer hunting season. At that time, I had never been on a deer hunt.

"I just can't believe you've never been deer hunting! Are you sure?"

"Nope, I sure haven't," I answered, "but I do want to go."

"Boy, I'm gonna take you on a hunt this fall," he declared, "and you're gonna get a big 'un!"

Killing a deer is not exactly paradise for me, but being intimate with nature while hunting, looking forward to seeing the deer, and perhaps getting a clean shot come mighty close. Listening to the squirrels' chattering complaints at an uninvited intruder, watching chipmunks wildly scooting about, and discovering that a sudden clamorous, leaf-stomping sound is being generated by a two-ounce bird and not a herd of panicking deer are all favorite sights and sounds of mine. Sometimes when I hear that telltale twig-popping noise and then feel the piercing chill slowly surge up my spinal column, I wonder whether or not I'll be able to pull the trigger if a gigantic twelve-pointer struts out into the open.

I learned to respect the woods, its animals, and all nature, in fact, from my dad, my Uncle Willis, and Happy Dupree.

The remainder of the early fall was spent in anticipation of the big November hunt, which was to be held in the Tensaw River swamp, some fifty miles south of the southern end of Choctaw County. It was to be a several-day event, with several organized hunts, plus the opportunity to squirrel hunt or fish if any of the attendees so desired. Unfortunately, Happy and I had other obligations at home, so we planned to stay only one night. Sleeping accommodations would be in a large houseboat and an old dormitory situated on the riverbank. Three meals a day would be served in the dormitory. Not only would there be hunting, there would also be card playing, impromptu gun and knife seminars, and big deer tales and lying contests, which are usually one and the same.

Happy called a few nights before the big hunt to "touch bases."

"Dr. John," he began, "now be sure to bring plenty of ammunition, a good raincoat, and a flashlight. Also, go by a shoe store up there and find yourself some Red Wing boots like the ones I wear."

"What kind of ammunition?" I asked.

"Why, buckshot of course," he replied. Then there was a brief silence. "You do have a gun, don't you?"

"No, I'm afraid not. Do you have one I can borrow?" It was not a disclosure that he took well.

"Dang, John, you've known for weeks now that this hunt was coming up, and you still don't have a gun? Why not? I thought everybody had a gun!" He was really peeved.

"Because I can't afford one. Everything we have is in this clinic and practice equipment," I declared. "Maybe I ought to just stay home. I ought to be working anyway."

"No, you're goin'! You can use one of mine. But you tell Jan to go to Sears and Roebuck down in Mobile and they'll sell you

one of those Belgian-made Brownings on time. She can pay a little bit on it every month until it's paid off. I never heard of a vet
that didn't have a gun. It's not good for your image." According
to Happy, I needed to wear a white coat in my clinic, keep a fishing pole stowed in my truck, and have a nice shotgun. My veterinary school professors did stress the white coat part, but said
nothing about the pole and gun.

~

A few days later, on the eve of the opening day of deer season, I drove south to the prearranged meeting point at the boat
landing on the Tensaw River, arriving in the late afternoon. During the hour's drive I reflected on the growth of my veterinary
practice back in Butler. It was hard to believe that it had only
been 350 days since Jan, Tom, Lisa, the pets, and I pulled into
town in a packed U-Haul truck and a station wagon for the purpose of creating a veterinary practice and doing our part to help
the community. It was a little scary to look back and realize that
we had had no family or friends or any other connection with the
county except for Mr. Sexton, the county agent. We must have
had a lot of faith to take such a giant step.

Now, a year later, I was working at the sale barn one day a
week, had a substantial base of clients, had tested a large number
of the county's cows for brucellosis, and had vaccinated several
thousand dogs against rabies. I was proud of what we had
accomplished and couldn't have asked to work with finer people, people who had immediately accepted us.

We had taken very little time off for ourselves since the move.
We had taken two days at Christmas to visit our parents, and Jan
had taken the kids back to the grandparents' for short visits on a
couple of occasions since then. I played golf occasionally, but my
clients knew where I was in case of an emergency, and some had
actually driven out onto the golf course to find me on at least two
occasions. I was still an amateur hunter who had never been on
a deer hunt in an area that was well-known as one of the finest

deer hunting places in the country. But I hoped this trip would change that. I was going to be away from the practice for almost forty-eight hours, and I was feeling a little guilty about being apart from my family and leaving Jan to look after the clinic, answer the phone, and try to help as best she could, since the nearest vet was thirty-five miles away.

About four P.M. Happy showed up, driving his dark blue, short-bed, 1962 Chevy pickup, just like mine, and towing a dark green jon boat and trailer. With a lot of eager chatter we quickly piled our hunting gear and other paraphernalia into the boat, parked our trucks side by side up on the bank, and finally pushed out into the river. The Tensaw River was fifty to one hundred yards wide, depending upon where you measured. Even though I was a little leery of big water, I felt fairly comfortable with Happy's boat-handling expertise. At least it wasn't dark and the river wasn't at flood stage, like the Tombigbee was when I had crossed it with Benny Lee, Mr. Campbell's hired man, back in February to save a wounded horse. But I was still glad I was wearing shoes that could be removed quickly in case the boat capsized. I wondered if Jan was worried about my safety in Happy's boat, but then decided that she knew that he had been boating in those waters for many, many years.

The cloudy and cool weather seemed perfect for deer hunting, I thought, even though I wasn't sure what kind of weather was best for that activity. As Happy expertly steered the boat out into the main channel and quickly accelerated the old Johnson outboard, I found that I relished the sudden chilly wind against my face and the occasional drizzles of rain that felt like darts puncturing the skin of my forehead and cheeks.

The twenty-minute boat ride was nature at its best. As we continued upstream, we saw raccoons, squirrels, birds of all sizes and shapes, and I'm sure I even saw an alligator or two. Happy suddenly tapped me on the arm and pointed toward the riverbank where we saw two deer scurrying away from the oncoming intruders and their noise. Fish would occasionally hurl themselves up and out of the water, and would disappear just as

quickly back into the murky depths. The elements of nature surrounding me gave me that rugged, natural feel that one is supposed to have on a hunting trip.

The river had taken a serpentine route, and it appeared to me
that we were traveling in a circle. Even though I was blessed with
a well-developed sense of direction, I was totally confused as to
the direction in which we were headed. In addition, we made
left- and right-hand turns at several tributaries, seemingly at random, which further complicated the route. Happy appeared to
be nonchalantly snoozing at the controls, and would make his
turns, robotlike, as if he had a radar outfit rigged up in his cranium. I hoped that I wouldn't have to find my way out of that
river swamp alone.

Finally, we rounded a bend in the river and I could make out
the ghostlike outline of a hunting camp appearing through the
light fog and the big oaks hanging heavy with Spanish moss. As
we drew nearer, I could see several men in red caps and leather
boots milling about, and others congregated in small groups,
apparently quietly conversing about the prospects of the upcoming hunts or slapping their thighs in obvious gaiety, probably in
response to the latest traveling salesman yarn. Some had their
meaty fists wrapped around beverage containers of some
description, and I saw a couple of men already slightly "toxic,"
no doubt from the consumption of certain fermented beverages.

Happy cut the motor, and we coasted into the landing area to
greetings of "It's about time!" and "Where y'all been?" and other
expressions of camaraderie and goodwill. One grinning and
glassy-eyed camper started toward our docking boat with long
but wobbly strides, only to slip on the muddy bank and glide,
wide-eyed, down to water's edge amidst gales of laughter from
his associates.

"Don't pay no 'tention to ole Shaky," Happy said, laughing.
"He don't come here to hunt anyway." I'm sure I looked puzzled.

Happy assured me that although there would be partying
that night, the hunting season didn't open until tomorrow.
Things would be different then.

We grabbed our gear and trudged to the houseboat, where we found a couple of unoccupied bunks. We exchanged greetings with the other hunters, most of whom I had never met before, and then Happy led me out through the thick woods to the kennels.

"That's Jack over there, and Sheba by the cypress tree," he pointed out. "Kate's that yeller one, and that's Black Cat settin' there beside her. I'm gonna put your name in the pot for one of her puppies next litter."

There must have been twenty dogs in the pen. I found out later that all of them would be needed over the duration of the three-day hunt, because there would be several "drives." A drive consisted of placing hunters on "stands" at predetermined and numbered points around the perimeter of the area to be hunted. Once the hunters were all on their stands, several dogs would be released across from the hunters. The dogs were accompanied by "drivers," who went through the woods making considerable racket, trying to drive the deer toward the hunters.

After formally inspecting the canines, Happy and I headed back to the houseboat for further socialization, followed by a supper of pork barbecue and all the trimmings. Big buck stories were told, each one bigger and more embellished than the one before. But the most amusing story we heard was something that had happened that afternoon shortly after our arrival.

Shaky, who was the most loopy of the drinkers at our arrival, continued to consume more and more of his alcoholic potions after he nearly fell in the water. In answering a call of nature, he went out into the woods and lost his sense of direction. After wandering about in the woods and swamp for a half hour, he came upon the south end of a camp, complete with friendly hunters and a kennel full of nice dogs. Shaky consumed several libations with the strangers, then staggered off to search for his own camp, which he thought was across the island. After wandering in the darkness for a considerable period of time, he approached his camp from the north side. When he finally arrived at his quarters, he related in great, slurry detail, the news about the camp across the way and how hospitable the people were. He said they had some fine-looking dogs, and a couple of them greatly resembled his own dogs.

Shaky's roommates were broken up by his recitation. One cardplayer threw his head back in a fit of laughter, only to turn his chair over and go sprawling on the floor. There was no other camp. Shaky had just been going around in circles and had stumbled into his own camp. I was again reassured that Shaky was among the nonhunters and would not be holding a gun the next day.

Although none of us slept very well or very much that night, we were up bright and early the next morning. It was the first day of deer season, which I soon found out was the most important day of the year in deer hunting circles. The hunters were all dressed in their opening day finery and were impatiently milling around and kicking at the ground. Finally, each hunter drew a little slip of paper with a number on it from a hat that was passed around. It was the number of his stand.

"Who's got stand number twenty?" shouted Happy.

"I have it!" announced a portly but distinguished older man, who appeared to be a prosperous banker.

"Lemme see it a minute," requested Happy.

He came over and handed me number twenty, then took the number that I had drawn and returned it to the banker. I didn't understand what was transpiring. He tried to explain.

"Just keep yo' mouth shut," he whispered. "You've got the best stand in the whole swamp. I guarantee you'll get yourself a deer on that spot."

We loaded into several boats and headed upstream several miles, since the morning hunt was going to be held on another island. My stand was located deep in the woods, about three quarters of a mile from the boat landing. Happy went with me every step of the way to be sure that I located and took up temporary residence beside the specified tree, and even faced the correct direction. Then he lectured me on the proper way to hold the gun he'd brought me.

"Now, when you hear them dogs acomin', look yonder way,

towards those cypress trees," he ordered, "and chances are he'll be coming right through there."

"What happens if I shoot but miss him?" I asked.

"You better not miss, after all the trouble we've gone to. I reckon you might as well stay here in this swamp if you do," he answered sternly. "And don't you leave this stand until I come to get you. Be still, be quiet, and don't go to sleep!"

"OK, I think I know what to do," I retorted. I was ready to get on with it, and do it by myself.

After he disappeared down the trail, I carefully sat down under the big oak tree that marked the stand, cradled Happy's old buckshot-filled Remington pump in my arms, and tried to get my bearings.

After getting relatively comfortable, I meditated on many things. I thought about how fortunate I was to have a friend and father figure like old Happy. He was a tough, gruff, to-the-point kind of guy who had a heart of gold and would do anything for you if he liked you. I wondered if five-year-old Tom, back at home in Butler, would ever be lucky enough to have such a good friend. What if I shot a doe by mistake? What if I shot at, but missed, a big buck? Would Happy really leave me in the woods?

Then I thought about some of my friends and clients who were against hunting and questioned whether a veterinarian should be shooting at wild animals. After examining my own ethics and sense of right and wrong, I decided I was comfortable with my legal right to hunt and the way I approached it. My two rules were to never pull the trigger unless it was a clean shot that I felt would kill instantly and to use the game for my family's dinner table or donate it to others. In addition, the deer herd was so dense in southwest Alabama that hunting was highly recommended by wildlife specialists as a population-control measure.

I must have been meditating for the better part of an hour about everything from hunting ethics to timber harvesting to the mating habits of squirrels, when I realized that the occasional bays and barks of the hounds somewhere in the distance were becoming more frequent and insistent. Now completely roused from my trance, I began listening more intently to the hue and cry. Even though I was a neophyte deer hunter, my fast breathing and thumping heart told me they must be on the trail of something interesting, and from their increasing baying it appeared they were fast approaching.

I peeked around the right side of the tree and actually saw the buck before I heard him make any sound. He was fifty or so yards away and quietly tiptoeing down the trail right toward my stand, occasionally stopping and looking backward with ears at full alert, gauging the distance of his sniffing pursuers. After a few seconds of apparent contemplation, he would wiggle his tail and recommence his forward motion, his head held low to the ground. He wore a beautifully symmetrical rack of antlers with a whole slew of points, and he was headed straight for me.

I think there is a point, when some hunters are face-to-face with the natural beauty of a majestic buck, that serious doubt about pulling that trigger creeps into their hearts. Such was my feeling at that point as I leveled the old shotgun at the base of his massive neck. As he grew bigger and bigger in my sights, I could just almost read the thinking in his eyes.

"I'll just slip over here by this big oak tree, then turn west, go through that patch of reeds, and lose those stupid bone chewers there," he was probably thinking as he rotated his ears as if they were radar dishes.

As with the scores of hunters before me, instinct took over, and I carefully squeezed the trigger. I'm sure the thunderous roar and concussion of the shotgun shell explosion was momentarily shocking, though at the time I didn't even notice the discharging weapon or its jarring kick.

The big buck reared up and fell over backwards a second or so after the load of buckshot caught him flush in the base of the neck. I pumped another shell into the chamber and cautiously stepped the few feet to where he was lying.

"That's strange," I remember thinking. "I know he's dead, but I can distinctly hear his heart pounding."

I quickly realized that it was my own heart that I was hearing, and it seemed as if it were trying to leap from my chest amid the excitement. With each beat, it felt like my hands had grabbed an electric fence. Then it occurred to me that I might be having some kind of excitement-induced cardiac arrest. Surely a grown man couldn't get that excited about killing a deer! Since that time, however, I have heard of many seasoned hunters who have suffered the same symptoms.

I carefully examined the beautiful specimen, then counted and recounted the points on his antlers. After my heart had quit its antics, I decided that I should field dress the buck before Happy came to see about the shot he had heard. I knew that because of his experience as a hunter, he would have surely recognized the sound of his own gun and zeroed in on the exact stand from which it came. But as I stood with skinning knife poised, all of a sudden I heard the sounds of limbs breaking, leaves shuffling, and more heavy breathing coming down the trail behind me. It was Happy, going at a fast canter. After all his warnings and lectures on the evils of leaving your stand before the hunt is over, here he came, crushing reeds and bursting through the bulrushes and thorny vines, stampeding toward stand number twenty.

"Did you get 'im, did you get 'im?" he panted. He was red-faced and bleeding from a forehead scratch, the result of his impatient dash through the swamp and woods. Then he spied the big buck.

"Lord have mercy!" he exclaimed. "What a fine 'un! Let's see how many points on these horns." He counted eight. I wanted to call it a nine-pointer, but Happy removed his wedding band to see if it would hang on that ninth point. "Naw, it's not quite long enough to call a point." I believe it was the first time I had seen him truly excited, and I'm sure his heart was pounding just as mine had been minutes before. Perhaps I didn't know it then, but I now know that true sportsmen get a bigger thrill when their children or guests get the prize.

Getting a big deer out of the woods was a job that I had not even considered up to that point. But it finally dawned on me just how deep we were in the woods and how heavy that deer was going to be while getting him to the boat. I knew he would be somewhat lighter after being field dressed, but I was still concerned about lifting and carrying something that must surely have weighed at least three hundred pounds.

"Quit worryin', hoss!" Happy ordered. "Just enjoy what's happened as we tote him out. There are people in New York City who'd give anything they own to be right here in your shoes."

"I know that, but isn't he going to be more than we can carry?"

"Aw, that ain't no hill for a stepper!" he exclaimed. That was one of his favorite sayings when we faced an arduous task. He produced a small army surplus hatchet from amongst the other hardware hanging from his belt and whacked down a small sapling. After trimming off the leaves and small branches, we turned the deer on his back and tied his feet to the pole. Then, with Happy on the lead end and me on the other, we started trudging down the trail, stumbling and staggering under our shoulder-gouging burden.

As we came upon each of the other hunters on their stands, we would stop and rest briefly and review the big event with them. Before long Happy took over the telling of the story himself and added considerable embellishment. As I stood open-mouthed, trying to work a word or two into the conversation, Happy would relate details of the kill, many of which were news even to me.

There was much discussion about the deer's size, how the rack compared with those killed on hunts in previous years, and whose fine talented dogs were responsible for bringing him to my stand. But I was disturbed about their obvious underestimation of the weight we were carrying. Most declared the deer's weight to be somewhere in the range of 150 pounds, while a few estimated 175. I couldn't believe something that heavy could weigh so little, and I felt a little wimpy for having so much shoulder discomfort. But the sympathetic hunters took turns relieving us of our burden, which allowed our numb shoulders to regain some of their feeling.

After what seemed like an hour and several miles, we arrived at the boat landing, draped the prize over the front of the boat, and shoved off. It was another cool, enjoyable ride, and I will always remember the big grin on Happy's craggy face when our boat finally arrived at the camp.

Several observers eagerly grabbed the deer, dragged him over to the hanging area, and lifted him up on the old cotton-weighing scale. Then Noah, called "Mr. Noie" by all the members, who had been weighing the daily kills at the hunt club since its creation, creaked up to the scale and slowly and meticulously placed the weighted pea way out on the 150-pound mark. All eyes were riveted to the scale to see if it balanced out level, but it was obvious that *my* deer was much heavier, as I had known all along. Noah gradually inched the pea farther out, at five-pound increments, until it reached the 170 mark and the scale began to approach the horizontal. Three more notches and he made his official and indisputable pronouncement.

"A hunnert and sebenty-three pounds," he declared as loudly as his eighty-year-old vocal cords would allow, but it wasn't much louder than a gravelly whisper. That meant the deer must have weighed about two hundred pounds on the hoof! When he was rehung over on the skinning platform, he made the other deer seem like runts. Happy was strutting around, inspecting, aging, and passing judgment on all the others, and being sure everyone who came within range understood what a "hoss" the big one was, plus who had brought it in.

Suddenly, Happy reached down, grabbed some deer blood from underneath one of the hanging deer, and started at me in a full run. At the same time, two burly hunters who had slipped around to my rear grabbed me in a double bear hug just as Happy smeared the clotted blood thoroughly all over my face, ears, neck, and hair.

"What are y'all doing?" I muttered and sputtered.

"Doc, that's our tradition here. When you kill your first deer, you get your face bloodied," said Happy. "Just be glad you didn't miss him, 'cause you would've gotten your shirttail cut off real high up." Everybody had a good laugh and enjoyed the moment, but no one loved it more than Happy.

The rest of the trip was anticlimactic. We had another deer drive, and then some of us went squirrel hunting in the afternoon but got lost. After an hour or so of worried wandering through the swamp, we found our way back to the river and flagged down a passing fisherman, who helped to find our boat. Being hopelessly lost and directionally confused in a strange land is a terrible feeling. I'll never know how we found our way out, unless there was a Higher Authority taking care of us.

The mounted deer head still hangs on my wall, and each time I look at it I think of my great friend, Happy Dupree, and that first hunt. I also remember fondly the short fishing trips we made together late in the afternoon when the bluegills and bass were biting. It was uncanny how he knew where the fish were active. It didn't matter whether we were fishing in the river or a small farm pond, he could always find the right spots.

From Happy I learned to enjoy life to the fullest, to respect and appreciate nature, and to live each day as if it was my last. Work hard, play hard, and ask no quarter.

Little did I know that the Tensaw River trip was the last time Happy and I would hunt together. One morning not long after that, he was approaching some nearby railroad tracks that he had safely crossed thousands of times. There were no safety gates or warning lights, and on that day Happy's truck and a train arrived at the crossing at exactly the same time. Happy lost his life instantly. But those of us who had the privilege of working and playing with him will never lose the memories of a good man and a great friend.

Twenty-two

~ Being away from the practice for two days was both a blessing and a curse. I thoroughly enjoyed being with Happy Dupree and his crowd of rowdies on the deer hunt in the Tensaw River swamp. There were no phone calls about colicking horses in the middle of the night or people knocking on the door of the sleeping quarters with sick dogs or cats. But the flip side of those two days freedom was that my work was piling up back at the practice, and I knew I was going to pay a price for it when I returned.

I also missed my family and felt a little guilty about being away and having fun while Jan was handling all the phone calls and explaining where I was and when I'd be back. I was sure Lisa had asked Jan a hundred times, "When will Daddy be home?" only to receive the same answer as the last time she asked. Tom was old enough to understand about deer hunting and how sometimes it's important for a man to get into the woods for a little while and refuse to shave and bathe, to observe the wonders of nature, and get a firsthand appreciation for life in the deep woods that few people ever experience. I didn't know whether Tom knew all this or not, but I knew it and it sounded good when I repeated it to him.

The next few days I arose earlier than usual, trying to catch up with all the requests for service that had come in while I was off playing. I spayed the dogs, altered the tomcats, dewormed the horses, tested a dozen herds of cattle, and worked as hard as I could from daylight until the phone stopped ringing at night.

"Honey, you sure are pushing yourself this week. Those two days in the woods must have given you inspiration," Jan declared.

"Oh, yes, no doubt about it," I replied. "Being out there among the trees and communing with nature, plus all that fellowship with hardworking men who have their heads screwed on straight, puts a different light on things. But you know I like to work hard, especially when I have a wonderful spouse and these lovely children behind me."

She took a long silent look at me, and I knew her highly developed sense of radar detected something that was a little amiss with what I had said. The words I had just uttered weren't exactly foolishness, but the phraseology didn't follow my usual speech pattern. After observing her baloney-detecting system up close for seven years, I had come to the conclusion that she had no equal in that department. Still eyeing me with one eyebrow raised, she consulted a sheet of paper stuck on the refrigerator.

"Uh huh, just as I thought. This is the week for the season's first big barbecue and hunt at Rudder Hill Hunting Club," she exclaimed, a wry smile crossing her face.

"Well, I declare. You're right as usual," I said, trying to act surprised. "And I really ought to be there, you know. What if a dog got gored or something? Plus, I think I should be there for business reasons. Can you handle the phone for a few hours?"

"Of course you should be there. You might even have some fun! And of course I can handle the phone," she agreed. "But don't hand me all that baloney about nature and gored dogs and fellowship with men who have their heads on straight. Save all that for your next speech at the cattlemen's meeting." She understood completely why I was trying to get as much work done by the end of the week as possible.

I smiled just wondering about what the inside of her brain must look like. I wondered if great scientists could look at brain tissue under their million-dollar microscopes and tell if it came from a man or woman. Maybe the female brain comes equipped with something like those little transistors that I had been reading about in the Meridian paper. I knew for sure that gender had to make a difference — Jan was always way ahead of me.

Rudder Hill was a large and prestigious hunting club located less than ten miles north of Butler's town square. Its leased hunting lands encompassed hundreds of acres of prime timber land in the heart of some of the finest Virginia white-tailed deer hunting in the universe. Carney Sam Jenkins had advised me to get my name on the Rudder Hill waiting list at our first confab, because, he said, "all the big shots belong." He must have been one of the big shots, because I had been invited to join by the time I had resided in the county six months.

There were several organized deer hunting days, complete with pork barbecue lunches, on the schedule for the year's deer season, which traditionally ran from the middle of November until early February. I was lukewarm about going on the hunt, but I really wanted to be there for that pork barbecue lunch.

There is no food more highly acclaimed in the South than barbecue. Grits, sweet potatoes, pecan pie, and collard greens are all wonderful delicacies when prepared the Southern way, but good barbecue makes everything else pale in comparison. It is very important for those hearing about the gustatory delight of a batch of barbecue for the first time to understand that the word *barbecue* is a noun, at least in the Deep South.

"Unca Bubba is takin' us all to town to eat barbecue!" would be a proper usage of the word. Also, it means that the meat used is pork and that it has been slowly smoked over hot coals, preferably from green hickory wood, for a period of hours, depending upon whether the entire hog is being prepared or just the hams, butts, or shoulders. In other areas of the South, it is perfectly acceptable to use the word *barbecue* as a noun to mean beef, or as an adjective, as in "barbecued chicken," but I am not aware of any true Southerner who would flop a couple of steaks on the gas grill out on the deck and have the gall to call it "barbecuing." That procedure is called "grilling."

Preparing true barbecue requires the person or persons in

charge to undergo hours and hours of physical suffering. Exactly how much suffering depends upon whether you have to do everything yourself, including raising the hog, butchering it, and butterflying it, to sitting up all night tending its cooking while being almost charred yourself from messing around the hot fire. Then there's the smoke. Since smoke seeks heat, it constantly torments your eyes and nostrils, regardless of where you are sitting or standing. Although the fire and smoke are givens, if you don't want to butcher your own, an easier meat procurement plan is to simply call Charlie Hale down at the supermarket, order the raw cuts you want, and pick them up the evening just before you start the fire.

The Rudder Hill barbecue committee, of which I was a newly appointed member, congregated at the "pit" in the middle of the night before the big barbecue lunch the next day. The pit was located adjacent to the clubhouse and was a concrete block structure about ten feet long, four feet wide, three or four feet high, and open on one end for the placement of the hot coals. It was under a roof for protection against the rain.

While a couple of us neophytes started the hardwood fire, others assembled all the meat and necessary equipment, such as pots and pans, an iron pot, and makings for the sauce. About midnight the meat was placed on the metal grills atop the pit and the hot coals were sprinkled underneath with a long-handled shovel. This is when a patient barbecue master gets serious and makes sure the amateurs don't put so much heat under the meat that it scorches. Too much smoke and sizzling meat are the clues that you've got trouble. At previous all-night cooking sessions I had seen old-timer barbecue masters get mighty riled up if an apprentice hot coal shoveler got too enthusiastic about his job. Such an old man is liable to start kicking people in appropriate places and using horribly vile language if the meat is burnt. Of course, that is understandable because the hundred hungry barbecue critics who will be arriving in just hours are expecting the very best and can detect the least iota of scorched pork in their serving.

In addition to the hot fire and smoke, I noticed there were

other forms of torture at Choctaw County barbecues. Since the cooking was done late at night, some of the cookers took to strong drink in ever-increasing quantities as the night wore on. When the pork got hot and the juices began to drip on the coals, store-bought liquor in skinny paper sacks twisted at the top and gallon Coca-Cola jugs of Choctaw County white liquor started to emerge from underneath and behind truck seats.

At first swill, I noticed, the imbiber's faces became twisted and grotesque, as if the fiery stuff they had just tasted was the most foul material that had ever passed between human lips, but several long seconds later they testified in raspy whispers to the smoothness and mellowness of the batch.

Then, because of the in-the-gut effects of the horrid brew, the imbibers would tell stories and jokes of all descriptions. Not only did these slurry recitations have to be tolerated, they also had to be laughed at, and with great thigh-slapping enthusiasm. If the teller didn't feel that the proper decibel level of laughter had been reached, he would tell the joke again, this time in more agonizing detail. In addition to the jokes, several hours of conversation covered every conceivable subject, from politics to Southeastern Conference football. As is to be expected, tempers flared between the Alabama and Auburn loyalists, but no physical injuries were sustained, probably because the barbecue master stepped in with his long-handled shovel raised high in the air.

"Whichever one of you jugheads that throws the first punch will get this here implement upside his skull," he announced. There seemed to be no doubt in anyone's mind that he was fully prepared to carry out his threat, and an uneasy peace was quickly restored.

At six A.M., I left the barbecue site, which was now beginning to smell as if the miracle of the hickory coals on hog meat was actually going to take place. The barbecuing process had proceeded so slowly I was wondering if we were going to have to find some fishes, loaves, and a preacher who was good with words in order to have something for the hunters to consume when they arrived back at the camp a few minutes before noon.

I knew they would not only be hungry, but most would be disappointed because the deer had eluded them, again.

As I sped the few miles south to the clinic, I met several pickups hustling north, probably on their way to the big hunt, which was to start about daylight. Once back at the clinic, I treated, cleaned up, and fed the half dozen patients there, then zipped the mile over to the house to check on Jan and the kids.

I tiptoed down the short hall, peeked in on Tom and Lisa, and saw they were sleeping soundly, sprawled crazily crossways in their beds. I followed my usual habit of quietly standing there, with head tilted for a square look at their faces, and drinking in the awesome beauty, perfection, and innocence of sleeping babes. I never tired of that view, but often wondered how such small, angelic bodies that were so still and peaceful at night could be up and roaring through the house or across the yard just hours later. I heard a rustling sound at the door.

"What are you doing here?" Jan asked sleepily. "I heard you drive up. I thought you were going to be hunting about this time."

"Aw, I don't know. I helped cook last night, and I'm just not in a hunting mood right now. Think I'll go back and help get the food ready to serve, see how many deer were harvested, then come back to the clinic. Do I have any calls?"

"Nope, not a one. I think everybody has deer hunting on their minds. Why don't you stay here, because I know you are bound to be tired. You don't want to go back up there with all those men, now do you?" She gave me that wry, one-side-of-the-mouth-turned-up female smile and a big hug.

"It's not all men. There are a couple of lady hunters up there," I declared. Another wry smile crossed her lips, but it exhibited none of the amusement of the previous one.

About mid-morning, when the barbecue was done and ready to be pulled from the bones, the heavy partakers of strong drink the night before were unavailable for work, much to the disgust of the head man, because they were down, scattered randomly around the pit area, one lying in a fetal position and two others prone under the front end of a truck, snoring away in open-mouthed comas. To prevent such an embarrassing state from befalling me, I quickly learned to politely refuse any offered potions that could induce stupefaction.

At lunchtime, I counted eleven bucks hanging upside down on the rails. I thought that represented an excellent morning's hunt, but some of the old-timers, including Carney Sam Jenkins, were bemoaning the fact that the kill was slimmer than back in the good old days, and saying that the deer seemed to be getting smaller each year. I was learning that this type of conversation is always heard wherever hunters or fishermen congregate. It doesn't seem to matter how successful the hunt or fishing trip has been, there are always a couple of loafing old-timers around who are quick to remind the younger people of better days. I have never gone into a bait shop without hearing such chitchat.

"Are the fish bitin'?" I ask.

"Boy, you oughta been here last week!" is the universal reply. "They were bitin' anything you throw down there at 'em."

I've even heard of fish jumping into the boat, but that was last month, of course.

Soon the hunters were seated at the long tables inside the old clubhouse, consuming their barbecue, slaw, baked beans, iced tea, and light bread. The standard bread to serve with barbecue is fresh, never day-old loaf bread, and the package should be torn in the middle for serving so that each diner won't have to go through the difficult procedure of sticking his hand down through an open end. Not only is the whole process of getting your bread easier, it is also more sanitary. Amid all the excitement, some careless hunters may forget to wash their hands at the well, and their filthy digits shouldn't be fingering the rest of the bread slices at the bottom of the sack.

Just as I raised the first plastic fork full of meat to my waiting lips, a man came rushing through the front door and shouted into the conversation of the hundred eaters, "Is the doctor here?" Immediately every head turned to peer at the shouter, then to scan back and forth across the room for one of the county's medical doctors. No doubt they were thinking that someone had suffered a lacerated hand while skinning a deer, or perhaps one of the older hunters had fallen.

"Poor doctors, they can't go anywhere and get away from sick or injured people, even for a few minutes," I thought to myself.

"Dr. Clark is supposed to be here in a few minutes," someone yelled. "'Course, he may have gotten an emergency over at the hospital."

"Naw, I mean the dog doctor. Charles's dog just got gored by a buck!" he yelled. "His entrails are hangin' out and everything!"

Immediately, forks were dropped, tea glasses slammed to the table, jaws ceased to move in mid-chew, and mouthfuls of meat were swallowed without the benefit of proper mastication. At the same time, at least half the crowd seemed to be pointing their fingers and forks in my direction, while the other half were pointing theirs toward my associate, Carney Sam Jenkins. Obviously a fine deer dog that has been gored is serious business. People might neglect a pot-licking, backyard cur dog, or perhaps their relatives, but a good hunting dog was another matter!

As Carney and I headed for the front exit, we were joined by a number of the other diners, some of whom were next of kin to Charles, and others who were potential assistants and supporters. Others were like rubberneckers at a highway car crash: they crave to see the wreck up close but are incapable of doing anything except stand in the way.

Charles, one of the deer hunt drivers, was sitting in his pickup with the dog in his arms and had the patient wrapped in flannel shirts and hunting vests. When he carefully started peeling off layers of shirts, we discovered a half-beagle, half-some-other-kind-of-hound cross that appeared to weigh about thirty pounds, which was considerably smaller than the average Choctaw County deer dog. There appeared to be a large tear in the left flank of the patient, but we couldn't be sure of its size because of the large red mass of abdominal contents that protruded, mushroomlike, from the poor dog's side. I could see no perforations or tears in the intestine itself, but there was a large blood clot in the middle of the spleen, which indicated a tear that had miraculously sealed itself over with a clot.

"Doc, is there anything you can do to fix him up? He's more'n just a dog, and he'll do anything for me. He thought that buck was comin' after me, so he jumped in front of 'im, and that ole deer must have thrown him fifteen foot in the air. I'd ruther it'd been me," Charles said, his voice shaking and his eyes watering. A mass of onlookers was peering through the windshield; some had jumped up into the bed and were gawking through the rear window, while others were pushing and jostling their associates around the open door in an effort to get a better look at the wounded canine soldier.

"Y'all git back now, ya hear!" exclaimed Carney. "You act like you've never seen a gored dog before. Go t' house!" As if the rebuke had come from the voice of the Lord, the spectators quietly eased away from the truck and, with hands in pockets and heads down, slowly trudged back to the clubhouse, occasionally sneaking peeks back at the dog and his attendants.

"What's his name, Charles?" I asked.

"Doc, we call him Dumpy, 'cause somebody dumped him out on the road by Daddy's house when he was just a puppy. When we found him he was nearly dead, but the kids took care of him like he was a baby."

"His gum color looks good, Doc," declared Carney. "Must've not lost as much blood as you'd think. And he seems to feel pretty good." A head rub or two produced some weak tail wags, but when the little beagle's eyes met mine, the message was clear.

"I hate to cause all this trouble, mister, and I hate to disappoint my master, but if there's anything you can do to help me, I'd be grateful," they seemed to say. If I had ever wondered why I'd wanted to become a veterinarian, at that precise moment I wondered no more.

"How long ago did it happen?" I asked.

"Ummm, about a half hour," he replied, checking his watch. "See, I heard him yelp and saw him flying through the air, but then he ran off. It took me that long to find him and tote him out of the woods to my truck."

"OK, here's what we'll need to do, Charlie. You sit right there and hang on to him, and we'll get somebody to drive you down to the clinic. We'll need to anesthetize him, then we'll see how much damage has been done to his viscera and then get him all sewed up."

"Doc, I'd drive, but I ain't supposed to, you know, on account of my eyes being so bad and all," Carney declared. Actually, he did drive some, but it was in his old 1941 International pickup truck, and he seldom exceeded twenty miles per hour. He obeyed few traffic signs, probably because he couldn't read them through his bad eyes. "But I sure do want to be there and see how you're gonna fix up Charlie's dog. I'll be on down there directly, if you don't mind me there lookin'."

"Sure, I'd like to have you there. You might need to help me, 'cause I reckon you've seen more of these than I have," I answered. I decided to ask my main man and pharmacist buddy, Loren Caudle, to help. He frequently rode with me on night calls and stopped by the clinic late at night while I was attending cases there.

"Main man, I hate to disturb your lunch, but I need you to help me. Can you drive Charlie's truck down to the clinic. I don't want him to turn loose of the dog."

"You got it, Main 'un, but I'm gonna make a sandwich and bring it with me. You go ahead and get things ready at the clinic."

Twenty minutes later Dumpy was lying on the surgery table under the anesthetic influence of pentobarbital sodium with Charles and Loren standing by, spectating and eager to be helpful. Examination revealed a four-inch laceration, but no damage to the gut other than contamination with dirt. The spleen would have to be removed, however, because of its laceration, which began to seep blood as I manipulated the organ in an effort to check for further injury. I wrapped the mass of viscera in a saline-saturated sterile towel, then commenced the time-consuming task of shaving, scrubbing, and otherwise prepping the skin around the injury.

The bulging mass of bowel had become so swollen with

edema that it was going to be impossible to place it back into the abdominal cavity through the lacerated opening. The swelling had made it very fragile, and any undue manipulation could cause a rupture of the gut, mesentery, or blood vessels. I took scalpel in hand and extended the lower length of the tear about two inches. Now I could remove enough of the remaining viscera to check its condition.

"Main 'un, scrub your hands right quick and put on a pair of gloves. I need you to help hold all this stuff while I look around inside here."

While Loren dutifully held the loops of gut aside, I probed around in the cavity, checking the other internal organs. When I checked the muscular wall, I found a large laceration on Dumpy's right side. Apparently, the antler had penetrated all the way through and had torn a small two-inch laceration through the peritoneum and muscle layers on the right side.

As I sutured the newly found laceration, Carney Sam finally arrived.

"Carney, did you go by way of Gulfport? What took you so long?" said Loren. He loved picking on Carney.

"Loren, you know I drive slow 'cause of my eyes. My eyes was plum awright till I started taking all them drugs you and that eye specialist give me. I don't know what's wrong with me, but if I was a cow, I'd split my tail and pour salt and pepper in it," he replied.

"Well, Doc'll do it. Main man, I'll hold 'im if you'll do the cuttin'," declared Loren.

"Let me finish what I'm doing here, and we'll see. I may not have any pepper here in the clinic," I said. "Carney, look over in here at this gash where that old deer's horn went all the way through and nearly came out the other side. You ever seen anything like this?"

He squinted his eyes, peered down into Dumpy's depths, and said just what I thought he'd say. "Yep, I've seen many a one just like it. He'll get well and be runnin' deer again before the season's over."

"Really! I can't believe it!" Charles exclaimed from the pass-through, where he was making phone calls, informing family and friends about the accident.

"Yes sir, and he'll do even better if you slip 'im two thimble-fuls of Kent Farris's liquor every day," Carney replied. From the aroma he gave off, I gathered that he had partaken of several thimblesful that morning himself.

"What does that do?" I asked, my head down in deep con-centration.

"It kills all them germs, especially the big ones," he answered. "Didn't you learn that over at the big university?" Loren and I exchanged looks, our heads shaking back and forth.

"All that tuition and book money thrown away, Main man. I wish I'd known that all we needed to do was get us a few gallons of white liquor," Loren said sadly.

"What we could have done was to put a different kind of dye in each jug. Then you could use the red stuff to treat pneumonia, green for nosebleed, and yellow following abdominal surgery. The possibilities are limitless!" I said.

"Y'all go ahead and make fun. One of these days you're gonna see all them high-powered wonderful drugs turn worth-less against these bad germs that's coming along, but some of the old-fashioned home remedies will still work. You'll see!" Carney declared.

Even though I had been engrossed in washing the viscera and suturing muscle layers, I had heard the front door open and close several times and the quiet whispers of additional specta-tors. Looking up, I saw folks standing in the door and peering through the pass-through, while others behind them were stand-ing on tiptoes in an attempt to see the veterinary surgeon at work. From the concerned looks on their faces I gathered they were family members who had heard about Dumpy from a phone call, or maybe at the barbershop, and had beelined it to the animal hospital to see the beloved family member.

While suturing the skin, I again heard the door open and the running feet and excited voices of small children, obviously recently released from a hard day at preschool. Suddenly, Tom, with Lisa close behind, forced himself between the legs of the onlookers. They came straight to the table and commenced their usual barrage of questions. When Jan appeared at the door, the crowd quickly became silent and then parted, as if they were the Red Sea and she was Moses. Many of the men, in classic old Southern style, even took off their caps and uttered the greeting that she frequently received, whether she was at the clinic, grocery store, or courthouse office.

"Hi you, Miz Doc," several said, while others nodded their heads forward in a show of respect. The word had gotten around very quickly that even though she was a very friendly person, she was a lot more businesslike than her husband and was the commander-in-chief when she was at the clinic. She didn't put up with any shenanigans.

"What happened? I'm sorry I wasn't here, but I picked up the kids and then we went to the Dairy Queen for a little lunch, then to Bedsole's for winter coats. Did you find everything you need? I should have been here to help. Hi, Loren, Carney. What do you want me to do?" Jan was also a world-class talker. She talked as she stalked around the surgery room, picking up sponges that had been tossed aside and the dropped instruments off the floor. Some of the spectators were even getting into the cleaning act, trying to assist by looking around on the floor for things to retrieve and tidy up their areas, scooping up chunks of mud and other debris that had fallen off their boots.

The children spent most afternoons at the clinic and had some of their toys in the back of the waiting room. We had found that many of our clients brought their children along with their pets, and they enjoyed having things there to entertain themselves. Some people think that youngsters shouldn't be hanging around the vet clinic, seeing kittens come into the world and all sorts of disagreeable samples being retrieved from various portions of dog anatomy, but I believe it gives them a better appreciation of the animal kingdom and an insight into the human-animal bond. Too many kids live in a television-created-animal fantasy land, where they are delivered a skewed portrayal of the realities of life.

After the surgery was finished and Dumpy had been taken to

his cage, the crowd quickly dispersed, some of the spectators dawdling about in the parking lot, no doubt discussing the surgical events of the past hour and a half.

"Did you see Doc tying them knots in that catgut with them little silver pliers?" one of them was probably saying. I knew that because someone always made that remark.

People in general seemed to think there was something sort of magical that went on in the surgery suite over at the West Alabama Medical Center, and they always had a yen to take a peek behind those No Entrance doors there just to see a man asleep on the table while the garbed-out doctors and nurses were working over him with "little silver pliers" and other strange instruments. The average person never gets to see such a sight in the human hospital, but he might get to see animal surgery if he happens along at just the right time when the veterinarian needs a helping hand. Perhaps observing animal surgery fulfills that need.

Later on that afternoon, I rushed out to my truck to make a large animal call. The aroma from inside the cab reminded me that I had not finished my barbecue lunch at Rudder Hill. There on the seat were two large plates rounded at the top and covered with aluminum foil. Without even looking I knew that some kind individual had noticed that I had not eaten my lunch and had prepared those plates for Jan and me. It was a simple gesture for which the preparer wanted no thanks, but it was the sort of act that spoke very eloquently: "Thanks for what you do for us and our animals. We appreciate you!"

Dumpy was alert and drank water when I checked in around ten o'clock that night. The next morning he ate some dog food and drank more water, and didn't seem to notice that he had very recently been through a major surgical procedure. A week later, he was at home with his loving family, although he didn't run after any deer until two months later, at the end of the season. Carney Sam Jenkins, the gifted seer, had been correct again. Of course, Carney said he would have been running deer two weeks earlier if I had just dosed him with two thimblefuls of Choctaw County "white lightnin.'"

Twenty-three

It was Christmas Eve, and it was late. The previous January I had vowed that I would plan my future Christmas gift giving in a more efficient and orderly manner, never again putting it off until the last possible moment. I had no desire to become quite as organized as Jan, who started her holiday planning and purchasing as early as the day after the previous Christmas, but I thought just maybe I could take off a couple of hours on a slow day in early December for a quick shopping spree. But December had been a busy month, with an unusual number of large animal calls, herd work appointments, and brucellosis testing, plus the small animal practice had also been busy, probably because of the extra days of vacation the schoolkids were having. Carney Sam had taught me that the health of dogs, cats, gerbils, and other pets gets a higher priority when the kids aren't in school. That's why there are so many sick pets on weekends, holidays, and snow days. So I again kept postponing the dreaded shopping chore until it was too late. Now I was in an eleventh-hour buying panic.

"What in the world can I get for Jan this year?" I asked myself while nervously rifling through various pieces of lingerie and funny-looking blouses. The slick, almost boiled-okra-like texture of the fancy feminine attire sure felt strange to my rough and callusy hands.

I knew Jan preferred a "personal" type gift instead of some small appliance or thingamajig for the kitchen. She always seemed to be pleased with a new mixer, an assortment of sharp knives, or salt and pepper shakers shaped to resemble Holstein cows, but little hints throughout the year indicated that she might appreciate a new nightgown from the ladies' store a lot more.

My problem with buying ladies' garments is twofold. First, there is the problem of size and style. I have always tried to keep a record of Jan's approximate sizes somewhere in my appointment book, but for some reason the recordings become illegible or I somehow scribble other information over them, such as "take worm medicine to Joe Ward the next passing" or "castrate horse south of Nanafalia—can't remember name—check at Compton's store." Usually I just ask the clerk which one she thinks Jan would like and then ask for the correct size. That way, I can blame her if the color, size, or style is wrong. That is another advantage to living in a small town.

The second problem is the embarrassment factor. It's very uncomfortable for me to have to discuss matters relating to ladies' garments, especially when speaking with someone to whom I am not married.

"Well, what size sweater does she wear?" the clerk always asks first. She usually appears to have just stepped off the page of an exclusive ladies' fashion magazine.

"I, uh, don't know exactly. I guess about medium or so," I stammer.

"Isn't she about my size?" she gushes, while clasping her hands to her sides and posing sideways, her head tilted provocatively.

"No, uh, she's a size or two bigger, and she doesn't wear her sweaters quite as tight as you do." Now I'm really embarrassed and wish I could be speeding away in the safety of my pickup truck. The other customers are looking my way and giggling as I shuffle in red-faced distress. That's why it's easier to just buy a waffle iron.

The store was owned by Mary Jo Jenkins, and was therefore appropriately named Mary Jo's. It was *the* ladies' store in town. Kate and Lois, as well as Mary Jo, clerked there, and the three were enthusiastic dog lovers. Actually, I didn't enjoy going into the store very much for that reason as well. The moment I walked through the front door and was recognized, the trio virtually attacked me and immediately began presenting long-winded, overlapping dissertations on the latest exploits of their respective beloved canines. When I tried to look at one of the ladies and make an appropriate response, the others would simply get closer and talk louder.

No subject was too sensitive to be discussed head-on. It might be Windy's ongoing bowel disorder or Duke's disgusting and exhausting nightly forays with that trashy little cur next door, or perhaps a terse question regarding Fluffy's continued scooting around on his rear end.

"I just had Fluffy up there last week, Dr. John," cooed Lois, "and he's doing it again! He's still mad at me about that shot you gave him!" This Pekingese ball of white fur and I were not good friends, in spite of his frequent trips to my office for his numerous ailments. In addition to his chronically impacted anal glands, he also had an infection of the left eye, brought on because it had popped out one Sunday afternoon when he challenged a German shepherd. It was only minutes later when we replaced the eye, but the cornea had been permanently damaged. Eyedrops three times a day were required to maintain some degree of normalcy. He also suffered from allergic dermatitis, bronchitis, bad teeth, and bad breath, and had a snoring problem. Lois frequently complained that she couldn't sleep because of his loud snoring and bad breath, but my recommendations of throat surgery and dentistry went unheeded.

Fluffy accompanied Lois to the dress shop every day. He spent much of his time in the front window snoozing among the mannequins and watching the shoppers tromping up and down the sidewalk. When he grew weary of being stared at, he would retreat to his store-bought basket bed, located adjacent to the cash register. Occasionally, if feeling depressed and especially antisocial, he would waddle into the back of the store and hide in the first "trying-on" room.

Just as I held up a frilly, silky, red nightgown for inspection, I felt a sudden sharp, penetrating, and excruciating pain just above my right heel.

"What in the world!" I yelled, whirling around and grabbing at my throbbing foot. My first thought was that I had been shot, stabbed, or bitten by a rattlesnake.

At the same instant, the corner of my eye detected Fluffy sprinting down the aisle toward the safety of the fitting room. He appeared to be grinning and snickering when he hung a right at the end of the aisle.

Kate and Mary Jo had heard my expression of pain and surprise and were by my side in seconds. After the proper hands-over-mouth demonstrations of shock and outrage, and a loud announcement that Fluffy had just bitten his doctor, they had me seated in a comfortable chair, my sock and shoe removed, and the profusely bleeding wound examined. Wet cloths and bandaging materials appeared from a back room while appropriate dog-scolding phrases were thrown toward the fitting room.

"Fluffy! Shame on you! Bad dog! You should be ashamed of yourself!" cried Lois, who had been busy at the cash register and had not seen the minor calamity. "Biting Dr. John is not acceptable!" Then she joined Mary Jo and Kate, kneeling at my feet, each talking full bore, and each elaborating on a plan of action for treating and bandaging my maimed extremity.

"Not acceptable!" I thought to myself. "Is that all? What about a rolled-up newspaper strategically placed upside his head three or four times?" I said nothing, but instead kept my lips zipped, like a good veterinarian should. It wouldn't be good public relations to say anything in my present state of agitation. Blood continued to ooze from the wound as the clerks-turned-nurses kept at their dabbing and wiping.

I stared daggers at Fluffy, who was now standing in the open door of the back room, his head thrown back, barking at his veterinary adversary and obviously gloating over his moment of triumph.

"Oh, I'm so sorry about this, Dr. John," cried Lois. "I just don't understand what came over him! He's never done anything like this before."

The embarrassing examination, wiping, and wrapping of my hemorrhaging heel continued. Now the other shoppers were also gathered around and making observations, stupid suggestions, and predictions about the eventual outcome of the injury.

"Ye need to put a mustard pack on 'nere," one said. "Gotta draw that poison outta there." She pronounced the word *poison* as "pison." "If you don't get that poison outta there you'll take the blood poisoning and die."

"Saw a bite wound just like that once," another added. "That feller's laig takened the gangrene and he wound up losin' it."

"Aw, there ain't nothin' much cleaner than a dog's mouth," declared an older gentleman who had quietly slipped in and selected a pair of bedroom slippers. "That's why dogs lick their wounds and they get well so quick. They's no need to take a bit-up dog to a high-priced vet. But take my advice, feller, and rub some lard on that leg when you get home. It'll keep it from swellin' up so bad." I could feel my temper about to get out of control, so I knew it was time to take my leave.

"Look," I growled, "just let me have my shoe. I can take care of this foot. Thanks anyway." Then I hobbled away, clutching the red nightgown under my arm. I heard Fluffy still barking furiously in the back as I passed the bargain rack.

"If it was me, I'd shoot that dog and get his brains checked," declared an elderly lady fondling a plastic purse. "I spec' he's got the rabbis, and you'll have to take those horrible rabbis shots in your stomach. Takes twenty-five of 'em, you know, and I hear tell they're 'bout the worse thing you can ever go through."

"No ma'am," I replied, "I know for a fact that a real good vet gave him all his shots recently. And by the way, it's only twenty-one shots in the stomach, not twenty-five." Then I fled out the door with shoe in hand, leaving a trail of blood in my wake.

As I reached my truck I heard Lois call out from the door, "I'm so sorry, Dr. John. And don't worry about paying for the gown tonight. I'll just put it on your bill and you can come by later when you're feeling better."

I sat quietly in my truck for a moment or two, seething and breathing hard. Finally the humor of the whole situation overrode the anger, and the laughter came, first in chuckles, then in guffaws. I was still giggling as I headed for the clinic to bandage up, thinking about being the only veterinarian in a small town. Knowing everybody in town and their dogs was great most of the time, but there were times when that was a liability.

It is an honor to be a trusted animal doctor and to have your friends and clients consult with you about their animals. But it is occasionally irritating not being able to go shopping without being surrounded by dog lovers seeking a diagnosis or bragging on their precocious pets. However, the worst part is getting dog-bit and being constantly barked at by dissatisfied patients themselves.

When I arrived home that night, Jan was busy shifting presents around under the Christmas tree.

"How bad is your leg, honey?" she inquired.

"What? How did you know about that?" I asked, surprised.

"Well, Loren called a little while ago from the drugstore to see if you needed him to bring something over for your wound."

"How did he know?"

"Clatis had been in there to get something for Betty Jo, and Lois had told her when they saw each other at the curb market."

"I don't believe this," I replied. "Why don't they save time and just put it on the air?"

"I hope you didn't act ugly to Fluffy, dear," she said. "I'm sure he didn't mean any harm. After all, he's real sickly."

"No I didn't, but I thought evil thoughts."

The worst part about the Fluffy episode was that within twenty-four hours the entire population of the town knew that Dr. John gave his Jan a frilly, silky, shorty nightgown for Christmas. A lot of them were shocked, and several thought it was a sin.

A number of my clients gave me strange looks after the news of the shorty nightgown made the barbershop and beauty parlor circuit. That and other happenings made me wonder what kind of reputation I was building. After all, I had been seen out front of a Mississippi honky-tonk, I had signed a petition calling for a vote on legal alcohol in Choctaw County, and I counted several distillers of homemade whiskey as clients and friends. Also, it was known that I played golf, had been stopped by the Butler police late one night for riding in a station wagon while wearing nothing but a pink pair of shorts, and made mysterious out-of-town trips up to Sumter County every Thursday, sometimes returning home in the wee hours of Friday morning. But all these things are just some of the enjoyable hazards of being a small-town country vet.

Twenty-four

⌒ "Honey, Mr. W. J. Landry called about an hour ago and wanted to remind you that next week is the week that he needs you to test those bulls and cows for his big production sale," Jan said when I returned from an evening call. "He wants you there the first thing Monday morning if at all possible. I told him it was on the book, and you'd be there just after daylight. Also, he said to tell you that your favorite patient is still doing fine."

Mr. W. J. Landry was our largest account, except for the Livingston Stockyard and the state and federal governments, which funded the brucellosis program. Mr. W.J., who was sometimes called "Mr. Double J" by his employees, was the owner of thousands of acres of prime timberland in the area that produced a steady supply of logs for his huge sawmill, which then shipped the quality lumber it produced all over the world. But my relationship with him and his family came about because of their large cattle and horse farm.

The Landry Hereford Farm consisted of several hundred acres of improved pastures, which fed four hundred head, more or less, of purebred Hereford cattle, as well as thirty quarter horses. Then there was a kennel full of fine redbone and blue-tick coonhounds, which served Mr. W.J. well when he decided to go on an occasional nocturnal coon hunt. Those valuable animals were his pride and joy, and he wanted the best health program possible for all of them. I was on the farm several times a week, sometimes on a daily basis, because Mr. W.J. spared no expense when it came to protecting his investment.

~

My "favorite patient" that he mentioned was a bull that had suffered a fractured forearm not long after we arrived in Butler. Mr. W.J. had found me on another farm in the area.

"Doc, one of the boys bumped our best calf with a tractor a little while ago and hurt his front leg. He can't put any weight on it. I'd appreciate it if you could come up and take a look." I learned later that every animal that he would call me about was always his best. Apparently, that is characteristic of all cattlemen.

When I walked into the barn, the three-hundred-pound Hereford calf was lying in a large pile of straw and was surrounded by four attendants who were carefully monitoring his every move with concern. Mr. Landry was nervously walking, pacing back and forth, and barking orders every other step.

"Careful with that leg, Eddie!" he warned. "Don't let the straw get in his eye, Fred! Watch out; don't hurt that leg! Uh oh! He's not bloatin' up, is he, Doc? Jimmy, go get water for Doc. That leg's really swole up bad. Can you give him a shot, Doc? Boy, that's the best calf we've ever raised on this farm. Why does this always happen to the best one?"

I was already half exhausted from listening to his constant chatter, and I had yet to touch the patient. When I knelt down and touched the calf's right front leg, he kept talking.

"Is it broke, Doc, is it broke?"

I said nothing, but just kept palpating the swollen area. When I picked up the foot with my left hand and manipulated it carefully, the calf flinched in obvious pain.

"Watch out! That hurts 'im, don't it? It's broke! I just knew it!" he said as he kept pacing, shaking his head, and redistributing straw with his feet.

"Yes sir," I said carefully. "I think it is broken. See right here just below the elbow? Feel that spot while I move his foot just a little. You feel that grating?"

"Oh, yeah, I feel it," he cried. "How bad is it?"

"Well, I can't tell for sure without an X-ray machine, and I don't have one of —"

"You need an X-ray machine?" he interrupted. "We got an X-ray machine! We'll just take him down to the West Alabama Regional Hospital in Butler and use the one down there. Let's get him loaded onto the school bus, boys."

"Mr. Landry, I don't believe they'll let us X-ray a bull's leg down at the folks' hospital."

"Well, I just reckon they will!" he retorted angrily. "I bought the thing myself, I hired the administrator, and I'm chairman of the hospital board. I don't like to pull rank, or anything like that, but when it comes to helping a helpless animal, I believe I can X-ray it if I want to." I would find out later that he was also chairman of the board of the bank and that there was no civic project in the county that he had not helped in some way. But I never heard him say anything about his community generosity except about that X-ray machine.

I was momentarily stunned just thinking about a bull's being wheeled into the emergency entrance of the human hospital for treatment. Then I realized that he was dead serious about his authority, as well as his concern for the sick animals.

"OK then," I said. "Why don't you go call and let them know we're coming, and we'll get the patient loaded into the back of the school bus." The old bus was used to transport timber workers to and from the woods, but the back few seats had been removed for storage of chain saws and other wood-cutting paraphernalia. That empty area would serve nicely as a bovine ambulance.

As I tranquilized the calf, Mr. W.J. made a beeline to his car, a beautiful Lincoln that he sometimes used to transport sick baby calves from the pasture to the barn for treatment. He retrieved a telephone from between the seats and quickly had someone from the hospital on the line.

"Yes, who is this please?" he said politely. After a short pause he continued. "Mrs. Moseley, this is W. J. Landry. Would you get Walter on the phone for me, please?" This time there was a more extended pause while Mrs. Moseley located the hospital administrator.

"I can't wait to hear this conversation," I thought to myself as I finished injecting the tranquilizer and then started a jug of IV fluids. "I wonder how Walter is going to get out of admitting a bull to the hospital."

"Hello, Walter. W.J. here," Mr. Landry said authoritatively. "I've got a bull here that the vet says needs X-raying. If you don't mind we're gonna—"

He stopped short at that point, while Walter apparently asked a question.

"Naw, naw, a BULL," he emphasized. "One of my calves. He's got a broken leg!"

Another several-second pause while Walter responded in detail.

"Good, good, I appreciate that," Mr. W.J. said. "But no, we won't need a private room for him. We'll just get him X-rayed and perhaps use some of your drugs and stuff if Doc needs it, but we'll try to avoid using the emergency room. I do appreciate you offering it, though. And no, we don't need the ambulance, 'cause we're bringing him down there in my school bus. See you in a few minutes."

I'm sure I stood there staring and openmouthed at what I had just heard, but I was quickly brought back to the task at hand as the large crowd that had gathered began to load the patient through the extra-large rear door of the bus. It was tedious work, trying to lift and push but at the same time protect the dangling leg and my intravenous apparatus, which was carefully attended to by one of the cowboy nurses.

"Be careful, be real careful!" ordered Mr. Landry as he hung up the phone and sprang from his seat. But with so many timberjacks and their bulging muscles under and around the snoozing patient, the loading was accomplished in short order.

The trip to the hospital was caravan style, with Mr. Landry and his Lincoln in the lead, his emergency lights flashing a warning to all the vehicles that we met during the ten-minute trip. Bringing up the rear were two pickup trucks, one from the farm and the other an interested neighbor who also had switched on his headlights. He had no idea what was going on, but whatever it was, he didn't want to miss seeing it.

When we arrived at the hospital, Mr. W.J. drove into the parking area reserved for the doctors, taking up at least three of the prime spaces since he pulled in crossways. As the bus made a wide turn and then started backing toward the emergency entrance, I noticed a mass of scurrying activity. There were at least three nurses stationed near the emergency room door, a clipboarded clerical worker was pacing back and forth, and a frowning orderly was standing with his arms crossed. As expected, there was a growing crowd of onlookers who just happened to drop by to observe the unusual scene after hearing about it over their CB radios.

Suddenly, the emergency room door burst open and a large rolling table being driven by two burly orderlies came barreling toward the bus. Mr. Landry was excitedly pointing and giving orders.

"Right there on the bus, boys. Get back, people, give us some room, this is an emergency, let 'im breathe. Doc, what's his pulse? Please don't let 'im suffer."

"Look out!" cried one of the orderlies as he smashed his cart into two spectators who had crowded in too close.

If the patient had been a famous quarterback or a popular president, no more fuss could have been created. As we wheeled the patient slowly to the emergency entrance, Mr. Landry went on ahead, clearing a path by parting the crowd with hand motions. A flashbulb popped in my face, and the local journalist directed asinine questions toward no one in particular. A policeman and a deputy sheriff drove up and screeched to a stop, exited their vehicles and donned huge dark sunglasses even though it was practically night, adjusted their weapon belts, and initiated crowd-control measures. The scene was getting a little chaotic.

"Who is your insurance with, sir?" the clipboard-carrying

clerk asked Junior, the young hired man holding on to the calf's head.

"My insurance?" Junior asked, pointing to himself.

"Yes sir, who is it?"

"My insurance is Mr. Double J — Mr. Double J Landry!" he stated proudly.

Some in the crowd were amused by Junior's pronouncement, while others paid it little attention. After all, in those days it was normal procedure for an employer to take care of his employees.

It seemed as if I was the only person there who knew that the calf would be denied entrance to the hospital. Sure enough, when we approached the open door, a large nurse blocked our forward progress.

"You can't bring that bull in my hospital, I don't care who his owner is!" she declared. Some discussion ensued, and it was agreed that the technicians would roll the mobile X-ray unit just outside the door and the picture would be taken there. That was all we wanted anyway, I never wanted to go inside and disrupt the tranquillity of the hospital.

While we waited for the technicians, I scanned the hospital wings. Faces were peering out nearly every window, enjoying the goings-on. I could see pajama-clad men standing with the aid of friends or crutches, taking in the strange activity. At other windows I saw frail, obviously very ill elderly ladies cranked up on their beds, craning their heads and stretching their oxygen hoses, gazing intensely at the scene. Across the way in the maternity ward, brand-new mothers in beautiful pink gowns were standing with their proud husbands, pointing at the snoring bovine patient and waving at their friends in the mass of observers. We had created a scene.

"Doc, Doc!" cried Mr. Landry. "Let me talk with you in private for a minute." We stepped over to the large oxygen tank, out of hearing range of the crowd.

"I want to ask you about my bull's reproduction," he whispered, looking all around to be sure no one was listening. "This X ray's not gonna hurt his breeding ability, is it? I mean, you know, I've heard that X rays will sometimes cause, uh, sterility."

"I don't think a couple of X rays will cause any problem, but just to be sure, we'll ask them to put a lead apron over his important parts," I said. "Then we'll be sure."

Presently, the technicians appeared with the machine, then proceeded to look at the calf warily from every angle for at least thirty seconds before they spoke.

"What do you want done here, Doc?" they queried as I placed the lead apron over the appropriate spot on the bull.

"Well, I think we should take lateral, AP, and oblique radiographs of the proximal forearm. Also, try to include the humero-radio-ulnar articulation in one of those radiographs," I requested. I noticed many of the observers dropped their jaws and rolled their eyes up in their heads as if in deep thought, trying to decipher my jargon.

"Yeah, and make it snappy," insisted Mr. W.J. "We want to X-ray him after you get through with those radiographs!" I decided to keep my mouth shut and not tell him that a radiograph was the same thing as an X ray.

Just minutes later we were in the viewing room poring over the radiographs, along with several hospital authorities. One young nurse was scratching her head over the strange anatomy that she saw.

"It's just a bull's leg," I said matter-of-factly.

"A bull?" she asked, wide-eyed.

"Yeah. You know, a boy calf. A little Sunday cow," I replied. "He's right out yonder on the emergency room patio." She exited the room still scratching her head with a pencil through a hole in her cap.

I studied the films carefully before I gave my diagnosis to Mr. W.J., who was by my side and becoming more and more impatient as the minutes ticked off. Both the ulna and radius were cleanly broken about two inches below the elbow, and I couldn't see any joint involvement. A young man who appeared to be an intern and a technician were also studying the pictures and talking softly between themselves.

"The ulna needs to be plated, of course, and…" the intern whispered. He rechecked the angle of displacement, looked closely at the cortices of the bones, and made several other calculations.

"Yes, the radius should be plated, also," he declared professionally. "The patient should be confined to a bed or wheelchair for at least two weeks."

"My bull in a wheelchair?" bellowed Mr. Landry. "Have you been grazing on buckeye sprouts, young man?"

It was obvious that the two neophyte medical men had thought they were dealing with a local football player's injury. They quickly left the area when the word *bull* was mentioned.

Mr. W.J. was on the verge of serious agitation. He had been waiting patiently at the hospital for at least an hour for a medical answer and solution to his prize calf's problem. I had decided what action to take, so I motioned for him to follow me outside.

"The breaks in those bones are clean, there is no splintering, and there is very little overriding," I told him. "I believe we can take him back up to the farm, make a modified Thomas splint, and set that leg. We can go to the shop and make a splint out of thick aluminum rods, some thin flat iron, and a lot of tape and padding."

"We can get the whole crew back in the shop if we need 'em," he declared.

Two hours later, with the help of a very handy man named Lee, we had fashioned a workable but unattractive splint. Even though the patient's sedative had worn off, he patiently allowed us to drill some holes in the outside walls of his hooves, loop some baling wire up through one hole and back down through another, then tie the ends together. Then we applied several rolls of four-inch plaster of Paris casting material around leg and splint, from toe to shoulder, and let it dry.

After cleaning up the calf and the stall area, things looked pretty nice. I felt good about the job we had done, but I was concerned about whether the splint was too heavy for the calf to get up and walk around. After a little prodding, the calf sat up cow fashion and sniffed the foreign contraption that had enveloped his leg.

"He needs to sit up like this all night so he won't bloat," I ordered.

"OK, Eddie," Mr. W.J. ordered. "You stay right here and watch him until daylight. B.J., you come on in and relieve Eddie the first thing in the morning. Just be sure this calf don't lie down flat on his side. He's got to be sittin' up like this all the time. Y'all understand?" Both young men nodded in the affirmative. They might not have understood the reason, but if Mr. Double J issued an order, they did understand that.

The next morning, I arrived at the farm about nine to find the calf standing and eating grain from a pan sitting on a folding chair. Mr. Landry was nearby, checking the feed for foreign objects that shouldn't enter the sensitive digestive tract of his prize bull.

Some of the crew had decided the bull's nickname should be Wheelchair, in honor of the comment made back at the hospital. Wheelchair tolerated his splint very well, and learned to move around so well that we had to add extra padding at the bottom of the splint.

About six weeks later we removed the splint, keeping our fingers crossed. When the last filthy piece of casting material came off, we found that a nice callus had developed at the site of the fracture. When we allowed Wheelchair to stand, he waved the leg around in odd fashion, probably wondering why it was suddenly light as a feather. Then he took a few slow and easy steps, and in spite of his obvious tenderness and a slight toeing out of the leg, we all felt he was on his way to recovery.

∼

Almost a year after Wheelchair's accident, the long-awaited sale day had arrived at the Landry Hereford Farm. The bulls had all been properly tested as required by the federal government, their fertility had been assessed, and they were all neat, clean, and perfectly coiffed. Even their hooves had been polished as painstakingly as the fingernails of a fine lady. All the cattlemen from miles around were present, wearing their finest boots and hats, each one carrying a well-used sale catalog.

As each tethered bull was inspected and evaluated by a potential buyer, the catalog was opened up and the vital statistics perused. Birth weight, adjusted weaning weight, yearling weight, and names of sires and grandsires were all carefully considered, and so noted in the pages. It struck me as amusing that folks down at the Dairy Queen had no inkling as to how much science, pedigree, and experience went into getting their hamburger steak on the table.

Finally, the sale kicked off with a welcome by Mr. Landry, who introduced his family and then told about the development of the herd. There were short speeches by two university animal scientists and some Hereford breeders from out west. I was shocked when I was called to attest to the health of the herd, but managed to mumble out something about leptospirosis and health certificates. Finally, the bidding started and Mr. Landry's dream began unfolding.

Some twenty minutes later, I was in the office when I heard the auctioneer's chant pause and Mr. Landry's voice come over the microphone.

"Y'all need to know about this fine bull," he said. "When he was just a calf, he broke his right front leg. With the help of the hospital down in Butler and the best veterinarian in the county, he has healed up so well that you can't tell it was ever broken."

Wheelchair topped the sale, and I was happy to have been called "the best vet in the county." I was on my way home several hours later when the thought hit me that I was the *only* vet in the county.

Twenty-five

⌒ I thought I had latched the corral gate behind the three wild bulls, but when I felt the sudden rush of cool winter air on the back of my neck, I suspected that I had not.

Whoppp! The loud noise made me sure of it.

Unbeknownst to me, the top hinge of the massive gate had broken, and the gate had fallen in my direction, barely missing my backside by inches. The next sounds I heard were the spine-chilling snorts of three angry Brangus bulls as they jumped to their freedom over the downed gate and speedily departed the corral as if they were late for a cow meeting. There are few things as embarrassing and distressing as the diminishing sounds of galloping bovine hooves bolting from the place where the owner and veterinarian want them to be, especially if that veterinarian is the one who allowed them to escape.

I stared at the prone gate and wondered whether I would have been permanently injured had I been standing four feet closer. It was made of green two-by-eight oak boards, and was seven feet high and ten feet long. No wonder the top hinge had snapped.

Eric and David, the two ranch cowboys, just stared at the gate from atop their horses. They simultaneously removed their cowboy hats and scratched the tops of their heads. It was the first time I had ever seen their heads uncovered, and I was surprised that Eric was baldheaded — except for a two-inch strip that extended from temple to temple just above his ears. David, who was a few years younger, had a full head of black hair.

"Dern, Doc, you can tear down more stuff in five minutes than we can build in two weeks," exclaimed Eric, now rubbing all around on his head with the palm of his left hand.

David just grinned and shook his head from side to side. I knew what he was thinking. He dreaded the thought of rehanging that heavy gate and repenning those wild bulls.

As I drove away, I thought about how farmers and veterinarians are exposed to so many dangerous things, from unruly animals and head bangs on the squeeze chute to falling or collapsing objects. Even spouses who are occasional assistants or observers are not exempt from injury. Jan had recently been hurt while on a farm call with me, and she was still suffering from the effects.

It happened at Colonel Zuber's farm. When he retired from the army, he and Mrs. Zuber had bought a small farm in the warmth, peace, and quiet of south Alabama. He soon had the place in shipshape condition. Each time I drove by, I always thought if a farm could stand at attention, the Zuber farm would have.

It wasn't long before he purchased a fine herd of Hereford cattle and had them on display in his well-groomed pasture. As expected, the cows were well disciplined, which made my job of vaccinating, pregnancy checking, and treating pinkeye much easier.

Because he was an orderly person, the colonel left nothing to chance. When the herd required routine veterinary service, he phoned the office, then followed that up with a very detailed letter outlining the various treatments, surgical procedures, and tests that were necessary, as well as the day and time that we had set. The letter always contained several complex questions that required some research on my part in order to write out the detailed answers, complete with references. Usually, he would send a confirmation letter a week or so before the appointed date. Jan was extremely impressed with all this letter writing, instructions, and questions, but I would have preferred a simple phone call without all that regimentation.

Jan occasionally accompanied me on large animal calls, and it was nice being alone together, driving through the country admiring the nice farms and fine homes. It was about time for us to build a home of our own, and we were constantly looking at houses, noting things that we liked and didn't like.

"Honey, would you slow down a little? The way you're going over these little rises and around these curves is making me feel a little queasy," she said a few miles outside of town. "I haven't felt that good all day."

"Sure, dear. Did you pick up a bug or something?"

"Probably. But you drive way too fast anyway, and you need to think about other people on the road. They may not know how wild you are behind the wheel, and how you read the mail as you drive."

"How do you know I drive and read the mail at the same time?"

"I was down at the IGA just yesterday and Charlie Hale told me he met you out on Riderwood Drive going real fast, right down the middle of the road. He said you were holding a newspaper up in front of the steering wheel and reading the sports page."

"Now just how did he know it was the sports page, huh?" I replied. "Besides, I was in kind of a hurry to get up on Scott's Mountain for that grass tetany case. The cow was bloated and all. You know how busy I am."

"John, I don't want to hear all that. Just slow down!"

"Yes, ma'am, I'll see what I can do. Now let's talk about something else."

"Okay. What did you say we had to do at Colonel Zuber's?" she asked.

"Have a couple of eye surgeries to do," I replied. "Of course, you can go in and visit with Mrs. Zuber if you want to. You know how unpleasant that eye surgery can be for spectators."

"Well, I'll not be a spectator, I'll be there to help. Maybe I can chat with her briefly and then I'll come on out. You should have the cow clipped up, scrubbed, and anesthetized by that time."

I knew that wouldn't work because Mrs. Zuber was a talking champion, just like Jan. Visitors were always treated to a tour of her poodle kennels and the detailed pedigrees of each dog. In addition, she would inform Jan of the medical history of each one as well. All that would take some time, since at last count there were two dozen of the long-pedigreed wonders.

Because of their lack of dark pigment around the eye, Hereford cattle are at an increased risk for eye problems, especially pinkeye and malignant tumors of the eye. After exposure to sunlight for a long period of time, one or more squamous cell carcinomas sometimes develop on the eyeball or eyelids of especially susceptible cattle. If the tumor is detected early, it can be surgically removed, frozen with liquid nitrogen, cauterized, or perhaps treated with a tumor-regressing drug. But if the cancer has spread into the eyeball or the tissues around it, the entire eye must be removed. It is not the most pleasant of tasks for bovine veterinarians. Because the surgery is performed with the patient in a standing position, good restraint in a squeeze chute and proper nerve blocks with local anesthesia are essential.

As I prepared the first cow for minor lower eyelid surgery, I could see Jan and Mrs. Zuber strolling down the walkway in front of the chain-link fence that enclosed the kennels. They were happily conversing, using lots of hand and arm gestures, and trying to make themselves heard above all the barking. Every few steps they would stop, poke their fingers through the fence, and scratch a dog's nose. Most of the dogs were standing on their hind legs, their funny clipped bodies almost upright as their front paws battered and shook the fence. It was hard to tell who was having more fun, the dogs or the two ladies.

I had finished the first cow and was half through removing the eye of the second before Jan arrived chuteside. The colonel had asked me at least two hundred questions about cow eyes, and I had been able to answer only about one hundred of them to both our satisfactions. As expected, he was scribbling notes in his ledger book on everything I said with the speed and dexterity of a court reporter. I was glad to see Jan arrive on the scene.

The colonel had created feeding troughs for the cows by obtaining empty government surplus fifty-five-gallon drums, splitting them in half longways, and then welding the two halves end to end. For some reason he had propped one of the troughs upright beside the fence, right next to where Jan was standing.

Suddenly, while she was making complimentary remarks about the condition of one of the cows, a sudden and sharp gust of wind toppled a heavy trough over, and it banged heavily onto the back of her head. She was cut off in mid-compliment and immediately crumpled to the less-than-ideal ground surface directly in front of the squeeze chute.

For a brief period of two or three seconds, I stood frozen with forceps in one hand and needle holder in the other, confused and not knowing what to do next. On one hand, there was my best friend in life lying unconscious in the barnyard muck, mud, and manure, but I was also at the most critical stage of meticulous eye surgery involving the colonel's top cow. I could almost hear the stern voice of my veterinary school surgery professor as he preached, "Do not break sterility! Do not break sterility!"

It was obvious that the operation on the patient would have to be interrupted. Instantly, I knelt beside Jan and asked the usual stupid question.

"Jan, are you all right? Jan? Jan?"

She said nothing, which was very unusual.

The closest thing I had to a towel was a surgical drape that I was using on the cow. I ripped it off the cow's head, quickly dipped it in a nearby water trough, wrung it out, and began dabbing it on Jan's ashen face. Bovine blood was splotched on the drape, and it was soon transferred onto her face. I wasn't concerned about a small amount of blood at that point since I was very concerned about my wife.

"Wake up, Jan! Wake up!" I pleaded.

The colonel was barking out orders, but I was blocking him out. He said something about an ambulance, then he hurriedly marched off toward the house.

"Ooh, my head," Jan began to mumble. "My head! What is it?" I could see a goose egg forming just above her right ear.

"I've got to sit up. I'm feeling sick at my stomach."

Slowly, I helped her to sit up. Her left side and back were covered with mud, muck, and other common barnyard material, but that was the least of my concern.

"Oh, my word!" she exclaimed. "I'm bleeding!" The first thing she had seen through her foggy vision was the cow blood on the wet drape and her hands.

"No, it's only cow blood. Just relax," I tried to say in a calm voice.

"Cow blood!" she replied, wincing in pain. "What happened?"

"It's okay, everything's all right. The ambulance will be here in a minute, and then we'll — "

"Ambulance? I don't need an ambulance! Help me to get up from here," she said, struggling. "Boy, my head really hurts! I'm just filthy! What happened?" Now she was drifting back toward normalcy, talking with both her hands and her mouth. "What's that cow doing in our yard?"

I tried to explain the accident while she glared at the offending trough and palpated the knot on her head. It was obvious she was still having trouble sorting out the events of the last several minutes.

"Who's that?" she asked, pointing toward an approaching figure.

"That's Colonel Zuber. We're at his farm, remember?" I said.

"Uh, yeah, I think so."

"The ambulance can't come," announced a puffing Colonel Zuber. "It's in the shop. What are we going to do? Do you think it would be safe to take her in the car?" He was nervously wringing his hands. Perhaps it is easier to lead troops into battle on foreign soil than it is to deal with a domestic emergency.

"Good! No ambulance is needed, 'cause I'm walking out of here," declared Jan. Now she was up, refusing assistance, and marching briskly but unsteadily toward the house in typical Jan-in-charge fashion, leaving two startled men in her wake. An aproned Mrs. Zuber and a brace of poodles jogged to meet her halfway to the house. When they met on the path she made the obligatory slow examination of the head wound and made all the proper sympathetic apologies about the injury and the fouled condition of Jan's attire. In no time, the ladies were talking animatedly as they headed for the house.

In all the chaos, I had forgotten about the cow until she rattled the chute, just to remind me that I had unfinished business there. In spite of the several-minute delay she seemed to be holding up well. I rescrubbed my hands and quickly took up suturing where I had left off, and completed the job in ten minutes. The only good part about the incident was that Colonel Zuber put his ledger away and asked no further questions that day.

I drove slowly and carefully on the way home since Jan continued to complain of head pain and nausea. We stopped by Dr. Paul's office for a quick but thorough examination, which indicated that she had suffered a concussion and could look forward to more headaches and nausea for a couple of weeks.

But Jan's two weeks of ill health turned into a month, and some mornings she felt so sick she didn't come into the clinic until nearly noon. She still had the headaches, and the nausea was worse. At the end of the third week, I suggested that maybe it was time to visit a specialist in Meridian.

"I'll take Tom and Lisa to Birmingham for a week's visit with your folks. That way you can have constant bed rest."

"No, not yet, I'll give it a few more days and if I'm still this sick on Monday morning, I'll go back to Dr. Paul and see what he thinks. He can refer me to someone else if he thinks it's necessary."

The following Monday afternoon I decided to stop at Chappell's barbershop for a much-needed haircut and all the latest news, plus some information on the status of the just-completed Southeastern Conference college football season and a complete rundown and critique of the recent New Year's bowl games. If you couldn't find the latest news and information at Chappell's barbershop, then it wasn't available!

"It's supervet hisself! Ever'body rise and greet the great

healer of hounds and horses." I had grown accustomed to Myatt's constant sarcasm, and actually looked forward to it. I was even learning how to respond to his insults and barbs. "Somebody told me you was wrote up in *Good Housekeeping* as one of the foremost dog tonsil removers in the whole US of A." The three customers waiting to be clipped giggled and looked up from the dog-eared magazines they were scanning, but apparently were not impressed with Myatt's loudmouthed greeting. They quickly scanned the coveralls-clad figure making his entrance but went back to looking at the pictures in their magazines.

"Myatt, you are a regular Bob Hope. I been wondering why you aren't on television late every night, sharing all that brilliant humor with the TV world. You'd be filthy rich in thirty days. But then I figured it out. You probably couldn't handle that long Trailways bus ride to New York, and especially that difficult layover and transfer at the Atlanta bus depot." The people waiting did enjoy that, and gave their approval by laughing heartily. They knew that few people ever had the last word on Myatt.

"Naw, I just don't like ridin' in airplanes," he replied. "I'll leave that to you and the other rich folks in town."

"I hear congratulations are in order, Doc," Chappell suddenly blurted out, looking directly at me. I noticed Myatt frantically shaking his head in negative fashion.

"Congratulations? Me? What'd I do?"

"Uh, just 'cause you, uh, saved that puppy for that little girl last week," Myatt stammered.

"Puppy? What are y'all talking about?"

"I mean about what somebody said they saw over at the drugstore an hour or so ago," Chappell exclaimed. "You know the medicine that he saw Tillman Wright sell Jan."

"Chappell, be quiet! You wasn't supposed to tell that!" Now the spectators were all ears, their magazines closed and placed in their laps. "Doc, you been home this morning?"

"No, I've been testing bulls all morning up at W. J. Landry's."

"Well, you better go home right away before Chappell busts a gut to tell you something you oughta hear from your wife," he stated seriously. I hit the door running, but hearing Myatt's admonishment.

"Dang, Chappell, sometimes you talk too much!"

Ninety seconds later I was walking in the back door of the house. Jan was in the rocking chair sipping on a 7UP. She had a big smile on her face. Obviously she was feeling better, probably from the medicine that she got from Tillman.

"You look like you're feeling a lot better," I stated. "Is it the new medicine?"

"How did you know about that?" she said, a shocked look crossing her face.

"I went to get a haircut and Chappell said something about the medicine you got at the drugstore, but apparently he wasn't supposed to tell."

She shook her head in amazement. "I can't believe the communication network in this town! You'd better sit down for this." I plopped down on the couch.

"You know how sick I was when I was pregnant with Tom and Lisa? And you know how last summer Tom was telling all his classmates that he was going to have a little brother or sister? Well, it's happened again. Dr. Paul said the rabbit died, which means we're going to have a baby in August!" She was still smiling.

I sat quietly for several seconds, not exactly shocked, but a little surprised while thousands of things raced through my brain. Things such as the health of both the new little one and Jan, the challenge of providing the proper environment and guidance, educational expenses, orthodontist's bills, and naturally, whether it was going to be a boy or girl. I believe most men when first informed of impending fatherhood, have nagging doubts in the backs of their minds as to whether they are up to the awesome challenge of properly raising a child. I also believe that most men rise to the occasion, perhaps because of pride, personal responsibility, or plain old panic. Nothing makes a man work harder than knowing there will soon be another mouth to feed and body to clothe.

"Well, I'm glad to know you have a reason other than a

smashed noggin that's causing all that upset stomach business," I declared, giving her a huge hug. "I know it won't make you feel any better, but at least you know why and perhaps it will be easier to tolerate. At least it won't last for very long."

"Dr. Paul said the same thing, but no man has ever had morning sickness or had a baby. If he did, I guarantee there wouldn't be but one child per family."

Nevertheless, we celebrated the discovery of the pregnancy and talked about how her absence from the clinic in the summer would affect the practice. Then, turning to a more pleasant item, we discussed names for baby.

"Do you want a boy or girl?" she asked.

"How about one of each?"

A wave of nausea overtook her, and she moved over to the edge of the sofa. Perhaps I shouldn't have mentioned twins.

"If it's a girl, let's name her Martha Christine, for both our mothers," I suggested.

"Since Tom already has your dad's name in the middle, if it's a boy, let's name him Milton Paul," said Jan. "After my dad and Dr. Paul. They've both been mighty good to us the past year."

As we explored the possibility of other names, the phone rang.

"Doc, is that 'chu? What are you doin' at the house this time of day?"

"Having a celebration. What are you doing calling here this time of day?" I was hoping for some hint that would tell me the identity of the caller, but I wasn't that lucky.

"Tried yo' shop, but nobody answered there, so just thought I'd call this other number," the voice said. "Looka heanh, Doc. I got this cow that's been tryin' to find a calf all mornin' and she's about tuckered out. What would you charge me to come over here and take it?"

"Where is she?"

"Same place as last time," was the reply. "We'll get on the tractor, cross the creek, then you can throw yo' rope on her, tie up to a tree, and deliver that calf. Now that won't cost much, will it?"

"It's gonna be ten dollars more than last time. I just raised my fees some thirty minutes ago!" I declared. Jan nodded her head very slowly in approval, and mouthed the words "It's about time!"

"My wife wants to know what your address is so she can go ahead and get your bill ready for you," I said, trying not to laugh. All of a sudden I was being more aggressive than usual, probably because of my excitement and newly found confidence.

"You tell that nice lady that I'll send you back with a quart of my pear preserves just for her. That woman is too good for you, Doc."

"Says he's gonna send you some pear preserves," I said, holding the phone away from my lips.

"Why that's my buddy, Mr. Yancey from over in south Marengo County," she said. "But I detest the thought of having to eat any kind of preserved fruit."

"How long you gonna be, Doc?"

"As Dr. Foreman used to say, 'Hang up the phone and watch for a cloud of dust!'"

Soon I was in the comfortable driver's seat of my Chevy truck, listening to the familiar buzz of the six-cylinder engine and the lonesome whine of the mud-grip tires as I sped eastward on Highway 10. I honked the horn when I passed Dr. Paul getting the mail out of his mailbox, and smiled when he pointed at me and clapped his hands. Folks working on the roadside recognized the sounds of the vet's truck and threw up their hands and waved in friendship and respect. In spite of the difficult task ahead of me, I knew this was what I was meant to do, and I was doing it in a friendly and close-knit community and county. My family was blessed with lots of good friends, lots of hard but honest work, and now with a welcome addition just eight short months away.

When I crossed the Tombigbee River at Ezell's Fish Camp, I decided I was going to enjoy thinking about all this for a few days. *Then* I would get nervous about the baby.

About the Author

Dr. John McCormack is Professor of Veterinary Medicine at the University of Georgia. He received his B.S. and D.V.M. degrees from Auburn University. He lives in Athens, Georgia.